POLITICS, SOCIETY AND DEVELOPMENT

POLITICS, SOCIETY AND DEVELOPMENT

Insights from Sikkim

Editors

Mohammad Yasin

Durga P Chhetri

KALPAZ

Politics, Society and Development
Insights from Sikkim

ISBN : 978-81-7835-931-1

Published in 2012 in India by
Kalpaz Publications
C-30, Satyawati Nagar,
Delhi-110052
E-mail: kalpaz@hotmail.com
Mob.: 9212729499

Laser Typesetting : Rajender Vashist, Delhi
Printed at : Chawla Offset Printers, Delhi

Contents

Preface

In Sikkim, democratic ethos is now nearly three and a half decades old. Until 1975, this Himalayan state was under the rule of Namgyal dynasty which lasted for more than 300 years. The centralised Namgyal administration came to an end in 1975 when Sikkim was finally merged to the Indian union. This event has led to the change in the political system of the state from centralised (theocratic) monarchical system to liberal democratic system. The politics in Sikkim thus, until the emergence of liberal democracy, can be characterised as containing not only undemocratic and non-participatory elements but also centralised, authoritarian and most unsuited to the conditions and needs of expanding populations, limited human resources, and contemporary demand for human and civic rights. This indeed had its impact on the society, economy and polity of the region.

Sikkim's progress towards democracy and stability is marked by two historic developments–first, the introduction of electoral system based on adult suffrage, and second, the abolition of the institution of monarchy in the 1970s. Inspired by the ideals of Indian national movement, the conscious and educated Sikkimese visualised democracy as the only dignified and perfect form of governance in which all the citizens in their humble way make their contribution to enrich the polity, society, culture and economy of the state. Further, they conceived the democracy as an ideal form of government where freedom and justice are institutionalised. The first important move toward democracy in Sikkim was the Government of Sikkim Act, 1974. This Act removed many of the worst inequities under the old political system where only few aristocrats and nobles were part of the governmental system.

The Act also established the right to vote based uniformly on the basis of universal adult suffrage.

Multidisciplinary in approach, the present volume is a modest attempt to portray the different socio-political and economic aspects of this tiny but unique state, and examine the range of issues surrounding the politics, society and development in Sikkim. The contributors of the volume with their rich insight as well as firsthand experience on the multidimensional aspects of the state, have penetrated deep into the issues that have over the years been critical to the overall development of the state. The volume in hand has been organised into fifteen sections each focusing on a specific theme. We hope this volume will contribute to the enrichment and enhancement of knowledge, and give fresh insights on the various developments in Sikkim thereby opening new windows of further research on the different aspects of the state.

The editors would like to thank all the contributors for their cooperation and commitment. The views expressed herein are those of the authors and do not necessarily represent the views of the institutions to which they are affiliated to. We are also thankful to all our colleagues and friends for their valuable support and guidance.

Last but not the least, we express our sincere thanks to Kalpaz Publications for bringing out the book in a record short period.

Editors

Abbreviations

ACT	:	Affected Citizens of the Teesta
AIR	:	All India Radio
ASHA	:	Accredited Social Health Activist
BJP	:	Bharatiya Janata Party
B-L	:	Bhutia-Lepcha
CARG	:	Compound Annual Rate of Growth
CBSE	:	Central Board of Secondary Education
CAA	:	Constitutional Amendment Act
CLOS	:	Concerned Lepchas of Sikkim
CMO	:	Chief Municipal Officer
CPR	:	Contraceptive Prevalence Rate
CPRF	:	Central Reserve Police Force
DESME	:	Department of Economics, Statistics, Monitoring and Evaluation
EC	:	Executive Councillor
FWPR	:	Female Work Participation Rate
GDI	:	Gender Development Index
GDP	:	Gross Domestic Product
GER	:	Gross Enrolment Ratio
GOS	:	Government of Sikkim
GSDP	:	Gross State Domestic Product
HDR	:	Human Development Report
HRDD	:	Human Resource Development Department
ICDS	:	Integrated Child Development Scheme

ICMR	:	Indian Council of Medical Research
ILP	:	Inner-Line Permit
IMR	:	Infant Mortality Rate
IPC	:	Indian Penal Code
IPR	:	Information and Public Relation
JAC	:	Joint Action Committee
JNV	:	Jawahar Navodaya Vidyalaya
KV	:	Kendriya Vidyalaya
LSI	:	Linguistic Survey of India
MBC	:	Most Backward Class
MC	:	Municipal Corporation
MIL	:	Modern Indian Language
MLA	:	Member of Legislative Assembly
MW	:	Mega Watt
NBA	:	Narmada Bachao Andolan
NFHS	:	National Family Health Survey
NGC	:	Namchi Government College
NGO	:	Non-Governmental Organisation
NHPC	:	National Hydro Power Corporation
NRHM	:	National Rural Health Mission
NTA	:	Notified Town Area
OBC	:	Other Backward Class
PDS	:	Public Distribution System
PHC	:	Primary Health Centre
PHSC	:	Primary Health Sub-Centre
SC	:	Scheduled Caste
SCP	:	State Congress Party
SDF	:	Sikkim Democratic Front
SGC	:	Sikkim Government College
SIBLAC	:	Sikkim Bhutia Lepcha Apex Committee
SLTJAC	:	Sikkim Limboo Tamang Joint Action Committee

SNC	:	Sikkim National Congress
SNP	:	Sikkim National Party
SSC	:	Sikkim State Congress
ST	:	Scheduled Tribe
TAR	:	Tibet Autonomous Region
ULB	:	Urban Local Body
UN	:	United Nations
UNESCO	:	United Nations Educational, Scientific and Cultural Organisation
UNICEF	:	United Nations International Children's Emergency Fund
WER	:	Women Elected Representative
WHO	:	World Health Organisation
WWF	:	World Wildlife Fund

List of Tables, Figures and Boxes

TABLES

FIGURES

BOXES

1

Introduction

Sikkim is a small, but stable and peaceful state situated in the north eastern part of India. The political stability coupled with a vibrant administrative system has helped this small state to be free from the problems of insurgency that has affected all other north eastern states. Indeed, the political stability of the state that has made the latter a unique model is the resultant outcome of a long tradition of social harmony. The kind of tolerance, bond of unity and social cohesiveness that exist among different ethnic groups in the state – the Nepalese on the one hand, and the Lepchas and Bhutias on the other - have contributed heavily to the social integrity in the state. All these have resulted to the building of a separate identity transcending the existing ethnic boundaries – the Sikkimese identity. Needless to say, the social cohesion and the political stability and the resultant sikkimese identity have been the important determining variables that account for the kind of development the state has been witnessing so far. The strategic location of the state also makes its developmental imperatives get sufficient attention from the Union of India.

Until recently, Sikkim was under the rule of Namgyal dynasty which lasted for 333 years. The centralised Namgyal dynasty came to an end in 1975 when Sikkim was finally merged to the Indian union. This event has led to the change in the political system of the state from centralised (theocratic) monarchical system to liberal democratic system. As many scholars from around the world argue that liberal democracy is the only suitable form of governance both for managing the modern state - which is now ubiquitous - and for mediating the forces of rapid economic and cultural change occurring in all the societies of the world. Fukuyama affirms that history has become one for all of humankind, and that liberal democracy constitutes the end of societal evolution. Whatever unfinished business of history may still remain will, according to him, soon be achieved with liberal democracy (Fukuyama 1992).

The emergence of liberal democracy as an alternative political model in Sikkim can be traced to the reformist movements of early 1940s. The acceptance of some aspect of liberal democracy gave birth to the institutions of party system, responsible government, local self-government and universal suffrage (Sinha 1975). The liberal state thus actually depends on the institutional mechanisms of representation to the political process, popular consent, protests and demands into state policies. Many developing countries of South Asia and South Africa after their independence from colonial rule switched over to this form of democracy. The most important attribute of liberal democracy is the competititon of ideas and views and the prospect of the inclusive politics.

The politics in Sikkim, until the emergence of liberal democracy, can be characterised as containing not only undemocratic and non-participatory processes but also centralised, authoritarian and most unsuited to the conditions and needs of expanding populations, limited human resources, and contemporary demand for human and civic rights. This problem with political structures manifested itself clearly in the sluggishness, lack of faith in, and conflict between the different levels of the political system. The electoral democracy was not institutionalised in the country. Even though the elections for councils had been held, democratisation was still very much an electoral issue, political parties were elitist and lacked internal democracy, institutions for popular participation were weakly embedded in society, and civic rights were not protected. The late 20th century has witnessed the breakdown of authoritarianism in many regions of the world. For some, the progress made in transforming authoritarian regimes into democratic ones corroborates the superiority of liberal democracy over alternative forms of government. Thus, the change in the system is not unique to this country; rather, it was a global order which culminated into the establishment of governments based on the principles of democracy.

The end of the monarchical system was for long represented as the beginning of the era of new form of nationalism, presenting an ambitious project of nation-building, development and democracy. In reality, however, much of those projects remained elite ambitions or sometimes just elitist propaganda. The elite undertook to promote democracy through the very composition and institutional structures of the state. For a long time, the nation-building exercise was conceived to be one that simultaneously led to greater unity of the nation, and greater involvement and participation for the citizen in the institutions of the state. But in the case of Sikkim, the task of building a single new identity called the 'nation' encompassing several identities and affiliations was the most ardous job. A nation as defined by Rupert Emerson (1970) is identified as a community of people sharing 'significant elements of a common heritage' and 'a common destiny for the future'. Going by this definition, Sikkim had neither a common heritage nor a common destiny (Sinha 1975). There has always been an inter-tribal and ethnic differences, and building single identity was always a big problem in Sikkim. This was mainly because of two reasons– firstly, the acceptance of the Lamaist traditional model by the Nepalese amounted not only to their political eclipse but also to their religious, cultural and economic subservience to the Buddishts, and secondly, adoption of the liberal democratic model by the Buddhists would have meant the loss of their grip over the decision-making process. Thus, the ethno-political polarity between Bhutia-Lepcha minority and Nepalese majority was the main obstacle to the growth of national identity and nation-building. The former was more interested in preserving the tenets of theocratic political structure of lamaist Tibet, while the later was for the establishment of secular democratic government in Sikkim. The proponents of secular government wanted to separate religion from the sikkimese politics and demanded broad participation of general public in the decision-making processes.

In this tug of war between theocracy and democracy, the Tripartitie Agreement of 1973 served as a solution to this dilemma of nation-building. The Agreement was signed between Chogyal, Foreign Secretary, Government of India and Leaders of political parties of Sikkim. The Agreement reduced the authority of Chogyal, appointed Chief Executive as a head of administration, and constituted State Assembly by replacing State Council. The May Agreement was followed by the passing of Government of Sikkim Act, 1974, which made the provision for the ruler to be the constitutional head of the state. In April 1975, the State Assembly finally passed a resolution that abolished the institution of monarchy in Sikkim, and declared Sikkim as a constituent unit of India. Accordingly, on the request from the Government of Sikkim, the Parliament of India enacted the 36th Constitution (Amendment) Act in 1975 which made Sikkim the 22nd state of Indian Republic, thereby ending the Lamaist theocratic rule of Namgyal dynasty. The entire power structure was re-organised where people, not the ruler, are considered supreme. The revolution which ushered in regimes of popular soverienty transferred the ruling power from the king onto a 'nation', or 'people'. Under a regime of popular soverienty, people are free, in a way that they are not under an absolute monarch or an entrenched aristocracy, for instance. In other words, a modern democratic state demands 'people' with a strong collective identity. Democracy obliges one to show much more solidarity and much more commitment to one another in the joint political project than was demanded by the hierarchical and authoritarian societies of yesteryears (Taylor 1999).

Like other developing political systems, the socio-political structure of earliest Sikkim is traditional and feudal in nature. The traditional society in Sikkim was characterised by three strata– the clergy, the nobles and aristocrats, and the commoners (Sinha 1975; 2008). Among the clergy, the monks were drawn from the Bhutias and Lepchas of high position. These monks played an important role in the management of monastery estates and administered justice, and in collaboration with Kazis, the clergymen also managed the affairs of the state.

The kazis and thikadars constituted the nobles and aristocrats of Sikkim's feudal society. The kazis were the regional lords and had authority to command the regional territories. They possessed the power to adjudicate minor disputes, and collected land revenue from people within their jurisdiction. They had no proprietory right in the land although they did have a kind of hereditary title to their office (Hope 1966). The peasants, wage earning people and skilled and semi-skilled workers, on the other hand, constituted the commoners. With the change of time, there was also a change in the social stratification in Sikkim. The present day society in Sikkim is characterised broadly by four distinct class - agrarian, business, wage-earning, and new (Datta 1991). The agrarian, comprises the big landowners, medium-sized land owners, small-sized landowners and landless farmers. The agrarian class is divided into these four classes depending on the size of land they possess. The big and petty businessmen, and also the owners of small scale industries are the main constituents of the business class. The agricultural labourers, manual workers including skilled, semi-skilled and unskilled belong to the wage-earning class. The educated members employed in the government services fall under the new class category.

The traditional and feudal society of early Sikkim gradually transformed into a modern and democratic society. The internal development and exposure to the wider world brought about some social and political changes. Contact with more advanced societies has been the principal force which has eroded the structure and values of traditional societies, and pushed it to a transitional process. In fact, the transition from feudal, peasant, agrarian society to a modern, democratic society cannot be accomplished without profound social changes. Among many issues, alteration of the class-structure deserves special attention because it involves entire incentive system of the society (Davis 1966). The post merger Sikkim paid special attention in this direction with necessary measures to make its society modern and developed. The contrast between the traditional and modern economy was not solely or perhaps even most significantly, a contrast in the standards of living and levels of consumption. In traditional societies, the normal thing was to accept one's status and frequently one's occupation as determined by inheritance and customs. Modern economic activity, whether colonial or indegenious, has taken people out of their conventional roles and put them in new situations both of work and of life, which have greatly broadened their perception of the range of alternative activities in which they might engage. This increased mobility, and widened perception of alternatives has markedly weakened the stabilising elements in traditional society (Badra 1992).

As the society start experiencing the process of modernisation, the profound changes take place in psychological, political and economic life of human beings. Psychologically, they must transform the old culture in ways which make it compatible with modern activities and institutions. The face to face relations and warm, powerful family ties of a traditional society must give way to a more impersonal system of evaluation (Weiner 1966). Politically, people start thinking about the new form of political organisation, which gives maximum freedom and choice in decision making. This condition prevails only in the democratic set up where the citizen involves in the formation of government through election. Economically, the occupation of the people shifted from traditional agricultural activities to employment-oriented services. The establishment of modern administration and small scale industries provided the new avenue of employment in various administrative, technical, professional and other industrial units.

Contemporary civil society in Sikkim consists of a large body of associations and civil institutions, most of which are modern, even though they take on traditional forms and symbols. They are mainly urban-based and include labour/worker unions, religious associations, ethnic associations, women's organisations, professional associations, employers' and occupational bodies, student and youth groups, cooperative associations, special interest groups such as human rights organisations, and a new range of NGOs such as community and neighbourhood groups and philanthropic and welfare associations. In terms of historical development, this wide range of associations and civil institutions can be broadly grouped into the conventional older groups (trade unions, community organisations, self-help groups, ethnic associations, women's organisations, professional bodies, religious groups) and the new groups, including some NGOs and human rights groups. It is the latter, with their new styles, global linkages, and heavily publicised advocacy that have prompted the much-trumpeted 'rediscovery' or 'emergence' of civil society. In reality, civil society has long existed in Sikkim but became dormant or stifled due to the authoritarian type of governance under Namgyal rule. Interest in civil society initiatives has been inspired in Sikkim by both the democratising impulses of nationalist leaders of India's independence as well as the neo-liberal interest in strengthening civil society as a counter-balance to the regulatory state. The political reforms being advocated today include the state withdrawing from some of the functions and responsibilities it had acquired under the influence of the planned development model. Civil society and social actors are being encouraged now to take up responsibility for the development and welfare functions which the state wants to shed.

These civil societies are mainly urban-based but not necessarily restricted to urban issues. Its effectiveness today is more or less tied up with the nature of the issues with which it is concerned; thus wider social justice or democratisation issues have broader constituencies and tends to have a larger impact than narrower. But the effectiveness of activities of civil associations depend on the role of leaders, their linkages with both the grass roots and the elite, the extent of the threat they pose to established interests, their links with effective power blocs both local and international, and their capacity to manage and sustain protests. Many civil associations lack effectiveness in running the organisations, and therefore, only few such societies/associations are active today in the state.

Political development of Sikkim is viewed by the authors as a changing political system– from authoritarian to democratic components (institutions, sructures, and practices) of polity that is in transition after merger. Daron Acemoglu and James A. Robinsonn (n.d) have identified three main paths of political development–first, there is a path that leads from non-democracy gradually but inexorably to democracy. Once created, democracy is never threatened, and it endures and consolidates. Second, there is a path that leads to democracy but where democracy, once created, quickly collapses. Following this, the forces that led to the initial democratisation reassert themselves, but then democracy collapses again and the cycle repeats itself. Logically, and third, is a path in which a country remains non-democratic or democratisation is much delayed. As far as the political development in Sikkim is concerned, it comes under the first category, that is, the path leads from non-democracy to democracy.

The change in the course of socio-economic development gradually leads to the reduction of the authoritarian component and to the growth and entrenchment of the democratic values. It can be viewed as the first and the major regularity of the process of democratisation in Sikkim. The authoritarian component is conditioned first and foremost by the absence of a competitive party system, less involvement of citizens in planning and decision making. The democratic component becomes increasingly indispensable for transitional society approaching developed, one which is a changing society and as such, it requires orderly changes of governmental policies and consequently, orderly changes of political leadership. Hence, it can be said that the progress of developing society requires a political system that contains democratic components at the initial critical stage of democratisation. The process of democratisation is far from unilinear. It suffered setbacks and interruptions by spells of increased authoritarianism. While eventually resulting from socio-economic development, democracy is achieved through political struggle. The 1973 agitation was vital for establishing the democratic governace in Sikkim. The popular agitation compelled the governemt to sign an agreement which was followed by the enactment of the Act of 1974 that made the monarch a constitutional head, and the Chief Minister, elected directly by the people, the chief executive. The tripartite Agreement was signed by the king, Foreign Secretary, Government of India and representatives from political parties. The provision of agreement includes, among other things, elected legislative assembly, voting on the principle of one-man-one-vote, election on the basis of universal suffrage, and ministerial collective responsibility. The Agreement is important for many reasons. For the first time in Sikkim's history, the people, represented by popular forces, became the acknowledged participants in the political process. Secondly, it has frustrated Chogyal's ambition to make Sikkim a soverign state (Rao 1978). These changes and growing consciousness of an autonomous political identity constitute the matrix of political development in Sikkim.

Sikkim's progress towards democracy and stability is marked by two historic developments–first, the introduction of electoral system based on adult suffrage, and second, the abolition of the institution of monarchy in the 1970s. Inspired by the ideals of Indian national movement, the conscious and educated Sikkimese formed various political parties to press their demand for the formation of democratic government. SSC in December 1947 was formed with the merger of three regional groups. Three main demands of the party were (i) abolition of landlordism, (ii) formation of popular government, and (iii) accession of Sikkim to India. Apart from formulating and presenting political issues of radical significance, SCP started to impart political education to the masses through campaigns and movements. The people, in association with newly emerged political parties, openly challenged the autocratic regime of the monarch and demanded the establishment of the popular government.

The constitutional changes that took place following the 1973 uprising and Government of Sikkim Act 1974 led to a dramatic change in the political and economic institutions that had important implications for the future of democracy. These changes emerged out of conflict between the monarchs' intent of maintaining and expanding their absolutist powers and the pro-democratic forces led by some educated leaders for the establishment of popular government in the state. The battle was won by the pro-democratic forces with the support from the masses. The outcome was the restructuring of political institutions that severely limited the monarch's powers and correspondingly increased those of Assembly. The change in political institutions led to the formation of a representative government which ensured greater participation of people in the decision making processes. The first important move toward democracy in Sikkim was the Government of Sikkim Act, 1974. This Act removed many of the worst inequities under the old political system where only few aristocrats and nobles were part of the governmental system. The Act also established the right to vote based uniformly on the basis of universal adult suffrage.

As a result of socio-economic development since merger, but first and foremost of competitive general elections and formation of democratically elected local government, the traditionally downtrodden increasingly turned assertive in overcoming the age-long depression. Before this, the feudal structure of state did not permit the masses to organise themselves for the democratic rights. Many different countries after the downfall of authoritarian or totalitarian regime witnessed extensive multiplication of political parties. Incidentally, this was the case in Sikkim too–First in the early years of 1970s and later, so to say, in 1979. In the election of 1979, there were more than eight political parties that contested the Assembly election. This was the first election held on the principle of adult suffrage, and under the provision of the Constitution of India. After this, there were continuous elections of legislative assembly with an interval of five years. The democratic governance and universal adult suffrage since 1975 has undermined the influence of the kazis and aristocrats, and opened the avenues for mass participation in the policy decision-making processes.

However, a serious observation of the politics of Sikkim shows a unique trend of one-party dominance in the apparent multi-party system. For a considerably longer period, Sikkim Congress Party ruled the state with virtually no viable opposition. Similar had been the case with Nar Bahadur Bhandari's regime. At present too, SDF of Pawan Kumar Chamling enjoys absolute command over the politics of Sikkim with no opposition party having any significant presence in, and posing challenge to the contemporary politics of Sikkim.

This book builds on a vast array of stimulating works in various fields that gives the insights of various developments in Sikkim. This volume is spread over fifteen chapters each focussing on a specific theme.

M. Choudhury in his paper titled 'Challenges of Urban Management and Sustainability of Towns in Sikkim' argues that urbanisation is an inevitable process in any country, state or province irrespective of difficult terrain or oppressive climate.

However, in the Indian Himalayas, according to her, urbanisation in modern sense did not happen as a natural process of evolution. It was introduced by the British colonial rulers for the first time in the 19th century. Therefore, urban centres emerged in the Himalayas only after the entry of British rulers who needed summer stations and sanatoriums for themselves. The paper highlights the issue of challenges of urban management, and sustainability of towns in the mountains with special reference to Sikkim. The author discusses in length the urbanisation process in Sikkim in two phases–pre-merger and post-merger. The paper concludes that this tiny mountain state has already discovered ways to sustain towns in spite of deficiencies in industrial development.

Vibha Arora in her article on 'The Democratic Challenge to Secularising Sikkim's 'Sacred' Landscape' has portrayed the contradiction that prevails in Sikkim's professed secularism that accompanied the democratisation process, and the opposition to state-led development process by ethnic groups on ethno-religious grounds, thus, posing a question on the very legitimacy of the developmental initiatives by a secular government. This contradiction has led the author to raise the question – does contemporary Sikkim reflect the successful transformation of a feudal theocracy in a secular democratic polity? The author delves deep into the ethnic imagery of the sacred landscape, and points to the difficulties faced by the secular state in implementing modern development projects, thereby 'fostering an economics-oriented definition of the landscape' and rooting secularism in the face of social movements by the indigenous Lepcha-Bhutia groups against the development projects in their perceived sacred land.

State Policies and Tribal Communities of Sikkim: An Ethnic Perspective by Gurung argues that there has been a steady growth in cultural-territorial identity and mobilisation in different parts of the country. According to the author, the dimensions of cultural-territorial identity and mobilisation included changing nature of cultural identity, structure of identity, political-economic foundations ranging from relative deprivation to internal colonialism of such movements, symbols and pattern of mobilisation, etc. Sikkim, like other parts of India, has been invaded by attempts on cultural-territorial mobilisation (popularly known as ethnic mobilisation) since the introduction of parliamentary democracy after the merger with India. The author argues that though the history does not appear to be a strong basis for emergence of ethnic or cultural politics in Sikkim, yet cultural-ethnic politics did not only emerge, it was sustained and proliferated further in Sikkim in recent past. It is in this context, Gurung's chapter tries to explain one aspect of this problem while focusing on the policies of the government on tribal issues in Sikkim.

Anjan Chakrabarti's article 'From Share Tenancy to Agrarian Reform: Sikkim in Perspective' attempts to review the changing trajectories of agrarian structure and land tenure system that was prevalent in Sikkim. It also takes stock of the agrarian reform initiated by the state government. The basic contention here is that the policy pursued by the state on the land reform since merger is still viewed as an unfinished agenda, at least in the distributive sense. The author argues that the state has failed to augment agrarian reforms despite the fact that various laws in this effect have been passed.

The essay by Padam Nepal is an earnest attempt to engage with and explores the nexus between the cultural/spiritual and the material by examining the ways in which religion and development interact and pose the issues of sustainability of development processes. It juxtaposes development dynamics, religio-cultural spaces, and the politics of ecology in the context of the protest movement of the Lepchas waged against the development project in Dzongu area of Sikkim under the plea of sustainability of development on the one hand, and of a community, as a response to the perceived threat of erasure of their religio-cultural spaces on the other hand.

Empowerment of women is central to human development. Human development, as a process of enlarging people's choices, cannot occur when the choices of half the humanity are restricted. Moreover, gender discrimination, unequal access to resources, and opportunities and decision making not only hinder the progress of women but the whole society and state at large. The article by Durga P Chhetri and Mohammad Yasin on 'Empowerment, Development and Status of Women in Sikkim' examines the socio-economic and political conditions of women. The chapter discusses three important dimension of empowerment– social, economic and political. The authors arrive at the conclusion that women in the state though enjoy relatively better position than their counterpart in the other states of India, are still deprived of many benefits of development. In the end, the authors have suggested some remedial measures to improve the status of women in the state.

In their paper titled 'Sikkim: A Historical Perspective on the Politics of Merger', K.R. Chakravarti and Y.P. Nepal present a comprehensive account on the politics of merger in Sikkim. The authors highlight several details of the events that lead to the end of Namgyal dynasty of about 333 years, and the change of political system from theocracy to democracy.

Vimal Khawas' contribution on the 'Agriculture in the Sikkim Himalaya: A Geographical Note' makes an attempt to understand agriculture in the context of larger Himalayan geography and environmental specificities. According to the author, the physiography of the region has made agricultural conditions extremely diverse. Agriculture is greatly impacted by altitude and slope aspect. The nature of terrain and varied micro-climatic conditions influences agriculture in Sikkim to a great extent.

Food security exists when all people, at all times, have physical and economic access to sufficient, safe and nutritious food to meet their dietary needs and food preferences for an active and healthy life. Food security depends on both the availability and access to food. The challenge of achieving food security for all remains a real one even today. Anjan Chakrabarti in his essay takes up the question of food security in Sikkim. He observed that the state is gradually moving from food-surplus to food-deficient State. He concludes that fall in cultivable land, fall in productivity and rise in population are among the major factors affecting the food grain production adversely.

Decentralisation and democratisation reflects genuinely the spirit and substance of local government all over the world. In recent times, there is an increasing realisation that genuine decentralisation leads to development. It is also felt that decentralisation of power to the local units of government is one of the best ways of bringing government close to the people, promoting public participation and increasing efficiency. According to Human Development Report (1993) where decentralisation has taken place, it has often been fairly successful in encouraging local participation, increasing accountability of local officials, reducing the costs and increasing efficiency. It is in this backdrop, the essay by Durga P Chhetri on Reinventing Municipal Administration in Sikkim dwells on the status of urban decentralisation in pre and post merger Sikkim. On the whole, an overview has been presented on the current status of urban decentralisation experience in Sikkim. The author opines that apart from legal backing, further changes in laws and attitudes of bureaucracy, implementation of citizen charter, transparency and political will are required for the success and empowerment of good municipal administration.

A.B. Subba in his article 'Multilingualism and the Development of Limboo Language: Contextualising the Language Policy in Sikkim' presents a comprehensive account of development of Limboo language in Sikkim. He tries to contextualise the development of Limboo in the broader framework of multilingualism practiced in the state. The author argues that the multiculturalism practiced in Sikkim is quite ambivalent in the sense that the languages which are on the verge of extinction with a very few speakers, have not been recognised; hence, the opportunity to bring the languages back suffers. This shows that electoral compulsions, among other things, underpin the process of recognition of languages in Sikkim. The author suggests the balanced linguistic policy for the development of the various languages, especially in a linguistic diversity state like Sikkim.

Chandrani Chhetri in her article 'Development of Education in Sikkim: The Changing Scenario' has highlighted the development of education system in pre-and post-merger Sikkim. She opines that over the last three decades, there has been a tremendous progress in the education sector in the state. Also there has been sharp increase in the literacy rate especially after 1980s, though a gap in the male-female literacy still persists. According to the author, in spite of this happy development in the field of education, the issues like dropout rates, inadequate infrastructures, quality education, etc. still remain the matter of concern in education scenario. She further observes that in order to overcome these problems and achieve an inclusive education in the state, more concerted effort by the government and the officials concerned is needed.

The paper by Navin Pandey 'Geography of Unmet need for Family Planning and Factors Non-use of Contraception' reports the results of a study undertaken in Dzongu, North Sikkim. His research was conducted in the reserved areas of Lepcha tribes, and attempt was made to estimate the total unmet need for family planning, and identify the major factors that are responsible for non-use of contraceptives. The study shows that the level of unmet need among the Lepcha society in Dzongu is recorded to be high as compared to other societies. It is due to the fact that this tribe is more isolated, and is not exposed to the influence of any social phenomenon of other social groups.

K.R. Chakravarti and Y.N. Nepal in their paper 'Sikkim: The Nathula Silk Trade Route: A Cradle of New Relationship between India and China' provides an account of reopening of historic trade route after 44 years in the border of India and China. The paper also presents a detailed list of export and import items. According to the authors, the reopening of trade route has led to massive development and helps in the bilateral relation between India and China.

References

Acemoglu, Daron and James A Robinson (n.d). *Origin of Dictatorship and Democracy*, Cambridge University Press.

Badra, M. (1992). *Sikkim: Democracy and Social Change,* Calcatta, Minerva Publication.

Datta, Amal (1991). *Sikkim since Independence*, New Delhi, Mittal Publication.

Davis, Kingsley (1966). "The Role of Class Mobility in Economic Development", in William J. Goode (ed) *The Dynamic of Modern Society,* New Delhi, Euresia Publishing House.

Emerson, Rupert (1970). *From Empire to Nation,* Calcutta, Scientific Book Agency.

Fukuyama, Francis (1992). *The End of History and the Last Man*, New York, Penguin.

Hope, N. (1966). "The Sikkemese Theory of Land-holding and the Darjeeling Grant", *Bulletin of Tibetology*, Vol. III, No. 2.

2

Challenges of Urban Management and Sustainability of Towns

Introduction

India is known to have many ancient cities, some of which are still surviving. But the Himalayas guarding the frontiers of the subcontinent are not known to foster towns or cities for long. The early history of the Indian Himalayas does not reveal much about formation of towns, let alone cities. It is not hard to imagine the reasons behind–urban management is a challenging task in a difficult terrain and harsh climate. But urbanisation is an inevitable process in any country, state or province that supports civil society. It happens as a corollary of evolution of state administration, trade and commerce irrespective of difficult terrain or oppressive climate. Be it a highland or lowland, the process of urbanisation cannot be avoided if there is a sizeable population that gets involved in tertiary economies. No state, even if it is located in remote mountains, can afford to be devoid of administrative and trading hubs, the two most vital factors for developing urban centres.

However, urbanisation in modern sense did not happen as a natural process of evolution in the Indian Himalayas. It was introduced by the British colonial rulers for the first time in the 19th century in a calculative manner to run the administration efficiently and open new avenues of trade. The heat in the plains of India, and the zeal of the British to expand their commercial territory beyond the mountains provoked the colonial administrators to select soothing as well as strategic spots in the Himalayas. They needed health resorts to recover failing health, particularly of their soldiers, and commercial centres to intercept trade routes leading to Central Asia. Thus, Shimla in the Western Himalayas and Darjeeling in the Eastern Himalayas happened in the 19th century. A series of hill stations were developed subsequently. It is to be noted that there was good number of small and medium-sized princely states all over the Himalayas from Kashmir in the west to Bhutan in the east much before the British stepped in the mountains, but the local rulers in pre-British India never consciously built cities or towns in their kingdoms, though they had the usual paraphernalia to rule their subjects from capitals which were basically citadels. The rulers of substantial princely states located in Kashmir, Garhwal, Kumaun regions in the Western Himalayas and Nepal, Sikkim and Bhutan in the Eastern Himalayas had places designated as capitals, but most of these were rudimentary townships or large villages; even the residences of the rulers were, in most cases, country houses made of stone, wood and mud. Other than these, there were well known places of pilgrimage which attracted sizeable population, but only seasonally, and there were never conscious effort to create townships in religious places. Urban centres emerged in the Himalayas only after the entry of British rulers.

Challenges of Urbanisation in Sikkim

There are many states in the Himalayas which present fine examples for the topics in question–what are the challenges of urban management in the mountains? How to sustain towns in the mountains? The state of Sikkim started urbanising from scratch, and is a perfect case to study the sustainability factor of towns in the mountains. What is unique about Sikkim is the fact that there were no urban centres in Sikkim even six decades back, although the hereditary monarchy of Sikkim dates back to 1642. For over three centuries, the kingdom of Sikkim remained completely rural in spite of the fact that Sikkim came under British influence in the early 19th century. The erstwhile kingdom of Sikkim became a protectorate of British India due to political reasons, and continued to be a

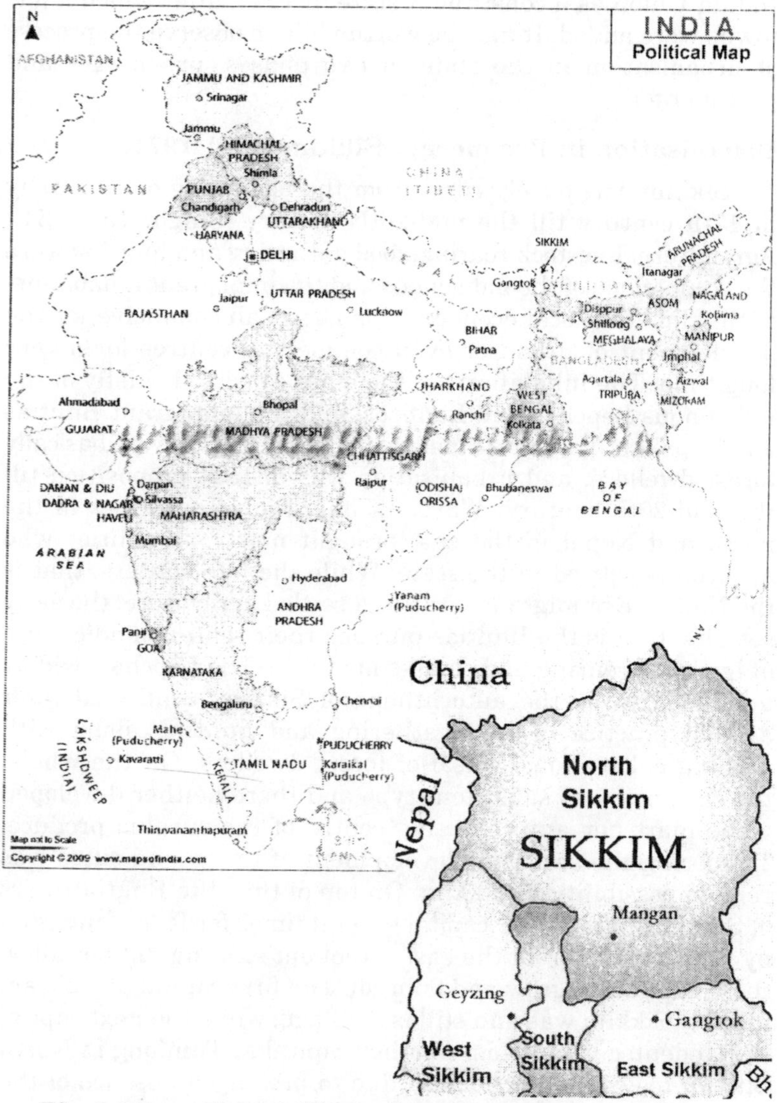

Fig. 2.1 Location of Sikkim in India Districts of Sikkim with Headquarters

(*Source*: www.mapsofindia.com)

protectorate of independent India, post 1947. Gangtok, the capital, got the designation of town only in 1951, and was the only town until the next decade. Sikkim was merged with Indian Union as a constituent state in 1975, after which a few towns were added. It may be worthwhile to observe the process of urbanisation in the state in two phases, pre-merger and post-merger.

Urbanisation in Pre-merger Sikkim (1951-1974)

Sikkim was purely rural from the beginning of monarchy in 17th century till the mid-20th century (Singh, 1985:151). Agriculture, livestock rearing, food gathering and hunting were the occupations of the indigenous and the immigrant inhabitants of Sikkim. The local economy was not at all conducive for the development of urban or even commercial centres for a very long time. The inhabitants of the state consisted chiefly of the indigenous Lepchas and Limboos, and the immigrant Bhutias and Nepalese. The state's indigenous communities were basically forest dwellers, and urbanisation was distant proposition till the mid-20th century. Waves of migration from Tibet in the north and Nepal in the east brought new communities who eventually settled in the state. While the late settlers, that is the Nepalese immigrants practiced settled agriculture, the early settlers, that is the Bhutias pursued their semi-nomadic habit of livestock rearing and small-time trade. The Lepchas, widely acclaimed to be the autochthons of Sikkim, continued their age-old practice of food gathering and hunting along with shifting cultivation, typical of forest dwellers. On the whole, the economy was subsistent type and there neither developed trade mart nor any collecting centre of the surplus produce. This being the scenario, development of towns and cities was remote possibility in Sikkim. On top of this, the Bhutia rulers of Sikkim shifted their capital several times for fear of invasion by the Gurkhas from the east. Frequent shifting did not allow these capitals to grow and flourish. The first capital at Yuksam in West Sikkim was and still is a village, while the next capital at Rabdentse is in ruins. Another capital at Tumlong in North Sikkim too could not flourish due to prolonged absence of the rulers who preferred to escape the state's steamy monsoon months and took refuge in the pleasant clime of Chumbi valley of Tibet, presently in China. Finally, the Maharaja of Sikkim found a safer and better place in the eastern part of the state and settled down at Gangtok, a place with equitable climate and away from eastern transgression (Choudhury, 2006:40).

It is somewhat intriguing that in spite of British influence for more than a century, not a single hill station emerged in Sikkim. The answer perhaps lies in the fact that with the accession of Darjeeling Hills from the Sikkim rulers, the British remained pre-occupied in developing Darjeeling as a hill resort and summer capital for the Viceroy of British India. The scene started changing as soon as India became independent and inherited the right from the British to protect Sikkim. The single most important factor that expedited the process of urbanisation in Sikkim is the construction of metalled road and entry of vehicular traffic. The process of road construction initiated by the British and expanded by the Indians brought Sikkim closer to India, and vice versa. The vehicles ferried not only the defence personnel who guarded the borders of Sikkim; they also carried brick, cement, iron and glass to construct buildings, and an array of processed food and manufactured consumer goods to lure the local inhabitants. Both white and blue collar professionals were brought from the plains of India to perform sundry jobs. The impact was immediate. Gangtok, as could be expected, sprang up as the first and foremost town of Sikkim. It enjoyed the status of state capital as well as the headquarters of East district. Along the National Highway 31A in the same district, two urban centres, namely, Singtam and Rangpo developed in quick succession. The administrative set up of the state required to have one urban centre in each of four districts. Gangtok remained the headquarters of East district while Namchi, Gyalshing (Geyzing) and Mangan were declared headquarters of South, West and North districts respectively. In addition, two more urban areas developed on the southern border of the state at Jorethang in South district and Naya Bazar in West district. It is interesting to note that, though the total number of urban areas in Sikkim rose to eight, none of them met the criteria of towns cited in the Census in terms of total population, density and percentage of male workers in non-agricultural pursuits. Therefore, all of them were given the special status of Notified Town Area (NTA).

The urban agglomeration around Gangtok grew at a fast rate due to the establishment of government offices, educational institutions, commercial establishments and hotels for tourists. The towns of Singtam, Rangpo, Jorethang and Naya Bazar owe their existence to the growth of industrial establishments and market places. The district headquarters at Namchi, Gyalshing and Mangan did not register any substantial growth in pre-merger Sikkim.

Urbanisation in post-merger period (1975-2001)

Sikkim's annexation with India in 1975 proved to be a major turning point in the administrative and urban scenario. The changeover of governance from a hereditary monarchy to democratic set up as a constituent state of Indian Union

Table 2.1: Urban Population of the Districts and Towns of Sikkim, 1981

District / Town	*Persons*	*Male*	*Female*	*Percentage of increase (1971-81)*
East District	43,232	25,387	17,875	154.20
Gangtok	36,768	21,388	15,380	176.28
Singtam	4,042	2,487	1,555	109.87
Rangpo	2,452	1,512	940	37.37
South District	5,866	3,193	2,173	399.12
Namchi	1,144	828	616	213.91
Jorethang	3,922	2,365	1,557	414.70
West District	1,702	1,013	689	55.29
Gyalshing	750	465	285	68.54
Naya Bazar	952	548	404	46.24
North District	780	512	268	135.65
Mangan	780	512	268	135.65
Total	51,110	30,105	21,005	159.86

Source: Census of India, 1981, Series 19, Sikkim.

necessitated establishment of various government departments at par with the other states of India. Employment of a huge work force consisting of bureaucrats, trained professionals for service sectors and all sorts of labourers for construction work contributed to the growth and development of urban centres in the district headquarters in general and Gangtok in particular. Since most of these activities were capital-centric, Gangtok grew very rapidly in the period 1975-1981. Within a decade (1971-1981) Sikkim registered an overall urban growth to the tune of 159.86 per cent. Gangtok alone had a growth of 176.2 per cent. Table 2.1 shows the rate of increase in urban population in the districts and towns of Sikkim during the first decade of statehood.

During the period 1981-1991, some of the urban areas including Gangtok registered negative growth due to reorganisation of boundaries. Substantial area under personal estates was excluded from certain town areas. While the urban population of the East district registered 25 per cent decrease, the same plummeted by nearly 50 per cent in the South District. The decrease due to reorganisation of territorial boundary was drastic in Gangtok and Namchi. Table 2.2 shows the district-wise as well sex-wise break up of urban population in Sikkim during the year 1991.

By 2001, the total population of Sikkim was 5,40,493 and the total urban population reached 60,005 of whom 32,831 were male and 27,174 were female. The urban population of

Table 2.2: District-wise Break up of the Total and Urban Population of Sikkim, 1991

Districts	*Total*	*Male*	*Female*	*Urban Total*	*Male*	*Female*
East	178,452	95,986	82,466	1,872	18,124	13,748
South	98,604	52,105	46,499	2,569	1,517	1,052
West	98,161	51,246	46,915	1,762	1,001	761
North	31,240	17,090	14,150	803	508	295
Total	4,06,457	2,16,427	1,90,030	7,006	21,150	15,856

Source: Census of India, 1991, Sikkim.

Sikkim accounts for only 11.1% of the total population of the state. The district-wise break up of urban population of Sikkim (2001) is given in Table 2.3.

Table 2.3: The Urban Population of Sikkim, 2001

District	*Persons*	*Male*	*Female*
East	52,986	28,893	24,094
South	3,946	2,144	1,802
West	1,824	1,026	798
North	1,248	768	480

Source: Sikkim Provisional Population Totals (Paper 1, 2 & 3) of 2001.

The disparity of urban population in the four districts is evident from Table 2.3. By all means, the urban population of the East district remained way above those of the other three districts of the state. While the urban population of the East district recorded an absolute increase of 21,114 persons 1991-2001, the West districts recorded an increase as small as 62 persons over the same period. Inter-district migration of urban population contributed to differential growth of urban population, especially in the West and South districts. Migration of people from Naya Bazar in the West District to the adjoining town of Jorethang in the South District caused negative growth in the former. In fact, Naya Bazar is facing problem to sustain on its own as a town. The situation is marginally better in the South and the North districts, The South and the North districts recorded increase of 1,377 and 481 persons respectively. The populations of Namchi, Gyalshing and Naya Bazar are yet to cross 1,000. It may be mentioned here that barring Gangtok, none of the towns in Sikkim satisfy the norms of census towns in terms of total population, density and workers' participation in non-agricultural activities. Primarily for the sake of administrative functions such Notified Town Areas (NTA) have been created. The district headquarters in the North, West and South districts are pre-determined; hence, are at a lower risk of haphazard growth. In terms of absolute numbers, the population of these towns may be abysmally low but in regard to conservation and planning, the slow rate of increase in urban population is welcome, especially in a state like Sikkim where the resource base is not strong enough to support a large population.

Table 2.4: Population of Towns, Sikkim, 2001

District	*Town*	*Male*		*Female*		*Total*	
		1991	*2001*	*1991*	*2001*	*1991*	*2001*
North	Mangan	508	768	295	480	803	1248
East	Gangtok	14,189	15,816	10,835	13,346	25,024	29,162
Upper Tadong*	–	–	–	–	–	–	14,670
	Singtam	2,259	3,049	1,609	2,382	3,868	5,431
	Rangpo	1,676	2,044	1,304	1,680	2,980	3,724
South	Namchi	389	573	241	405	630	978
	Jorethang	1,128	1571	811	1,397	1,939	2,968
West	Gyalshing	441	489	276	339	717	828
	Nayabazar	560	537	485	459	1,045	996

* Upper Tadong, the southern extension of Gangtok, has been added as a Census Town.

Source: Sikkim: A Statistical Profile, 2002. DESME, Gangtok. Census of Sikkim, 2001.

It is noteworthy that the number of towns in Sikkim remained more or less static in post-merger period, barring the case of Upper Tadong, a township grown as a southern offshoot of Gangtok, which has been designated as class IV Census Town. In 1971, the total number of towns was eight and after nearly thirty-five years, the number is nine. However, over the last three decades, a number of markets emerged all over Sikkim and many of them developed rurban characteristics. To name a few, Tadong, Ranipool, Pakyong, Rhenock, Rongli, Dikchu in the East district, Chungthang, Phensong, Phodong in the North District, Melli, Ravongla, Majhitar, Temi, and Kewzing in the South District, and Legship, Sombaria, Soreng, Pelling in the West District are steadily graduating to rurban areas. With the boom in tourism business in this Himalayan state, many villages in the interior are getting connected with the towns within and outside Sikkim. According to an estimate of the state tourism department, more than 1,00,000 people annually visit Sikkim. To accommodate this huge floating population, the housing and urban development sectors are already on fast track. The demand for hotels and resorts in the rural areas, courtesy village tourism and ecotourism, has made the rural folk conscious of modern infrastructure. Need of good housing, power supply, water supply, telephone, transport, etc are no longer priorities of urbanites only. Such privileges are in great demand in all four corners of Sikkim. The large seasonal influx of population that include tourists, tour operators and transport providers from outside have necessitated construction of not only hotels, lodges, restaurants, resorts but also roads, bridges, parks, water reservoirs and power plants. Thus, what the kings and merchants could not do in three hundred years, has been easily accomplished within three decades by the magic word called 'tourism'. In the years to come, Sikkim is likely to experience robust growth in tertiary sector and urban development, again thanks to tourism.

Concluding Remarks

The process of urbanisation in Sikkim has been facilitated by two operative forces–administrative and commercial (Dasgupta, 1992:23). The capital town Gangtok developed due to administrative forces. Namchi in South district developed as a nodal town due to its location at the junction of two major routes connecting neighbouring city of Darjeeling with state capital Gangtok, and Pemiongchi, the headquarters of a local religious order with Gangtok. The other force behind the emergence of small towns in the state is commercial activity. The state witnessed the emergence of 'bazaars' or market centres at nodal points. Two major market centres, namely Geyzing or Gyalshing in the West district and Mangan in the North district were made district headquarters in 1963 (Dasgupta, 1992:23). However, poor accessibility, difficult terrain and highly dispersed population did not allow them to grow at the required rate. Comparative isolation from external influences kept the size of population minimal (Mangan : 1248, Gyalshing : 828 in 2001); Yet, migration from outside Sikkim played an important role in the development of towns. In the first decade after merger with India (1971-1981), 64% of total population was migrants from other Indian states.

The service areas and sustainability of the towns in Sikkim depend largely on spatial location. The north-south alignment of the main roads has given rise to unidirectional pattern of commodity flow (Dasgupta, 1992:24). The towns located in low altitude valleys (Rangpo, Singtam, Jorethang and Naya Bazar) are sustainable due to their service area extending upwards along roads leading from south to north. The towns located on comparatively higher altitudes (Mangan, Gyalshing, Namchi and Gangtok) have their service areas downhill. Of late, a few places located in the north, such as Chungthang, have acquired urban characteristics and shown tendencies to extend the service areas uphill further north due to heavy flow of defence and tourist traffic.

There is one aspect common in all the towns of the state all these towns have strategic location in a land-locked territory. The small size of population in these towns has restricted haphazard growth, and, barring Gangtok, they still have scope of planned development. Gangtok is too well known now in India for its tourism-related functions, in addition to usual administrative, economic and cultural functions. The town started as a class VI town in 1951 with a measly population of 2,744. In 1971, the town was classed as a class IV town with a population of 13,308. It has been accorded class III status in 1981 and is yet to graduate to class II level. All other towns in the state are still at basic stages (IV to VI). Over the last three decades, Gangtok has grown in somewhat haphazard manner, but corrective measures have been taken to check unplanned growth during last decade. The town accommodates an additional 1,00,000 floating population every year due to its attraction as a tourist centre. The Urban Development and Housing Department has taken steps to make the town sustainable for a larger population by concentrating on urban sanitation, drainage, parking areas, vehicle free areas, shopping areas, amusement parks, etc. The local authorities have also planned for integrated development of small and medium towns.

One major problem of the mountain towns has always been of waste disposal. However, due to sloping terrain there is no dearth of streams in the mountains to carry waste materials far away from the towns. But clogging of drainage is still a problem. Besides, open streams carrying wastes can be an eyesore in a place of tourist attraction. After all, much of the state's revenue earnings come from tourism sector. To overcome the problem, the state authorities have acquired around 13 acres of land at a place called Marchak for dumping and segregation of biodegradable and non-biodegradable garbage. In an innovative manner, some of the streams used to drain wastes have been converted into underground sewers and the covered sewers are serving as thoroughfares. To make the towns of Sikkim sustainable, the state has already enacted the following Acts: (i) The Non-biodegradable Garbage Control Act, 1997 and its Rules, (ii) The Sikkim Urban Regional Planning and Development Act, 1998, and (iii) The Sikkim Building Construction Regulations, 1991 and its amendments. If these Acts are implemented in right earnest, the towns of Sikkim will not only be sustainable but also be exemplary.

Realising the value of Gangtok as a tourist centre, beautification programmes have been undertaken to make the capital more attractive for promotion of tourism. Ropeways and flyovers have been constructed to decongest the town. Stringent traffic regulations have been effected in the town, particularly regarding parking. Besides, zoning regulation has also been introduced so that the vehicles coming from a particular direction are not allowed to enter the main business area. To make the town more environment and tourist-friendly, the civic authorities have planned to keep some stretches of roads vehicle free for pedestrians and converted them into a mall. There is also a proposal to upgrade the drainage system along the National Highway passing through the urban area, and construct the drainage in such a way that it becomes part of the road itself to ease traffic.

Sikkim is generously endowed with places fit to develop tourist destinations into small towns. A number of leisure and adventure tourism destinations have emerged in last one decade or two, even at high altitudes. These destinations are nucleuses of future towns. In addition to leisure and adventure tourism, the state is an ideal place for regional, national and international conferences/seminars/symposiums, etc. The local authorities have already taken initiatives to develop Gangtok as a Convention Centre which will also help in promoting tourism and creating a cultural hub. Apart from scenic beauty and cool climate, one major reason for the popularity and sustainability of new destinations in Sikkim is the nature of its people. The mountain communities, generally speaking, are peace-loving and civic abuses, if any, are at a very low level. The resident communities have a distinctive lifestyle which help preserve the sanctity of places, particularly, landscapes. Thus, Sikkim has already discovered ways to sustain towns in spite of deficiencies in industrial development.

References

Government Reports

Census of India, 1981, Series 19, Sikkim. Directorate of Census Operations, Government of India.

Primary Census Abstract, Census of India, 1991, Sikkim. Directorate of Census Operations, Government of India.

Primary Census Abstract, Census of India, Sikkim, 2001. Directorate of Census Operations, Government of India.

Sikkim: A Statistical Profile, 2002, Directorate of Economics, Statistics, Monitoring and Evaluation, Government of Sikkim, Gangtok.

Books

Choudhury, Maitreyee, (2006). *Sikkim: Geographical Perspectives*, New Delhi, Mittal Publications.

Dasgupta, Manas, (1992). *Sikkim, Problems and Prospects of Development,* New Delhi, Indus Publishing House.

Singh, O.P. (1985). *Strategic Sikkim*, Delhi, B.R. Publishing.

3

The Democratic Challenge to Secularising Sikkim's 'Sacred' Landscape

According to a press release issued by the Information and Public Relations Department of the Government of Sikkim, democracy not only exists *but reigns supreme* in Sikkim. There "is total freedom of self-expression and the right to criticise the government both through the press and speech, equal opportunity to all the citizens in all walks of life without any discrimination on the basis of caste, creed, and faith, no ban on forming associations and holding of public meetings and rallies, including hunger-strike" (Now, 17 August 2007: 1-2).

Historically, democratic development and secularisation were perceived as complementary processes that would culminate in the participatory human development and evolution of the former Buddhist Kingdom of Sikkim into a state of secular democratic India. The Governor of Sikkim in his speech delivered on 5 March 2008 in the Sikkim Legislative Assembly lauded Sikkim to be a peaceful insurgency free state with no communal and religious tensions. On the contrary, 'ethnic' opposition to state-directed development projects such as the Rathongchu and Teesta hydropower projects during the last decade testifies to the historic failure of government policies to make Sikkim's polity secular and transform its 'sacred' landscape into a profitable natural resource. The ongoing Teesta hydropower protests explain the emergent urgency to issue repeated 'official' declarations of government of Sikkim's secular and democratic credentials. Rather than conferring legitimacy to government and development planning, hydroelectric projects have required to be legitimised by the modern state. Klingesmith's (2007: 252) assertion that a challenge to a dam can be a challenge to much more than just a dam, is quite relevant to the Sikkimese context where the legitimacy of governments has been undermined by public opposition to what they perceived as desecration of their sacred land (Arora 2009: 110). It is the credit to the people of Sikkim that their opposition has not taken a violent route unlike the Gorkhaland movement of the neighbouring Darjeeling Hills.

The inseparability of politics and religion in Sikkim's feudal theocratic heritage makes it not merely unique but integral to any debate on the peculiar nature of Indian secularism. Sikkim has experienced merely three decades of constitutional democracy and people's response to formal democracy and government directed at development makes it additionally interesting. Does the principle of secularism counter the rights of the indigenous minorities in Sikkim? Does contemporary Sikkim reflect the successful transformation of a feudal theocracy in a secular democratic polity? Are the ethnic fissures widening as identity politics and cultural rights over resources coalesce? The paper begins by discussing the meaning of 'Indian' secularism in theory and constitutional practice, and its extension and contested application with special reference to Article 371F of the Indian Constitution, which made Sikkim both democratic and secular and facilitated its 'controversial' incorporation into India. The second section focuses on Sikkim's representation as a sacred landscape in the Lepcha-Bhutia ethnic imaginary both in the past and into the present. The social movements by the indigenous Lepcha-Bhutia groups against hydropower development projects planned and implemented in Sikkim's 'sacred' landscapes clearly point towards the difficulties in rooting secularism and fostering an economics-oriented definition of the landscape. Development projects are increasingly becoming sites for the expression of ethnic conflict over the appropriation and distribution of resources, and these exchanges have deepened the divide between the 'indigenous' who mobilise themselves to protect their dignity, livelihood, and cultural heritage embodied in their sacred landscape, as opposed to the others who are migrants/outsiders/Indians, and treat the land merely as a resourceful commodity and source of profit.

Can 'Democratic' Sikkim become 'Secular'?

The words 'Socialist Secular' were inserted into the Indian Constitution (the 42nd Amendment) in 1976 on the recommendation of the Swaran Singh Committee (Jain 2000: 753). On 16 May 1975, the former Buddhist kingdom of Sikkim was incorporated as the 22nd state of India with the 36th Constitutional Amendment Act. These two dates 1975 and 1976 mark the turning points in the democratic political history of India and Sikkim. Secularism does not imply the negation of religious beliefs or an inculcation of religious scepticism among the Indian citizens. It implies state impartiality between all religion's and neutrality towards religion. It was construed in terms of religion being excluded from the political domain, and largely the private concern of individuals and social groups. Given the considerable ambiguity in defining secularism, I will briefly explain its usage within India. As a secular state, India does not have any state religion but neither it is opposed to religion altogether–it is neither irreligious not anti-religious. If there is any conflict of interest between religion and the public order, then it is argued that religion has to yield.

The Indian Constitution does not define secularism, and there is considerable ambiguity around its meaning and usage. As a fundamental principle of the Indian Constitution, secularism is reflected in Articles 25-26, 29-30, 44, 51-A and 14-16 prohibit the establishment of a theocratic state. Article 14 guarantees equality before law to every person. Article 15 prohibits discrimination *inter alia* on grounds of religion. Article 16 guarantees equality of opportunity in matters of public employment irrespective of the religion of a person. The Constitution of India also recognises the religious freedom of individuals and groups. The cultural and educational rights of religious minorities are enshrined as justiciable fundamental rights in the form of both individual rights as well as minority group rights. These rights enable the state to protect and preserve cultural pluralism. Not only does each individual have the freedom to profess, practice and propagate his religion

(Article 25), every religious group or denomination has the right to establish and maintain institutions for religious and charitable purposes, to manage its own affairs in matters of religion, to own and acquire movable and immovable property and to administer such property in accordance with law (Article 26). Further, any section of citizens of India that has a distinct language, script or culture has the right to conserve the same (Article 29.1). All minorities, whether based on religion or language, have the right to establish and administer educational institutions of their choice (Article 30.1).

Since the Indian Constitution does not reflect a single definition of secularism, hence, the Supreme Court's readings of it become critical. Cossman and Kapur's argue: "We see law neither as an instrument of liberation nor one of oppression; but rather as a complex and contradictory site…the courts can guard against any further legal erosion of the principles of toleration and the rights of the minorities" (1999: 94-96). Based on an in-depth analysis of Indian Supreme Court judgements on secularism, Padhy (2004) concluded, "Judicial pronouncements on secular issues have thus been marked by contradictions. While in cases it has promoted majority interests, by eroding the rights of minority groups, in others, it has privileged minority groups." The court's definition of secularism is actuated by practical necessities (Jain 2000: 757). The Supreme Court judgement of 1993 on Sikkim in this paper established that context takes centre-stage in judicial decision-making.

The failure to distinguish between the religious and the irreligious prompted sociologist Andre Beteille (1994: 559) to suggest that "we should, in the interest of intellectual clarity, stop using the term altogether".[1] In sharp contrast, other Indian scholars argue that secularism is 'a gift of Christianity', which should not be imposed upon Indian society (Madan 1987: 754, 1991, see also Nandy 1998). Ashis Nandy and T.N. Madan emphasise the need to define secularism in terms of an inter-religious understanding. They argue that the rigid separation of the church and the state originates in Protestant doctrine and western societies,[2] which cannot be prescribed for non-western societies such as India where the separation between political and religious spheres has been impossible. P. Chatterjee

(1994) argues for a reconfiguration of the 'problem of secularism' to one of toleration and recognition of minority rights while Rajeev Bhargava (1998) emphasises the need of 'contextual secularism', which does not require strict non-interference or equi-distance, but rather a policy of principled distance. Still other scholars stress the need to replace the vacuous concept of secularism with an alternative theory of cultural pluralism (de Roover 2002). Whatever may be the argument, a divorce between religion and politics is impossible in the Indian situation. As Hansen emphasises, "Communal consciousness and stereotypes are ... integrated parts of the social and political imaginary in many parts of India" (1999: 215). Historically, this has been the case with Sikkim.

Special provisions were inserted into the Indian Constitution under Article 371F to meet the special needs and circumstances of Sikkim in 1975 when it became a democratic state of India. Differences based on religion, ethnicity and migration histories, caste, gender, and class deeply fission and stratify Sikkim's population. Demographically, the Buddhists comprise a large minority of 27 per cent in Sikkim while 68 per cent of its total population are Hindus, and 3 per cent are 'converted' Christians with some Muslims who settled recently (Census 2001). The majority of the Hindus of Sikkim have ethnic-national origins in neighbouring Nepal and considered to be migrants by the indigenous Lepchas-Bhutias (20.6 per cent) who define themselves as the Sikkimese.

Ethnically, Sikkim's population is categorised into three groups–the Lepchas, the Bhutias and the Nepalis. There are cultural, religious, and linguistic differences between the Lepcha-Bhutia and the Nepalis that provide the objective basis for the persistent ethnic boundaries between them. These broad categorisations underplay the competing definitions, the internal variations, and the intersections between the diverse ethnic groups in Sikkim. Barth (1969: 9-38) emphasises that it is the boundaries between these groups that transform them into ethnic groups. The main ethnic boundary is between the Lepchas and the Bhutias who are united in their opposition towards ethnic groups categorised as Nepali, and termed as migrants by them. Ethnic relations are neither harmonious nor have ethnic tensions escalated into any secessionist demands or led to an insurgency. Identity politics and conflict over resource-entitlements establish the contours of faultlines in this Himalayan borderland (Arora 2004, 2005).

Formal democracy and elections were introduced in Sikkim in the 1950s but confined only to *bona fide* Sikkimese citizens, and guided by a policy of preferential treatment for indigenous Lepchas and Bhutias.[3] Sikkim can be described as a young democratic society balancing the claims and the aspirations of the diverse social groups residing in it.[4] Historically, authority was traditionally vested with the ruling family, the nobility, the lamas, and the shamans in Sikkim. Full-fledged modern democracy with adult suffrage was introduced after Sikkim's incorporation into India in 1975. Nonetheless, the moral basis of temporal authority was never completely decimated. The Buddhist sangha elect a representative in the Legislative Assembly. The Ecclesiastical Department of the Government of Sikkim is responsible for the administration of the Buddhist monasteries and preserving Sikkim's cultural heritage (as enshrined in article 371F of the Indian Constitution). Sacred landscapes such as Pemagayantse, Tashiding, and Tholung monasteries have functioned as arenas legitimising political authority in the former Buddhist kingdom and continue to do so in the present. In 1978, the Lepchas and the Bhutias were recognised as Scheduled Tribes and 12 seats are reserved in the legislative assembly to safeguard their political interests and quotas in government employment and educational institutions. These safeguards were justified in order to protect the interests of the Lepchas and the Bhutias who were rendered a political minority with the incorporation of Sikkim into India. However, the Nepali are numerically and politically the dominant ethnic category in contemporary Sikkim.

The competition over resource entitlements is intense, which is aggravating ethnic tensions in Sikkim. Some Nepali politicians challenged these provisions and the matter was hotly debated for more than a decade in the Supreme Court until 1993. Even in 1984, Justice Bhagwati stated that under Article 371F(f), reservation of seats for the Bhutias-Lepchas and the sangha in the Sikkim assembly were justified (cf. Kazi 1993: 128-131).[5] Therefore, the matter was kept pending until the Supreme Court (3:2 by a 5 member bench) made a landmark judgement on 10 February 1993 upholding reservation of the Bhutia-Lepcha seats and one seat for the sangha in the legislative assembly. Justice Venkatachaliah argued that "historical considerations justified a differential treatment" (cf. Kazi 1993: 337). The Supreme Court judgement explicitly acknowledged that these provisions were necessitated since a nation was being incorporated into a state.

It is true that the reservation of seats of the kind and the extent brought about by the impugned versions may not, if applied to the existing states of the Union, pass the Constitutional muster. *But in relation to a new territory admitted to a Union, the terms and conditions are not such as to fall outside the permissible constitutional limits.* Historical considerations and compulsions do justify inequality and special treatment. We are of the view that the impunged provisions have been found in the wisdom of Parliament (that were) necessary in the admission of (a) strategic border state into the Union. The departures are not such as to negate the principles of democracy (cf. Kazi 1993: 338, emphasis added).

These special provisions were intended to overcome disruptions by ensuring a smoother integration of Sikkim into India while continuities with its theocratic heritage were maintained. Nonetheless, the Supreme Court judgement of 1993 emphasised the transitional character of these provisions:

The provisions of clause (f) of Article 371F(f), and the consequent changes in the electoral laws were intended to recognise and accommodate the pace of the growth of the political institutions of Sikkim, to make the transition gradual and peaceful, and to prevent the dominance of one section of the population over another on the basis of ethnic loyalties and identities. These adjustments reflect the political expediencies for the maintenance of social equilibrium. The political and social maturity and of economic development might in course of time enable the people of Sikkim to transcend and submerge these ethnic apprehensions and imbalances and might in future – one hopes sooner – usher in a more egalitarian dispensation (cf. Kazi 1993: 337-38).

Sikkim is the only state of secular democratic India (excepting Maharashtra with its 1%. Buddhist population) that acknowledges the minority rights of the Buddhists. Admittedly, democratic governance and universal adult suffrage since 1975 has undermined the influence of the lamas and monasteries and other religious functionaries including the shamans, nevertheless not completely displaced their political influence (Arora 2006a). We cannot ignore the historic fact concerning Sikkim that Buddhism was neither merely a matter of religious practice nor separate from its politics and self-presentation. The political representation of the Buddhist monasteries in the sangha seat implies not merely protection of minority rights but entitlements that are unparalleled within India. Even the Supreme Court judgement of 1993 acknowledged the sangha to be historically a political and social institution and not merely a religious institution (cf. Kazi 1993: 341). The religious divide and the ethnic boundaries between indigenous and migrants were supported by Sikkim's theocratic polity until 1975, and have long historical trajectory in social practices and in law, hence making it quite difficult to displace them in contemporary Sikkim which professes to be secular and democratic.

Struggles against Hydropower Projects to Preserve Sikkim's Sacred Landscape

Anthropologists argue that we sense the place through our own body that this is how we are placed in the world: "The landscape is a contextual horizon of perceptions, providing both a foreground and a background in which people feel themselves to be living in their world" (Stewart and Strathern 2003:4). The landscape is not a physical backdrop but reflects and is part of a socio-cultural process (Hirsch and O'Hanlon 1195: 5-23). In contemporary Sikkim, 'sacred' landscapes reflect and materially represent the politicisation of culture and ethnic identity, indicate the processes of conflict and integration between groups, and constitute the locus of ethnic-competition over resource-use in the context of state-directed development (Arora 2006).

Sikkim being a sacred landscape can be traced to Lepcha-Bhutia cosmologies and their ethnic history, the historical myths about the founding of the Buddhist Kingdom of Sikkim, sacred Buddhist texts, and the Rathongchu project movement of the 1990 (Arora 2006a, 2006b). Broadly, the term 'sacred landscape' includes a range of sites and landscape formations such as peaks and mountains, waterfalls, rivers, valleys, big rocks, caves, trees and forests, which are either historically and culturally significant for the indigenous Lepchas-Bhutias of Sikkim or are religiously consecrated Buddhist sites including Buddhist monasteries, stupas, and sites associated with famous shamanic and Buddhist saints (Arora 2006c). During a fieldwork, many Sikkimese Buddhists (both Lepchas and Bhutias) remarked, "Being Sikkimese is indissolubly linked to the worship of Mt. Kanchenjunga, and the Nepali groups neither worship nor regard it to be a sacred mountain (Arora 2004)." According to the Lepchas and Bhutias, the landscapes embodies their culture and knowledge. The Lepcha and Bhutia alliance is expressed in their common worship of Mt. Kanchenjunga representing their sacred knowledge, and regarded the source of all food, medicine, fecundity, wealth, knowledge, and divine protection. The ethnic alliance of the Lepchas and the Bhutias is traced to the blood-brotherhood treaty of 1366 enacted at Kabi village by keeping Mt. Kanchenjunga as the witnessing deity. Sikkim's Tibetan Buddhism regards Mt. Kanchenjunga (its Tibetan name is *Gangs chen mdzod lnga*) to be the guardian deity of *'Bras mo ljongs'* (Tib.: Sikkim). The name literally means the five repositories or ledges of snow, and it is physically descriptive of its five great peaks. According to the pilgrimage guide to Sikkim (*gnas yig* in Tib.), Padmasambhava made this mountain deity into guardian of Sikkim's treasures and wealth in the 8th century. The sacred text *gnas bsol* is the ritual manual for the worship of Mt. Kanchenjunga and the other protective deities of Sikkim. Regular offerings to propitiate these protective deities are an integral part of the cultural calendar of the Lepcha and the Bhutia groups. Mt. Kanchenjunga is the owner of the land, the people, and the guardian of Sikkim's hidden spiritual treasures (Tib.: *gter*).

Sikkim enjoys a special status as a place of Buddhist pilgrimage, a land blessed by the great Buddhist saint Padmasambhava,[6] and significantly with the Rumtek monastery being the seat of the Karmapa[7] who will be the spiritual heir to His Holiness the 14th Dalai Lama Tenzin Gyatso. These religious perceptions of Sikkim exist and persist not only in the oral tradition or as revelations, but are inscribed in sacred scriptures such as the pilgrimage guide to Sikkim and advanced by texts such as the 'History of Sikkim'.[8] The pilgrimage guide to Sikkim is regarded a sacred text that was composed by Padmasambhava and passed to his disciples in order to guide his followers regarding the route to enter the hidden valley of Sikkim, describe the location of the various treasures he had hidden in the land, and instructions about propitiating the protective deities and secure their blessings. The 'History of Sikkim' contains rich descriptions of places of historical importance, the monasteries and sacred sites of Sikkim that are associated with eminent shamans and Buddhist saints and the role of the Namgyal dynasty in maintaining the sanctity of the kingdom. That Sikkim is a Holy Buddhist land is indisputable and beyond any debate.

The representatives and ideologues of the Lepchas and Bhutias assert that need and support Sikkim's economic development, but it should not undermine their cultural heritage and privileges as the indigenous groups of Sikkim. The extract given below is cited from the memorandum that the Buddhist monastic order submitted to the Chief Minister of Sikkim (dated 29 July, 1995).

> *"We, the monks of Sikkim, hereby demand that the Rathongchu hydroelectric project located at Yoksum be stopped immediately. We oppose the project because it will have severe negative consequences for the most sacred area of Sikkim...The gnas bsol text is to the Sikkimese Buddhists what the Ramayana is to the Hindus, the Koran to the Muslims, and the Bible to the Christians. If the Rathongchu Hydroelectric project is not stopped and abandoned, we, the lamas of Sikkim are ready to burn our gnas bsol texts as its meaning and purpose will be lost..."*

This memorandum provides an evocative image of lamas, who are forced to rise up in protest and threaten to burn their sacred texts on the perceived defilement of their sacred landscape. This image significantly influenced the public perception of the Rathongchu hydel project, articulated public protest, and organised dissent with the state government. The idea of a defiled sacred landscape was the chief argument used by the Lepchas, Bhutias and Buddhist activists protesting against the implementation of Rathongchu hydroelectric project in West Sikkim during 1993-97. The project was implemented in Yoksum area of West Sikkim, which was identified as being a biodiversity hotspot by the WWF in 1992-93. Nevertheless this project was given environmental clearance by the Ministry of Environment and Forests in 1992 while specifying some conditions under the Forest Conservation Act of 1980 and Sikkim's Forests, Water Courses and Road Reserve (Preservation and Protection) Act 1988. The project was widely accepted as being ecologically viable since it did not entail any large-scale displacement of people or any submergence of land. The activists argued that the project infringed their indigenous rights in land and violated Article 371F of the Indian Constitution under which the kingdom of Sikkim was incorporated into Indian Union in 1975.

The battles between the Lepcha-Bhutia activists and the state over the implementation of the Rathongchu project divided Sikkimese society and spilled initially into the High Court of Sikkim, and then the Supreme Court of India where they were concluded in November 2002.[9] In sharp contrast to the Supreme Court judgement of 1993, the High Court judgement of 1995 on the Rathongchu project gave a different perspective of minority rights. The High Court judgement of 1995 argued:

> "*...no doubt the region is of value to the Sikkimese of Buddhist faith of this area. No doubt that the area is covered with religious monuments and their ruins. No doubt that the observance of religious faith will be affected. But on the overall it is a viable project. Tolerance for the benefit of all expected should culminate in maximum benefit to the maximum people...* (M. Sengupta and Bhargava 1995: 21)."

The High Court of Sikkim dismissed the petition filed by the activists who approached the Supreme Court of India where the case was fought on their behalf by the eminent lawyer, Rajeev Dhawan. The Supreme Court was hearing this case when the political decision to close the project was taken in 1997, and the matter was accordingly closed on 15th November 2002.

The Chief Minister of Sikkim, Pawan Kumar Chamling, was forced to shelve this ecologically viable and economically profitable project in August 1997 in order to avert an ethnic imbroglio within Sikkim. The main reasons cited by the Sikkim government for the closure of the project were escalating ethnic tensions, preserving Yoksum as a sacred landscape and respecting the religious sentiments of the Buddhists, checking environmental destruction caused in the area by frequent landslides, the escalating costs of construction, and gaining favourable public opinion before the general elections scheduled for Sikkim in 1998.

The rising number of controversies around sacred sites impressed the government on the need to document all religious sites and shrines of Sikkim. It was believed that such a listing would enable them to maintain the *status quo* and prevent any religious conversions in the future (Arora 2006a). Hence, the Home Department of the Government of Sikkim issued a notification in November 1998 "prohibiting the conversion of sites, the defilement of sacred lakes and the scaling of sacred peaks such as of Mt. Kanchenjunga" (No. 59/Home/98 published in the Sikkim Gazette). The notification conforms to the legislation issued by the national government on 'Places of Worship (Special Provisions) Act, 1991' that prohibits the conversion of any place of worship and instructs the administration to maintain the *status quo*. Hence, the State government declared: "No conversion or alteration or new construction or any developmental activity shall be undertaken at the site or in the close vicinity of any place of worship or religious institution or sacred lakes or of sacred peaks." A comprehensive list of sacred peaks, sacred caves, sacred rocks, sacred lakes, stupas, and hot springs was included in this notification. The Ecclesiastical Department was given the responsibility of identifying and preparing a comprehensive report, which appeared in 2001 while I was undertaking fieldwork in Sikkim (see Committee 2000). For preparing the report, the researchers used both *gnas yig* and the *History of Sikkim*.[10] The report also certifies their status as historically significant sites that have existed in Sikkim for the last hundred years. Yet, current government policies disregard these completely.

Clearly, development planning and the government have already forgotten the lessons that they should have been imbibed from the Rathongchu controversies. Currently, the Sikkim government has pinned high hopes on cascade development of the River Teesta in six-stages through 26 hydropower projects to generate an estimated capacity of 3635 mW. Various private developers of national and international (dis)repute are involved in implementing these. The Teesta cascade projects are advertised as environmentally benign and largely run-of-the-river projects located in low-density population areas and therefore would not displace people at a large scale. The larger of these projects do entail construction of large dams and diversion of the river waters through longhead race or underground tunnels (HRTs) where they pass through a powerhouse before being dropped back into the river at a downstream location. Teesta III in Chungthang envisages the construction of a 60 m high concrete dam and a reservoir of gross capacity of 5.08 m^3, and Panang in Dzongu involves the construction of a 56 m high concrete gravity dam. Teesta V stage under NHPC has already constructed a 95 m high reservoir and 17 km long underground tunnel.

However, many of these projects are located in areas of historical, religious, and cultural significance, and thus, being resisted. Dzongu in North Sikkim enjoys the status of being an exclusive Lepcha reserve and contains a number of important sacred sites such as caves where Guru Rinpoche meditated, the Keshong lake, the Kongsa hot springs, the Tholung temple revered not merely by the Lepchas but by all Buddhists of Sikkim. The Panan Hydel project harnesses the waters of the Tholung River. The sanctity of this area is well documented in historical and religious texts including the pilgrimage guide to Sikkim and anthropological literature (Arora 2006c). The activists have argued that these projects violate the safeguards enshrined in Article 371F of the Indian Constitution. The projects violate their minority rights and their protective entitlements as the indigenous people.

On 20th June 2007, three Lepcha youth affiliated to the Affected Citizens of the Teesta (ACT) and the Concerned Lepchas of Sikkim (CLOS) with the support of the Sangha of Dzongu began an indefinite relay hunger strike on 20 June

2007 at Bhutia-Lepcha house in Gangtok to pressurise the government into revoking the power projects on Teesta river in Sikkim and North Bengal. River Teesta is assigned religious significance in Lepcha folklore and cannot be regarded merely as an environmental and economic resource by them. The activists protest narrative draws heavily on their folklore and mythology to establish their position as protectors of sacred sites and environmentalists. They have argued that their sacred river is weeping at being raped in the name of development. Vociferously protesting the desecration and alienation of their ancestral roots, the activists beseeched, "(I)n the name of development, do not make us refugees in our own homeland." One of their banner declared, "They are all set to Dam(n) you!" These activist concerns are not new, and were raised as far back as 2001.

More recently, with the formation of an organisation front in 2005, these protesting activists who are largely Lepchas and Buddhists have filed legal petitions in the National Appellate Authority at Delhi to question the grant of necessary environmental clearances. They have repeatedly sent delegations to convince the state government to commission a review of the ecological impact of these projects, generated debate during hearings and public-meetings, and demanded a better relief and compensation package for the affected and displaced families.

The emergence of protests against Teesta III and Teesta Low Dam projects located in North Bengal with an ethnically diverse population, Teesta II project in Lachen and Lachung in North Sikkim that are inhabited mainly by Sikkimese Bhutias does substantiate the activists' claims that they are generally concerned about Sikkim and not merely Lepchas (Arora 2009). On its part, the state government maintained that only a politically influenced minority of the Lepchas were opposing these projects and hence they declared these activists to be both anti-national and anti-Sikkimese. This is precisely how the Chief Minister, Pawan Kumar Chamling framed the Affected Citizen's of the Teesta and their leaders during his public speech on the occasion of the Indian Independence day celebrations on 15th August 2007 at Gangtok. This rationalises the need of their recent August 2007 declaration.

Both pro- and anti-hydropower project constituencies have divided Sikkim. Development gains and possibilities of employment have prompted some villagers to sell their land and visibly maintain pro-project positions. Lepcha legislators including Sonam Gyatso Lepcha (the MLA of Dzongu) assert that the development prospects offered by Hydel projects are being welcomed by the Lepchas of Dzongu wherein the majority of the residents have accepted them. Pressurised by these activists the government constituted a review committee in September 2007 but its composition was totally unacceptable to the protesting activists.

Determined to agitate against the arbitrariness of the government, these activists have sent numerous delegations to Delhi to appraise ministers in the central government. A thirty-member delegation successfully staged a *dharna* on 5-6 December 2007 at Jantar Mantar in Delhi in collaboration with other human rights activists. The visit of the Review Committee to Dzongu on 5 February 2008 was greeted by peaceful show of protest and banners opposing the projects. On 10 March 2008, about three hundred Lepchas of Dzongu staged a rally at Gangtok carrying placards and banners demanding the closure of all Hydel projects in North Sikkim. Dawa Lepcha and Tenzing Lepcha commenced a second round of an indefinite fast on 10 March 2008. On 14 April 2008 nearly 500 Lepchas living in Kalimpong and Darjeeling marched from Triveni in North Bengal to Sikkim to show support and express their solidarity with the protesting Lepchas and offer prayers in Dzongu. They were on a pilgrimage to their holy land, Dzongu and had obtained formal permission from the Sikkim government to undertake this *padyatra*. Their banners declared, "Dams in Dzongu shall be built over our dead bodies". However, these Lepcha pilgrims were not allowed to enter Gangtok where the government imposed Section 144, which prohibits the assembling of more than three people in order to maintain law and order. At Dikchu, these anti-dam protestors clashed with pro-dam supporters and aborted their pilgrimage to Dzongu. The government declared that, "these groups have now attempted to create fear and alarm amongst different sections of the people on grounds of religion, race and caste for their narrow self interest." It goes to the credit of the anti-dam activists and their leaders who have decided against a confrontationist strategy. In April 2008, *Narmada Bachao Andolan* (NBA) activist Medha Patkar also went to Gangtok to extend a warm support to these struggling Lepchas after their pilgrimage to Dzongu, the affected sacred land was abandoned.

If democracy was merely about the show of strength and numbers, then these struggling environmentalists and Lepchas would never be able to win or successfully pressurise the government. Nevertheless, democracy is centrally concerned with engendering debate and conferring legitimacy on governance; undoubtedly these agitations are undermining the moral basis of the political order and become central to circulating discourse of Sikkim's democratisation and participatory governance. The 'Save Teesta, Save Sikkim' banners along with the faded prayer flags flapping in the wind, and the khada-garlanded Gandhiji's inspiring picture stand mute witness to the prolonged nature of these protests. The footpath leading to Bhutia-Lepcha (B-L) house on Gangtok's Tibet road which is the public site of ongoing hunger-protests stands transformed into an altar-shrine of non-violent resistance. Slogan bearing banners hanging outside B-L house intermingle with Buddhist prayer-flags to declare the moral basis of their resistance to everyone.

On 12 June 2008, just a few days short of the first anniversary of the indefinite relay hunger strike initiated by Lepcha activists on 20 June 2007, the Sikkim government announced the shelving of 90mw Ringpi, 33 mW Rukel, 120 mW Lingza and the 141 mW Rangyong projects located in Dzongu in North Sikkim. Dawa and Tenzing finally broke their indefinite Satyagraha on 13 June 2008 after being hungry for 96 days. At the height of their protest hunger-strike, they had declared that they were ready to sacrifice their life for this 'holy' cause. Amidst all arguments for and against the hydropower project over River Teesta, debates in corridors of the state government and in corporate boardrooms, Dawa and Tenzing have been transformed into true Gandhians (see Arora 2007). With the support of others who valiantly pray and organise opposition, Dawa and Tenzing have emerged as youth leaders demanding the rooting of morality, consensual politics, people-centred development, and a strong democratic ethos within Sikkim. There are other unsung heroes and Buddhist lamas who are participating not merely in these relay hunger strikes at Gangtok but also in neighbouring Kalimpong and Darjeeling.

Inspired by the Rathongchu agitations and swift government response, the Teesta activists had not expected to engage in a protracted battle with the government of Sikkim, nor did they mobilise sufficient financial and human resources to support their movement. This was clear to me repeatedly during my fieldwork in 2007 and 2008. Leaders such as Dawa Lepcha and Tseten Lepcha often admitted to me that they had only expected their protests to go on for a couple of weeks at the most! Ironically, now these Teesta protests have become the longest in Sikkim's political history and quite inspirational for other ethnic groups and environmentalists. During numerous interviews, Tseten Lepcha and Dawa have remarked how these protests became a learning context enabling many of the Lepchas and other Sikkimese to remember what they had forgotten in their hunger for modernisation and development, namely the value of their home-land, the sanctity of their sacred-land, and a renewed respect for their cultural heritage and existence of indigenous knowledge (Arora Forthcoming).

Supported by other Indian civil society organisations and people's movements resisting arbitrary imposition of development projects in India, these agitations reflect the strengthening and deep-rooting of democracy in Sikkim and in India. In July 2008, citing technical and administrative reasons the government of Sikkim announced the scrapping of another three projects and the activists welcomed this decision. The battles over controlling and taming the Teesta River are ongoing and frame its ecological nationalist discourse. These political performatives will shape the identity politics and the development discourse of Sikkim.

Conclusion

The Sikkim Human Development Report published in 2001 declared Sikkim to be close to being a 'model' state in terms of development interventions, social harmony and political stability despite its political institutions being very young and inexperienced (Lama 2001: 90-91). More recently in his message introducing the Sikkim Development Report published by the Planning Commission in 2008, the Chief Minister of Sikkim declared that "peace and tranquillity in the state has been a catalyst resulting in development..." The state government controls the political economy of Sikkim as a major employer and distributor of subsidies and development funds. This is a partial explanation of why law and order has rarely been disrupted and escalated into violence even when motivations have been strong. My discussion above outlined how political processes ranging from elections to political representation, the voicing of dissent, and the organisation of resistance have facilitated and enhanced the normative desirability of democracy, while simultaneously challenging state-directed development in Sikkim. The absence of ethnic conflict and armed insurgencies is credible given Sikkim's proximity to Nepal which has witnesses a tumultuous decade of blood-shed and violence with the Maoist people's war *jan andolan*, ethnic insurgency in neighbouring Darjeeling Hills where the Nepali are demanding a separate homeland, and the Lhotsampa crises in neighbouring Bhutan. If the indigenous people have not taken opted for disruptive means, then the credit goes largely to the ideologues of these protest movements, and other ethnic organisations and civil society organisations with whom they network and partner. The leaders of both Rathongchu and Teesta hydropower protests not only adopted and believed, but consistently followed a democratic route of expressing dissent with the state government and constantly appealed for redress from the central government.

Constitutional democracy is merely only three decades old, but Sikkim has been lucky to beget a legacy of cultural pluralism. The 'peace' pervading in Sikkim should neither taken for granted nor should people's dissent representing warning signs be ignored for a prolonged period. This journey is appreciable despite the tumultuous interpellation of secularism and democracy in the contemporary context. Sikkim has not become progressively secularised and ethnic-religious divisions have not lessened but *are* becoming sharper and additionally acquiring an environmental idiom (Arora 2007). Secularism flowing into Sikkim under Article 371F has affirmed ethnic minority rights while preferential reservation in seats in Sikkim's Legislative Assembly to the Buddhist *sangha* and the indigenous Lepchas and Bhutias has ensured they have an 'official' voice in decision-making and internal administration (Arora 2006a). However, this formal public voice is not representative or authoritatively unambiguous. We beget divergent voices and there is evidence of intensive contestation within the indigenous communities and others residing in Sikkim and with other Indians over the meaning and process of democratic development and secularism. The Lepcha and Bhutias and other indigenous activists that oppose hydropower projects in Sikkim constantly iterate that they are not against micro hydro-projects and development *per se*, but that they oppose development projects that would vanquish their unique culture and destroy their sacred sites. Religious myths have become raw materials for protest narratives and ammunition for waging battles against state-sponsored mega-development (Arora 2009). Hence, the spread of democracy under an elected 'popular' government has not displaced the idea of the ethnically sacred land, but ironically facilitated emergence of peaceful opposition to development projects on socio-cultural and environmental grounds. The combination of Gandhian *satyagraha* and Buddhist values as part of social protest narrative has undeniably rooted democratic values within Sikkim, albeit not secularised its political discourse.

To end this paper, the rise of social movements opposing hydropower projects in the last decade point towards, on the one hand the strengthening of democratic consciousness and availability of opportunities to voice resistance and on the other hand contour the weaknesses in state-directed development planning and other formal institutions that are unable to promote participatory development in Sikkim.

Acknowledgements

This paper is dedicated to the people of Sikkim engaged in democratic struggle. It is a much revised version of my presentations at two international conferences namely the 20th European Conferences of South Asian Studies organised by the University of Manchester in July 2008 and Rethinking Religion in India-II organised by Ghent University, Kuvempu University, and Karnataka Academy for Social Sciences and Humanities at Delhi in January 2009. I thank the participants of both these conferences for comments and suggestions.

Notes

1. de Roover (2002) raises an important question: "How to explain the persistence of the idea of secularism, while this idea is not intelligible in the first place?"
2. "We have come to equate secularity, the disengagement and differentiation of the public sphere from religion, with modernity. In fact, the emergence and form of the western secular nation-state have everything do with Christianity, and Protestantism in particular" (Friedland 1999: 315).
3. Discriminatory treatment towards the Nepali groups brewed acute discontent and contributed to political instability in Sikkim during the 1970s, thereby justifying Indian government's intervention to stabilise the region after Tibet was annexed by China.
4. Democracy comprises more than an institutional context for decision-making by a majority but emerges as a site of tug between competing forces and ethnic groups to ultimately facilitate accommodation, opposition, and reconciliation of demands and interests.
5. In 1984, the judged concurred that that the matter was not for the courts to decide as it was of a political nature and they were wary of an Assam like situation developing in Sikkim. So the issue was kept pending until 1993.
6. Padmasambhava (8th century) is credited with spreading Buddhism in Tibet.
7. It is associated with the Karma Kargyu school of Mahayana Buddhism that was founded in the 12th century by Dagpo Lharje Gampopa based on the teachings of Naropa and Milarepa. There is much controversy around the Karmapa legacy. H.H. the Dalai Lama recognises the Karmapa claimant H.H. XVII Gyalwa Karmapa Orgyen Drodul Trinley Dorje. However, the government of India is not permitting him to enter Sikkim.
8. *Brasmo ljongs gnas yig* or the guidebook to the sacred places by Lhatsun Jigmed Pawo (1682-1717) is the most commonly referred version and is available as a block print text at the Namgyal Institute of Tibetology, Gangtok, Sikkim.
9. For detailed analysis of the Rathongchu movement refer to Arora (2004, 2006b).

10. Sonam Gyatso and N. Dorjee of the Ecclesiastical Department, Government of Sikkim during an interview in April 2002 in Gangtok.
11. Paper presented at the International Expert Meeting 'Conserving Agricultural Heritage System in Mountainous Landscape' organised by United Nations University, Sikkim University and Kyoto University, 4-6 November 2007, Gangtok, Sikkim, India.
12. Mention should, however, be made here that the Himalayan environment supports and affects a much larger geographical area, covering India, Pakistan, Afghanistan, Nepal, Bhutan, Bangladesh and Burma, than its actual geographical stretch.
13. The term Nepali does not connote social group in the technical sense but a nationality of Nepal. It is also that all the Nepali language speakers residing in different parts of the world are called Nepali. There are, however, several social groups within the larger Nepali community.
14. Sandeep Tambe, D.K. Pradhan, Nakul Rai, Sangam Rai, Sonam Rinchen Lepcha, Karma Gurmey Bhutia, Abhina Thapa.
15. This exercise was primarily a part of Monitoring and Evaluation Training imparted by the Council for Social Development, New Delhi to the Officers of the Government of Sikkim. It was a field exposure to the trainees to supplement classroom lectures on Monitoring and Evaluation delivered by relevant experts.
16. Such irrigation system is called *Kuhl* in Himachal, *Gul* in Uttaranchal and *Kulo* in Darjeeling-Sikkim. Further, in regions like Uttaranchal and Himachal Pradesh it also provides water for small water mills.

References

Arora, V. (2004). Just a Pile of Stones!: The Politicisation of Identity, Indigenous Knowledge, and Sacred Landscapes among the Lepcha and the Bhutia tribes of contemporary Sikkim, India. Unpublished D.Phil Thesis, University of Oxford.

—. (2005). Being Nepali in Sikkim, *Contemporary India*, Vol. 4. No. 1-2, Jan-June 2005.

—. (2006a). Text and Context in Sikkim, India in *Reading Religion in Texts and Context: Reflections of Faith and Practice in Religious Materials* edited by Elisabeth Arweck and Peter J. Collins. Aldershot: Ashgate.

—. (2006b). The Roots and the Route of Secularism in Sikkim, *Economic and Political Weekly*, 23rd September 2006, Vol. 41, No. 38.

—. (2006c). The Forest of Symbols Embodied in the Tholung Sacred Landscape of North Sikkim, India. *Conservation and Society*, Volume 4, No. 1.

—. (2007). Assertive Identities, Indigeneity and the Politics of Recognition as a Tribe: The Bhutias, the Lepchas and the Limbus of Sikkim, *Sociological Bulletin*, May-August, Vol. 56, No. 2.

—. (2008). Gandhigiri in Sikkim, *Economic and Political Weekly*, 20th September 2008, Vol. 43, No. 38.

—. (2009). 'They are all set to dam(n) our future': Contested Development through Hydel Power in Democratic Sikkim, *Sociological Bulletin*, Jan-April, Vol. 58, No. 1.

—. In Press. Walking the 'Shangri-la' Sikkim Trail in *Globalisation, Marginalisation, and the Marginalised: The Emerging Context* edited by Debal K. Singha Roy, Manohar, Delhi.

Barth, F. Editor. (1969). *Ethnic Groups and Boundaries: The social organisation of cultural difference*. Oslo: Scandinavian University Press.

Beteille, A. (1994). Secularism and Intellectuals. *The Economic and Political Weekly*, Vol. 29, March 5.

Bhargava, R. (1998). *Secularism and its Critics*. Delhi, India: Oxford University Press.

Chatterjee, P. (1994). Secularism and Toleration. *The Economic and the Political Weekly*, Vol. 29, July 9.

Cossman, B and Kapur, R. (1999). Secularisms' last sigh? Hindutva and the (mis)rule of Law. Delhi, India: Oxford University Press.

de Roover, D. (2002). The Vacuity of Secularism: On the Indian debate and its social origins. *The Economic and Political Weekly*.

Hansen, T.B. (1999). *The Saffron Wave: Democracy and Hindu Nationalism in Modern India*. Princeton: Princeton University Press.

Hirsch, E., and M. O'Hanlon. Editors. 1995. *The Anthropology of Landscape: Perspectives and Places.* Oxford: Clarendon Press.

Friedland, R. 1999. When God Walks in History. *The Institutional Politics of Religious Nationalism in International Sociology*, Vol. 14.

Jain, S. K. 2000. *The Constitution of India: A Commemorative Edition of 50 years of the Indian Constitution*. Delhi: Taxmann Publishers.

Kazi, J. N. (1993). *Inside Sikkim, against the tide*. Gangtok, Sikkim: Hill Media Publications.

Klingesmith, D. (2007). *One Valley and a Thousand: Dams, Nation, and Development*. Delhi: Oxford University Press.

Lama, M.P. (2001). *Sikkim Human Development Report*. Delhi: Social Science Press.

Madan, T. N. (1991). "Secularism in its place," in *Religion in India*. Edited by T. N. Madan. Delhi: Oxford University Press.

—. (1997). *Modern Myths and Locked minds*. Delhi: Oxford University Press.

Nandy, A. (1998). "The Politics of Secularism and the Recovery of Religious Tolerance," in *Secularism and Its Critics*. Edited by R. Bhargava. Delhi: Oxford University Press.

Padhy, S. (2004). Secularism and Justice: A Review of Indian Supreme Court Judgments. *The Economic and Political Weekly*.

Planning Commission, (2008). Sikkim Development Report. Planning Commission, Government of India and Academic Press, Delhi.

Stewart, P. J., and A. Strathern. Editors. (2003). *Landscape, Memory and History*. London: Pluto Press.

4

State Policies and Tribal Communities of Sikkim: An Ethnic Perspective

Introduction

There has been a steady growth in cultural-territorial identity and mobilisation based on it in different parts of the world since the late 20th century. Such cultural-territorial movements have been described or conceptualised with reference to different terms such as ethnicity, tribalism, cultural-nationalism, internal colonialism, regionalism, etc. The lack of unanimity among the scholars may be due to the nature of mobilisation itself as well as due to divergent disciplinary background of scholars. However, among various factors, a great deal of primacy is assigned to economic reasons and the issue of cultural identity. Sometimes, the theme of elite manipulation of economic and cultural issues is emphasised and sometimes discussions on such cultural-territorial movements expose multiple dimensions of such mobilisations which are generally conceptualised as ethnic mobilisations. The above dimensions of cultural-territorial identity and mobilisation included changing nature of cultural identity, structure of identity, political-economic foundations ranging from relative deprivation to internal colonialism of such movements, symbols and pattern of mobilisation, etc. Very often, researchers also focus on integrative / disintegrative role of such movements.

Sikkim, which had been a tiny Himalayan kingdom before 1975, is at present one of the smallest and most performing States of North East India. Sikkim is inhabited by multiple cultural-racial groups like Nepalis, Lepchas, Bhutias, etc. of which Nepalis constitute the majority. Apart from them, there exist some smaller groups like Sherpas, Tsongs (Limboos) etc., who are also identified as Nepalis in Sikkim.

Sikkim, like other parts of India, has been invaded by attempts at cultural-territorial mobilisation or popularly known as ethnic mobilisation since the introduction of parliamentary democracy after the merger with India. Before the merger, the ruling Namgyal dynasty belonging to a minority Bhutia racial community was ruling over subjects belonging to different racial-cultural communities; this helped the Bhutia community to acquire a predominant position though members of other communities also occupied important positions in the monarchical administration. Cultural-territorial mobilisations or ethnic mobilisations were not altogether unknown under the monarchical form of government in Sikkim. Incidents of Lepcha or Nepali, including the Tsongs (Limboos), protests against the Bhutia dominations did occur, but such mobilisations though had community orientation were not cultural or ethnic mobilisations in the modern sense–they were primarily directed against the State or its agents. Attempts at cultural-ethnic mobilisation became discernible with the emergence of political parties during the second half of the 20th century. There were political parties like Sikkim National Party (SNP), formed in April, 1948, which articulated interests of a particular community. Such community interests, however, were never presented as the interest of any particular community. Rather, such community interests were aggregated and presented as the general interests of Sikkim. Even when the general subjects of whom Nepalis constituted the majority, protested against the discriminatory and oppressive rule of the Bhutia king and elites, the protest movement was not known as the movement by Nepalis. Rather it was the grievances surfaced in the form of movement for introduction of democracy in Sikkim.

After the merger, Parliamentary democracy and notions of equality, individual freedom, and modern legal system have come into existence. It was hoped that the cultural differences and ethnic politics would be gradually marginalised with slow permeation of notions of individual rights and equality. But, contrary to general expectations, cultural or ethnic consciousness and the political actions based on cultural or ethnic identity have become more frequent. New political parties and organisations have been formed with community oriented claims and demands, and are competing with each other for the ethnic space. A cursory look at the manifestoes of various political parties since 1977 generally reflect attempts at mobilisation of ethnic categories by raising community oriented issues either in isolation (i.e. emphasising a particular community interests) or in conglomerate form (i.e. common issues concerning more than one group). By raising community oriented issues, political parties have facilitated the process of articulation or aggregation as well as legitimisation of demands of various cultural categories.

Apparently, cultural and/or ethnic mobilisations process in Sikkim cannot be regarded as an expected development. As mentioned earlier, Sikkim does not have a long history of conflict among different communities though some communities were discriminated against. There are evidences showing cultural exchanges and inter-community marriages among the members of the three major communities in the past as well as today. The Bhutias and Lepchas are Buddhists while Nepalis are predominantly Hindus (certain sections of the Nepalis, particularly Tamangs, Gurungs and Shakyas are Buddhists). But there is no history of religious conflict or a history of ethnic violence and social conflict among the groups apart from the resentment expressed sporadically against the rulers and their agents. In other words, history does not appear to be a strong basis for emergence of ethnic or cultural politics in Sikkim. Yet, cultural-ethnic politics did not only emerge, it is sustained and proliferated further in Sikkim in recent past. The present article tries to explain one aspect of this problem while focusing on the policies of the Government on tribal issues.

Politics and Tribal Communities

As mentioned earlier, Sikkim became a part of India in 1975. A significant development which came along the merger was that the erstwhile ruling community of Sikkim, that is, the Bhutias, became ordinary citisens of a larger Indian nation. This they had been contemplating ever since the movement for democracy began in 1949. By the time the merger took place, the Chogyal had accomplished whatever was possible in the capacity as a ruler to safeguard political and economic interests of the ruling community. The 36th Constitutional Amendment Act, 1975 made these measures a part of the Indian Constitution.

However, in pursuance of the spirit of the Constitution of India, certain modifications in the existing rules governing the affairs of the minority community of Sikkim were felt necessary. Accordingly, the Chief Secretary of Sikkim, T.S. Gyaltshen, asked his central counterpart to furnish norms for the specification of the Scheduled Castes and Scheduled Tribes communities in Sikkim. The norms approved by the Government of India for this purpose and communicated to the Chief Secretary, Government of Sikkim, were :

A. Scheduled Castes (SCs): Extreme social, educational and economic backwardness arising out of the traditional practice of untouchability;

B. Scheduled Tribes (STs): Indications of primitive traits, distinctive culture, geographical isolation, shyness of contact with the community at large and backwardness.

The letter also revealed that earlier the Lhendup Kazi government had proposed for Scheduled Tribe status only for the Lepchas and Bhutias: the Bhutias were classified into three sub-groups (i) Sikkimese Bhutia, (ii) Bhutias including Dopthapa, Tromopa, Chumbipa and Drukpa, and (iii) the Tibetans. The proposal of the State government seeking to recognise the three sections of the Bhutias as Scheduled Tribe (ST), however, seemed to have created lot of confusion at Shastri Bhawan. Hence, the Ministry of the Home Affairs sought a clarification from the State Government stating, "It appears that there are no great cultural differences between the Sikkimese Bhutia and other sub-groups of Bhutia. It is also not clear whether inclusion of only these terms would cover all the sections of the Bhutias or some sections would be left out. Information available here also seems to show that the term 'Tibetan' is used to denote those Bhutias who have been preserving their tradition of having migrated from Tibet. Altogether it might be best not to include the term 'Tibetan'. The Sikkim Government may consider whether it could be sufficient to mention only the generic term Bhutia in the Schedule to cover all the sub-groups, including Tibetan."

Further, the central government also categorically wanted to know from the state government as to why Limboos (also called Tsongs) could not be included in the Scheduled Tribes list. Under para no. 5, the letter stated, "It would also appear that there is another primitive tribe namely the Limboos who have social affinity with the Lepchas and some of them are animists. The Limboos have been mentioned as autochthonous inhabitants of Sikkim and are sometimes considered as Limbuan (Limbuwan) Lepchas .... The status of the Limboos will have to be spelt out clearly and if necessary they may be grouped with Lepcha, and the entry could be "Lepcha Limboo". The letter also highlighted the inability of the State government to include other tribal communities i.e., Gurung, Mangar, Tamang and Rai, and instructed the state government "to review the case of these communities and also other communities which may have been left out."

The then ruling party, however, did not seem to have pursued the matter seriously. However, when the Constitution (Sikkim) Scheduled Tribes Order, 1978 was promulgated, only the Lepchas and Bhutias (including Chumbipa, Dopthapa, Dukpa, Kagatey, Sherpa, Tibetan, Tromopa and Yolmo) were declared scheduled tribes of Sikkim. The Scheduled Tribes Order, 1978 included all Bhutia sub-groups into a single generic term 'Bhutia' while other groups like Limboos, Tamangs, Gurungs, Rais, Mangars, etc. were denied scheduled tribe status.

Logically, from ethno-cultural point of view, the Sherpas, Kagatey and Yolmos should not have been included in the category of Bhutias though by tradition and religion they are mostly Buddhists. Sikkimese Bhutias are originally refer to as Denzongpa who migrated to Sikkim in the late 16th century from Tibet and other Bhutias like Chumbipas, Dopthapas, Tromopas, Drukpas and also Tibetans came from Tibet and Bhutan considerably after the establishment of the Namgyal dynasty in Sikkim. Sherpas and Yolmos are believed to have come from Nepal while Kagatey is a synonym of Yolmos. Besides, Sherpas and Yolmos, though included as Bhutias, are not recognised as Bhutias by the Revenue Order No. 1 of 1917.

Socially, various socio-cultural groups of the Nepalis community like the Rai, Limboo, Gurung, Tamang, Mangar and others (Bhujel, Sunuwar, Thami) should have been included in the Scheduled Tribes list of Sikkim in view of their distinct culture, language, religion and overall backwardness. Besides, the Ministry of Home Affairs, Government of India, had also expressed desire for their inclusion in the Scheduled Tribes list of Sikkim and accordingly had instructed the state government to review the case of these 'left out' communities.

The policy of the Sikkim government in tribal affairs was not only ambiguous but also discriminatory. If the period of settlement had been the criteria for being included in the Scheduled Tribes then the Drukpas and Tibetans do not merit inclusion but the Limboos, Mangars, Gurungs, Rais and Tamangs should have been included on this ground. On socio-economic grounds these communities were far more backward, possess elements of primitive traits, distinct culture and living a hard economic life than the erstwhile ruling community. And if religion was the criteria (for the Nepalis are basically Hindu and Scheduled Tribes are, at least officially, Buddhist), then at least Tamangs and Gurungs who are basically Buddhist should have been recognised as scheduled tribes.

SSP Government and the Tribal Policy

N.B. Bhandari, after coming to power in 1979 Assembly election, took up the issue with the central government. In 1981, he wrote to the then Prime Minister of India recommending inclusion of the Limboo community in the list of Scheduled Tribes of Sikkim. In June 1987, he further wrote to the central government recommending inclusion of Limboos and Tamangs of Sikkim in the list of Scheduled Tribes. The response of the central government was positive, and expressed desire to have a comprehensive revision of the list of Scheduled Castes and Scheduled Tribes. Accordingly, in 31 July 1987 the Secretary, Ministry of Welfare, Government of India, sent a telegram to the Secretary, SC/ST Welfare Department,

Government of Sikkim, requesting him to present positively in the meeting of the Ministers scheduled on 13 August 1987 at Parliament House, New Delhi, to discuss on the issue of comprehensive revision of the list of Scheduled Castes and Scheduled Tribes.

As scheduled, the meeting was held under the chairmanship of the Union Minister, Shri Buta Singh. One of the agenda of the meeting was inclusion of Limboos and Tamangs in the list of Scheduled Tribes of Sikkim. Mr. Pasang Namgyal, Secretary, SC/ST and Welfare Department, Government of Sikkim, submitted a favourable report to the Committee of Ministers for SC/ST regarding inclusion of Limboo and Tamang in the Scheduled Tribes list. Later in his report, dated 19 August 1987 to Shri Sanchamana Limboo, the then Minister SC/ST and Welfare Department, Government of Sikkim, Mr. P. Namgyal noted that the 'deliberation indicated sufficient recommendation in favour of the above two communities. It is further learnt that sitting of the group of Ministers was final scrutiny in the process of the comprehensive revision of the lists of Scheduled Castes and Scheduled Tribes'. But the then SSP Government did not recommend for the inclusion of Limboos and Tamangs in the Scheduled Tribes list. Bhandari's view was that the demand for Tribal status for Limboo and Tamang communities should not be isolated from the issues of citizenship, seat reservation and recognition of Nepali language in the Eighth Schedule. His official note dated 22 August 1987 on the report of the Secretary, SC/ST and Welfare Department, stated 'we cannot separate the demands. We do not want divide and rule policy. All Sikkimese are one'.

It seems that there had been a major shift in the priorities of the State Government after June 1987. Mr. N. B. Bhandari who supported recognition of Limboos and Tamangs as Scheduled Tribes was now opposed to it. Bhandari Government was apprehensive that recognition of the Limboos and Tamangs as Scheduled Tribes might split the Nepali community and subsequently weaken the demands for constitutional recognition of the Nepali language, citizenship to 'left-out' Sikkimese and reservation of Nepali seats etc. which the State Government was pursuing so vigorously at that time. In fact, the pressure from the existing tribal communities (Bhutia and Lepcha) was politically too cumbersome for Mr. Bhandari that he had very little option other than to deny inclusion of Limboo and Tamang communities in the Scheduled Tribes list. The decision of the State Government was not only contradictory to its earlier stand but also confusing to the Central government as well. The Bhandari government's position on this issue became more evident when Mr. Bhandari sought explanations from two of his legislators (Mr. Sanchaman Limboo and Mr. Birbal Limboo) for participating in the delegation of Akhil Sikkim Kirat Limbu Chumlung which met the Prime Minister of India, P.V. Narashimha Rao, on 14 June 1990. There was no doubt that Mr. Bhandari had reservation regarding inclusion of the Limboo and Tamang communities in the list of Scheduled Tribes of Sikkim.

SDF Government and the Tribal Policy

The Sikkim Democratic Front (SDF), led by P.K. Chamling assumed power in 1994 and with it, the tribal issue attained a new height and dimension. On the eve of Assembly elections, the party promised to work for the protection of the rights and privileges of the Bhutia-Lepcha tribals together with recognition of five different socio-cultural groups – Limboos, Tamangs, Gurungs, Mangars and Rais – in the list of Scheduled Tribes of Sikkim. Interestingly, had there been a consensus between the Central and State governments, these communities could have been declared Scheduled Tribes much earlier.

In June 1995, the Chief Minister, Shri P.K. Chamling, wrote to the Union Home Minister, Shri S.B.Chavan, to include the Limboo, Tamang and Gurung communities in the Scheduled Tribe list of Sikkim. Later, some other communities namely Mangar, Rai, Sunuwar, Bhujel and Thami were also included in the proposed list of tribal communities. In December 2002, the Bill seeking to amend the Constitution (Sikkim) Scheduled Tribes Order, 1978 (Bill No. 62) was placed in the Union Parliament and was passed by the Rajya Sabha on December 18, 2002 and Lok Sabha on 19 December 2002. The Bill received Presidential assent on 7 January 2003. Thus with the Presidentail assent the two communities–Limboos and Tamangs – were included in the Schedule Tribes list while the communities like Gurung, Manger, Rai and others were once again denied the tribal status.

The Sikkim Bhutia Lepcha Apex Committee (SIBLAC) in its first ever convention held on 23 September 2001 adopted a resolution demanding not to grant ST status to the Limboos and Tamangs in the interest of the Bhutias and Lepchas. The Committee believed that government's proposal to grant Scheduled Tribes status to them would have detrimental effect on the rights and privileges as well as identity of the Lepchas and Bhutias. There were rumours about the fall of the Chamling Government. Even P.K. Chamling contemplated worst for his government, "'My government will go on 19 December 2002. Let it go if it has to but I'm not afraid. I will work for the Limboos and Tamangs". But nothing unprecedented happened. Rather Chamling returned to power with 31 seats in 2004 Assembly election though, according to some reliable sources, majority of the Bhutia-Lepcha had refrained from voting Sikkim Democratic Front party led by P.K. Chamling.

Tribal Communities and the Question of Seat Reservation

A new dimension was added to the tribal issue with the inclusion of the Limboos and Tamangs in the STs list of Sikkim. As Scheduled Tribes these communities deserved reservation of seats in the State Assembly under article 332 (1) of the Indian constitution. It must be noted that as of now no seats have been reserved for the Scheduled Tribes in Sikkim Legislative Assembly. Though the Bhutias and Lepchas were declared Scheduled Tribes in 1978, the 12 seats reserved in the State Assembly continued to be the ethnic seats meant exclusively for the Bhutias and Lepchas. No change or amendment was thought necessary in the Representation of the People Act, 1950/51 (as amended in 1976 and 1980), basically on the impression that the groups for whom seats were reserved on ethnic ground earlier were alone scheduled tribes requiring no separate provision for reservation. There is also no evidence to show that the Lepchas had ever resented hitherto to seat sharing scheme though, of late, the Lepchas as well as the Sherpas have expressed dissatisfaction loudly and strongly over the nature of the seats, and the manner in which they are to be shared.

The Sikkim Limboo Tamang Joint Action Committee, P.R.Subba group and supported by the state unit of the Indian National Congress (I), submitted a proposal to the central government and the State Delimitation Commissions demanding to carry out special census of the two communities immediately to provide seat reservation and to reserve seats in the same way or method as was followed to reserve seats for the Scheduled Tribes earlier. The Committee also demanded amendment to the Representation of the People Act, 1980 and expedite the process for seat reservation for the two communities before the commencement of the Assembly election scheduled in 2004. The Sikkim Limboo Tamang Joint Action Committee for Tribal Status (Birbal Subba group) also demanded reservation of seats before the completion of the work by the Delimitation Commission 2002. These organisations also urged the visiting President of India, A.P.J. Abdul Kalam, to grant the political rights to the Limboo and Tamang tribal communities before the implementation of the Delimitation Commission proposal. The memorandum submitted by the Sikkim Limboo Tamang Joint Action Committee (SLTJAC) to the President Kalam read, "if the delimitation proposal in the present form is allowed to see passage, the Limboo and Tamang communities will be deprived of their political rights for another 25 years." They expressed resentment over the discriminatory treatment meted out to the communities by the central government.

SIBLAC, on the other hand, made it clear that the 12 seats reserved in the Assembly were exclusively meant for the Bhutia-Lepcha community and any attempt to dilute the existing provision would be viewed as a threat to the rights of the minority Lepcha-Bhutia by the majority. Similar view was also expressed by Ven. Lama Chosphel Zotpa, Vice-Chairman of the National Commission for Scheduled Castes and Tribes, Government of India, in a letter entitled 'Threat faced by Bhutia and Lepcha Tribes in Sikkim from Nepalis', addressed to the Chief Secretary, Government of Sikkim. After the inclusion of the Limboo and Tamang communities in the Scheduled Tribes list the State Government had revised its policies on reservation both in employment and higher professional educational institutions. Earlier, the scheduled tribes (Bhutia and Lepcha) enjoyed 23 per cent reservation. In September 2003, the percentage of reservation for the Scheduled Tribes had been increased to 33 per cent which also included the share of the Limboos and Tamangs. Since then the Bhutias had been expressing resentment over the possible domination of the Nepalis in the area monopolised exclusively by them earlier. Thus apart from the tribal seat, there is a deep seated apprehension for possible deprivation among the Bhutias and Lepchas in terms of employment and resource distribution which they had to share with the Limboos and Tamangs tribes now.

In fact, as early as September 2001, the state government clarified that the seats reserved for the Bhutias and Lepchas would not be disturbed. While alleging the Opposition parties and organisations for fomenting communalism on the issue, Mr. Chamling assured, "My job as the Chief Minister is to protect the people of Sikkim and the day I am not able to do so I will not only retire from politics but will excommunicate myself from Sikkim". The issue being ethnically contentious, the government also sought legal advices from the constitutional experts. The major points expressed by these experts (Shri K.K.Venugopal, Shri Soli Sorabji and Shri S.S. Nariman) were:

(a) Limboos and Tamangs could not claim any of the 12 seats reserved for the Bhutia-Lepcha in the State Assembly.

(b) The total percentage of reservation to the Legislative Assembly could exceed 50 per cent without affecting the provision of article 14 of the constitution.

(c) Article 332 would proporio vigour operate on the reservation of seats for the Limboos and Tamangs.

(d) On the basis of available population data about 16 per cent of the 32 seats, that is at least 5 seats, could be reserved for the Limboos and Tamangs.

(e) The State government would retain the right to make a demand for readjustment of seats before 2006 provided that the Union Parliament deems it necessary to take decision in the matter.

In July 2003, the Chief Minister P.K. Chamling in a letter to the Prime Minister, Mr. A.B. Bajpai, expressed his intention to increase the number of Assembly seats from existing 32 to 40 to enable a provision of reservation of seats for the two newly included tribal communities. The discussion in the Rajya Sabha over the issue reaffirmed that the Chief Minister, P.K. Chamling proposed for reservation of seats for Limboo and Tamang tribal communities without effecting the reservation provided to the Bhutia-Lepcha community. The state government also requested for conducting a special census of the Limboo and Tamang tribal communities in order to fulfill the constitutional obligation mentioned under article 332 (1) and (3) of the constitution. In response to the Chief Minister's letter to the Prime Minister of December 2004, the Joint Secretary, Ministry of Home Affairs, Government of India, informed that the matter was being examined by the Ministry in consultation with the Union Law Ministry and, in the meanwhile, the state government was requested to choose one of the three options short listed by the Ministry and communicate to it immediately. The options were– (a) Reservations to be carved out of the 17 unreserved Assembly seats arrangements in Sikkim on the basis of proportion of their population...without increasing the size of the State Legislature; (b) Strength of the State Legislature be increased to 40 and reservations be considered out of 25 seats (i.e. present 17 plus 8 additional seats) subject to the condition that in the event of any more communities being declared as Schedule Tribes in future they may also be accommodated within the overall size of 40 without having to request further increase in number of seats and (c) The size of the Legislative Assembly be increased to 60 to bring at par with other States and in conformity with article 171 (1) and reservation from Limboos and Tamangs be considered in proportion to their population out of the 45 seats (17 + 28) subject to the condition that in the event of any new communities being declared as Scheduled Tribes in future they will also be accommodated within the overall strength of 60 without having to ask for any further increase in the strength of the Assembly.

A high level delegation of the state government, including some senior bureaucrats and citizens, called upon the Prime

Minister and the Home Minister among others in November 2005. It was learnt that apart from talks on Limboo and Tamang seats, discussion on other communities like Gurung, Rai, Mangar, Thami and Bhujel for tribal status was also figured prominently in the meeting. But nothing substantive happened after that. The issue also did not come in the Budget Session of the Lok Sabha in 2006. In the meanwhile, Shri H.R. Pradhan, President of the State Unit of the Bharatiya Janata Party (BJP), lodged a writ petition in the Supreme Court seeking clarification as to why the seats for the Limboos and Tamangs could not be reserved in the State Assembly. In its preliminary hearing dated 20 March 2006, the Supreme Court issued show cause notices to both the central and state Governments asking why the prayer of Shri H.R. Pradhan, the President of the Sikkim Unit of the BJP, should not be granted. On behalf of H.R. Pradhan, the former Union Minister, Arun Jaitley, assisted by Advocate Ranjit Kumar, represented the case.

In view of the State government's recommendation for enhancement of Assembly seats to 40, the Ministry of Home Affairs, Government of India, asked the state government for further clarification on two fronts – (a) convincing justification as to why Assembly seats be enhanced to 40, and (b) whether the seats reserved for B-L (Bhutia-Lepch(a) should be correspondingly enhanced if the Assembly seats were raised to 40. The second explanation was sought in view of the memorandum submitted by the Sikkim Bhutia Lepcha Apex Committee (SIBLAC) to the Welfare Ministry, Government of India, demanding corresponding enhancement of B-L seats if the Assembly seats were raised to 40. This demand for corresponding enhancement of B-L seat further complicated the issue. There had been a general apprehension among the members of the Sikkim Bhutia Lepcha Apex Committee that if seats for the Limboo and Tamang were reserved outside the 17 open seats, the domination of the Nepalis over the affairs of the state would increase. In other words, the 12 Bhutia-Lepcha seats would no longer remain as decisive as it has been at present in the making and unmaking of the government. The problem with the tribal issue is that even if there is reliable criterion or policy for determining 'tribe-ness', the question of determination of various communities as schedule tribes of Sikkim has been addressed arbitrarily and very often politically motivated.

Conclusion

Considering the socio-cultural and political peculiarities of the state of Sikkim, the government of India has been rather lenient and accommodative in its dealing with Sikkim. After the merger Article 371F, as a special provision, is incorporated in the Constitution of India extending legal-constitutional sanctions to the laws and institutions prevailing just before the merger. These old laws had been designed to maintain politico-cultural identity and administrative convenience of the ruling community and, therefore, had been community oriented and discriminatory in many respects. As a matter of fact, most of these laws are incompatible with the democratic and secular spirit of the Constitution of India. The continuation of these old laws has been the major cause of social division at the community level and very often the source of ethnic tension. For example, in 1989, the Sikkim High Court judgement allowed L.D. Kazi, a Lepcha, to gift a piece of land located in the prime urban area to his foster son N.B. Khatiwada, a Nepali. The Bhutias feared that it would facilitate further alienation of Bhutia-Lepcha land and an appeal was lodged in the Supreme Court of India. Khatiwada, a veteran politician and a Supreme Court lawyer, on the other, believed that the plot being in the urban area the jurisdiction of Revenue Order No. 1 (one of the old laws) could not apply. This had been the opinion of the honorable Sikkim High Court also. Though the Supreme Court upheld the judgement of the Sikkim High Court in 2006, the affidavits submitted by both the parties in defense of the case became the source of ethnic tension. It is to be noted that the Revenue Order No. 1, 1917 does not allow Bhutia – Lepcha land to sublet or sell to any other community other than themselves. At present, this Order has been also the source of discontent between the Bhutias and Lepchas on the one hand, and between the Bhutia and Other Bhutias on the other. This Order in its present form is considered bias towards the erstwhile affluent ruling community. The present imbroglio regarding reservation of seats for the two new tribal communities is also rooted in the existing legal – political structure which is founded upon the ashes of the feudal legacy of pre – merger era.

Notes and References

D.O. No. 18 (3)/Home/75, dated 19th April, 1976.

D.O. No. BC-12016/24/75-SCST, dated 21.07.1976.

Sikkim Government Gazette, Ex. Gazette No. 93, dated 12.07.1978.

NOW, Vol. 1, No. 34, dated 19-25 February, 2003.

Copy of the letter of the Chief Minister, N.B. Bhandari, to the Prime Minister of India, Mrs. Indira Gandhi, dated 14th November, 1981.

D.O. No. 155/SC/ST WD, dated 02.06.1987.

D.O. No. 12016/28/87 – SCD (R. Cell), dated 22.07.1987.

D.O. No. 12016/28/87 – SCD (R. Cell), dated 31.07.1987.

Copy of the Report submitted by the Secretary, SC/ST Welfare Department, government of Sikkim, to the Minister, SC/ST Welfare Department, Government of Sikkim, dated 19.08.1987.

Official noting of the then Chief Minister, on the Report submitted by the Secretary, SC/ST Welfare Department, Government of Sikkim, dated 20.08.1987.

D.O. No. 120616/17/810 SCD (R. Cell), dated 18.12.1991.

Copy of the explanation letter of N.B. Bhandari, to B.B. Subba, Ref. No. 291/SSP/90-91, dated 30.06.1990.

Draft copy of the Scheduled Tribes Order (Amendment) Ordinance, 1994.

D.O. No. 26/CMS/95, dated 17.06.1995.

Memoranda dated 25th August, 1995; 19th December, 1995; 18th July,1997; 30th March, 1998; 10th November, 1999; 22nd April, 2000.

The Gazette of India, Ex. Gazette Part II, Section I, No. 10, New Delhi, dated 08.01.2003.

Hamro Prajashakti, September 26 – 02 October, 2001.

Birbal Subba (Tamling) 2004: "Sikkimay Limboo and Tamang Birodhi Narbahadur Bhandari ko Kalo Kartutharo",Tamling Family, He Gaon, West Sikkim, p. 33.

Memorandum of the Sikkim Limboo Tamang Joint Action Committee, dated 30.04.2003.

Sikkim Express, dated 27.09.2005.

Copy of the letter of the Jt. Secretary, National Commission for SC/ST, Government of India, to the Chief Secretary, Government of Sikkim, No. 17/11/2003 (C-CELL), dated 15th October, 2003.

Sikkim Government Gazette, No. 130, dated 6th July, 1995.

Sikkim Government Gazette, No. 307, dated 17th September, 2003.

NOW, dated 18-24 December, 2002.

Weekend Review, dated 25-27 February, 2004.

Memorandum of the Chief Minister of Sikkim to Prime Minister of India, dated 23rd July, 2003.

Reply given to unstarred question no. 1325 in the Rajya Sabha by the Minister for State for Law and Justice, Shri K. Venkatapathy, dated 14th March, 2005.

D.O. No. 405/CMS-2003, dated 05.05.2003.

D.O. No. 1021/CMO/SKM, dated 27.12.2004.

D.O. No. IV/11015/1/2005-CSR-11, dated 30.05.2005.

NOW, Vol. 5, No. 7, dated 22.03.2006.

Letter of Shri A.K. Srivastava, the Joint Secretary, Ministry of Home Affairs, to Shri N.D. Chingapa, the Chief Secretary of Sikkim, dated 01.05.2006.

5

From Share Tenancy to Agrarian Reform: Sikkim in Perspective

A Brief Note on Share Tenancy

In the large contour of agrarian structure, land is considered a primary productive asset in any agrarian society, and land tenure system is one of the important determinants of land productivity. While dealing with land tenure system, share cropping which is considered as integral part of feudal society has emerged as one of the most dominant agrarian relation and was in prevalence in some pre-capitalist and pre-socialist societies from ancient period. It was and it is most prominently visible in most of the third world countries. From the historical perspective, in feudalism, the lords who received land directly from the 'Crown' were called 'tenants in chief'. They doled out portions of their land to lesser tenants in exchange for services, who in turn divided it among even lesser tenants. The process of granting subordinate tenancies is known as subinfeudation. Therefore, all individuals except the monarch were said to hold the land of someone else. And in the process, a mechanism of forcible reciprocity of various types between lord and tenant had allowed been to evolve. However, in the words of Rodney Hilton, "Marx used the term feudalism to describe a whole social order whose prime feature was the domination of the rest of the society, mainly peasants, by a military, landowning aristocracy. Here, once the producer's subsistence necessities had been fulfilled became the income of the ruling class. The essence of the feudal mode of production in the Marxist sense is the exploitative relationship between landowners and subordinated peasants, in which the surplus beyond subsistence of the latter, whether in direct or in rent in kind or money, is transferred under coercive sanction to the former" (Hilton, 2006). Even though share tenancy has always been identified as inefficient system[1] by the early neo-classical economists like Adam Smith (1937:367) and Alfred Marshall (1948:648), to them peasants are a homogeneous category and consists of owner and tenants. As a result, the process of class differentiation and class formation within peasant society has mostly been looked into from Marxist perspective. The high degree of variability of effective resource endowment among the peasantry gave birth to labour-hired capitalists and rich peasants, self employed middle and small peasants and poor and hired peasants (Patnaik, 1994:156). Pearce (1983) had explained share cropping from the Marxist perspective. According to him, share cropping is a method of surplus appropriation by which surplus labour is transferred to the landlord in the form of surplus product. He went on adding that share cropping is transitional mode of surplus appropriation 'between forms of agrestic servitude and the full commoditisation of rural labour itself'. As a dominant parlance in history and anthropology, the term peasants has been used that when cultivators are governed by an organised state apparatus or more precisely, when the cultivators pay taxes or tribute in the form of labour services or goods in kind or cash to superior right holders on land or to the state authority are identified as peasants (Bagchi, 2002:156).

By and large, share cropping (either in share tenancy/ share cropping contract or fixed rent tenancy) has mostly been used as a means of surplus appropriation for the dominant class, and it also allowed the dominant class to maximise labour input, land productivity, and surplus. And insecure relationship between land and tenants worked as a deterrent in raising the standard of living of small farmers and agricultural labourers and worked as a hindrance for economic development, both by preventing the expansion of the food supply and by causing agriculture – usually the major economic activity – to stagnate (United Nations 1951: 89).

Various Facets of Land Reform and its Relevance

On the contrary, the term land reform has many connotations and is interpreted and implemented in various ways in different countries. In broader perspective, land reform means redistribution or reallocation of rights to establish a more equitable distribution of farm land (Boyce *et. al.* 2005:1). In addition to this, state sponsored land acquisitions, communal or collective forms of farming, and changes in land tenure pattern, that is, changes in the rent sharing arrangement between land owners and actual tillers of the land are considered as different variants of land reform (Griffin *et. al.* 2002: 3-4). In recent past, 'market led agrarian model' (Deninger and Binswanger, 1999:247-76) and 'negotiated' land reform that relies on voluntary land transfers between buyers and sellers with government's role restricted to establishing necessary framework for negotiation and making land purchase grant available to eligible beneficiaries is gaining importance (Deininger, 1999:3, Ghonemy, 1999, Reidinger *et.al.* 2000).

In India, to achieve greater productivity and production and to ensure distributive justice for landless farmers in the post independence period till pre-green revolution period, (1964-1965) major policy thrust revolved around land reforms.

Sen (1962), Bardhan (1973), Berry and Cline (1979), on the basis of their findings, have shown that small sized farm shows higher productivity. Banerjee, Gertler and Ghatak (2002), based on their field surveys in the mid-1990s, have concluded that a 17-18 per cent increase in productivity in West Bengal has been observed in the plots operated by registered sharecroppers and this is in conformity with the hypothesis that security of tenure and fair crop sharing to sharecroppers ensure incentive to increase production. It has also been observed that if poor farmers cultivate their own land they would not compete with full time landless agricultural workers in the rural labour market and in the process it will raise rural wages. In addition to that, having a piece of land of their own will save them from various restrictive practices imposed by the landowner (Ghimire, 2001). International evidence overwhelmingly endorses a rural growth strategy based on the dynamism of small, family farms because small farms are demonstrably more poverty-reducing than large holdings and are typically more productive per unit area (Handstad *et.al.*2001).

If it is accepted that land reform has direct bearings on agricultural production and productivity, then rise in production and productivity certainly contribute towards achieving food security. The degree of success in implementing land reform has varied significantly from state to state. As a result, especially in many less development countries capitalist mode of development made successful inroads but feudal elements in the agrarian structure still had its root and by and large agrarian community as well as agriculture had continued to suffer.

Sikkim in Perspective

Along with many Indian states, Sikkim, the 22nd State of India which is located in the Eastern Himalayas had similar experience. Sikkim up till 1975 the state was under hereditary monarchy for over three centuries (Subba, 1989a:80). However, from 1861 to 1947, the British had a de facto control over Sikkim. Prior to the integration of Sikkim with India, the migrant Bhutias were the ruling class and they ruled over indigenous Lepcha tribes and migrant Nepalese. The general notion that Nepalese were solely brought by the British from Nepal was partially correct because the Limbus (a tribe belongs to Nepalese community) did have presence in Sikkim from very ancient period. Majority of the Nepalese, however, did not have any land rights and they were either landless agricultural labourers or tenants.

In Sikkim, around 70 per cent of the population still depends on agriculture (Census of India, 2001), and its importance can also be traced from popular Nepalese saying in Sikkim, '*Padhi guni ke kam, halo joti khayo mam*' which means what is the use of reading and writing, as ultimately you have to plough the field (Sinha, 2009). Therefore the land tenure system, agrarian structure and relations in Sikkim demand special attention.

In this context, an attempt has been made first to review the changing trajectories of agrarian structure and land tenure system that was prevalent in Sikkim under the monarchy. Further, the agrarian reform initiated after Sikkim became the 22nd state of India, has closely and critically been scrutinised.

Agrarian Structure in Sikkim and Land Tenure System under Monarchy

Lepchas were supposed to be the original inhabitants of Sikkim (White, 1909). One school of thought believes that the Lepchas might have come from the east of the mountains from Assam and Upper Burma, but the other view proposes them 'as migrants from hilly mountain of Kailasa, way up in Tibet' (Singh, 1993). Prior to any infiltration into Sikkim from outside, the life style of Lepchas was marked by a high degree of mobility subsisting on roots, tuber, fishing and hunting (Das, 1978). Among the Lepchas, a few also used rotational method of cultivation or slash and burn method to grow rice, millet and maize (Thapa, 1966).

Recorded history of Sikkim began from 17th century, precisely in 1642, when three monks consecrated Phuntsong Namgyal (at Yoksom, in western part of Sikkim) as the first 'religious and temporal ruler' of Sikkim (Singh, op.cit).

Later, a treaty was signed between Lepchas and Bhutias, wherein the former accepted the latter as a spiritual and secular head of Sikkim kingdom. Through this treaty, Bhutias established their supremacy over the Lepchas. This marks the beginning of the unbroken rule of Namgyal dynasty in Sikkim (Das, 1983). During this period, when the Lepchas and the Bhutias were coming closer, a small group of Limbus, known as Tsongs, who were believed to be migrants from Tsangpo valley in Tibet, were also visible in disperse hamlet. Towards the South-West, the Mangars (according to Risley, their original homeland was in Western Nepal from where they migrated to Eastern Nepal and finally came to Sikkim) used to live by occupying a small territory there (Risley, 1928). Both the Limboos and Mangars extended their solidarity with the Bhutia ruler and accepted the Chogyal as spiritual and temporal head of Sikkim kingdom. Phuntsong Namgyal, after being consecrated, divided the territory of Sikkim into twelve dzongs or districts each under a Lepcha dzongpen or district chief. A symbolic surrender of lands by the twelve dzongpen to the Bhutia king created the notion that all lands belong to the

Bhutia ruler, and the Lepchas were mere occupants, who could be evicted at the will of the ruler. This marked the beginning of the cultural and economical marginalisation of Lepchas and the Limboos *per se*, at least in pre-Britsh phase in Sikkim.

Consolidation of Feudalism

At the top, there was *Chogyal* or the King and according to traditional Sikkimese economic system, all land belonged to him (Sinha, 1975:47). The king would lease out portion of land to the *kazis* and *thikadars* as gift who were primarily the absentee landlords.The *kazis* and *thikadars* finally leased out the lands to peasants under different exploitative terms. They would employ *mandals* (the headmen) and *karbaris* (account assistants of headmen or *mandals*) to collect rent from the tenants and were also entrusted with responsibility to settle disputes of the tenants. For collecting revenue, the State of Sikkim was divided into 104 estates and out of that 61 estates were leased out to the *kazis* and *thikadars* and they were assigned to pay a fixed sum to the State. Five estates belonged to the monasteries and 15 estates, which formed his private estates, exclusively belonged to the king or *Chogyal*, (Report on Agricultural Census, 1976-77:13).

As per the Revenue Circular (No.8554/G) of 1924, a *kazi* could hold up to 100 acres of land. However, with special permission, they could hold up to 200 acres of land and for *mandals* it was settled at 30 acres. The landlords enjoyed and exercised enormous magisterial power relating to civil and criminal matters and they generally used this power to evict the tenants or subjects according to their wish. Generally, four types of tenants could be found–*adhiadar / adhiawal*, *kutdars/tanam*, *pakhureys* or *sukumbasis,* and *chakureys* (ibid:9).

An *adhiawal/adhiadar,* though a sharecropper and had to pay half of the produce as rent, did posses a sizeable amount of land. A *kutdar* had to pay a specific amount of grain (minimum half of the produce) as rent to the landlord at the end of the harvest. In case of *tanam,* rent was paid in cash and tenure was for one year subjected to yearly renewal which was at the discretion of the landlords. Landless agricultural labourers were identified as *pakhureys* or *sukumbasis*. The *pakhureys* had to pay rent in terms of labour as well as packet of gift or '*koseli*' which consisted of milk, butter eggs and fowls (Subba,1989.b:73-79). It was mentioned in the Census of 1891 that about 1% of the then population was slaves. As mentioned by Subba, *chakureys* and slaves were probably the same group of people (Subba op cit: 83). In addition to rent, landlords (*kazis* and *thikadars*), *mandals* and *karbaris* forced the raiyats to render free service to them. This system was, however, scrapped vide notification number 5874/G dated 15 August 1924 and instead cash payment was introduced and rates to be paid were Re. 1 to landlord, 50 paise to *mandal* and 25 paise to *karbari* respectively. This system was in place till 1949, and thereafter, it was abolished (Subba, 1985:37).

The amount of rent to be levied was fixed on ethnic line and was discriminatory in nature. Nepalese had to pay higher rent than Lepchas and Bhutias. It was only in 1956, the king abolished the discriminatory rent system and declared that Lepcha-Bhutia and Nepalese would pay rent at equal rate.

The Revenue Order No. 1 of 1917 was an act to protect land possessed by Lepchas and Bhutias, it prohibited the alienation of the land of Bhutias and Lepchas in favour of non hereditary subjects (Nepalese). But, gradually as the number of Nepalese immigrants increased and nearly outnumbered the Lepcha-Bhutia population, the King of Sikkim through a notification (No: 5063/F), in 1948, prohibited the Nepalese people from acquiring land especially in North Sikkim.

Land Reform Measures in Sikkim after it became a State of the Indian Union

After Sikkim became an Indian state in 1975, the first measure taken by the Government was the abolition of intermediaries. And it subsequently created the provision of land rights to the landless tillers, enforced ceiling laws of landholding, distribution of surplus land and protection of tenancy rights through legislations like The Sikkim Cultivators Protection Act, 1975, The Sikkim Agricultural Land Ceiling and Reforms Act, 1978, and The Sikkim Land (Requisition and Acquisition) Act, 1978.

Land rights of the indigenous Lepchas and Bhutias, which was protected earlier by the Revenue order No. 1 of 1917, (it was mentioned there that the land owned by the Lepcha and

Bhutia community can not be transferred to other communities), continued to be so after the merger of Sikkim with India because of the tribal status of those two ethnic groups.

Imposition of land ceiling on agricultural holdings helped the State to acquire a substantial amount of agricultural land, demarcated, as 'vested land', however, complete abolition of feudal agrarian structure remained unfulfilled (Chakrabarti, 2010). Because of that, the ceiling was applied only to the agricultural land; no ceiling was imposed on non agricultural holdings. The *kazis* still hold considerable amount of land and many *kazis* are reported to have 1500 acres of land even today.

In 1996, the Government of Sikkim introduced a land redistribution mechanism through land bank scheme. According to this scheme, land owners were supposed to surrender their surplus land voluntarily and landless labourers (known as *sukumbasis* in Sikkim) were free to choose the plot of land they wanted for cultivation. Landless labourers were identified by the government and would be given permanent land rights and each land- less family could choose a land up to the amount of 1000-2000 sq. metre at a cost not exceeding Rs. 52,500 (including registration and stamp duty). In 2004-05 and 2005-06 alone, 114 families received land under this scheme (Economic Survey, 2006-07: 124).

But few pertinent questions need to be raised here–first, in the absence of any governmental measure, what would prompt the landowners to surrender the land? Second, how would the landless labourers accumulate the money to purchase the land if it is not financed by the state? and third, and most importantly, according to the constitutional arrangement, the land possessed by the Lepcha and Bhutia tribes is non-transferable and given that how much surplus land will be available for redistribution is also matter of concern (Chakrabarti, 2009, 2010). From Table 5.1, it is evident that land distribution is skewed in Sikkim. The skewness is highest in North District where around 22 per cent of the people hold 66 per cent of the land. The plausible reason for this is that the majority of the people are from Bhutia and Lepcha communities and their land is non-transferable to any other

Table 5.1: District wise size/class wise distribution of Land Holdings (1991)

Category	NORTH DIST.		EAST DIST.		SOUTH DIST.		WEST DIST.	
	Holding		*Holding*		*Holding*		*Holding*	
	No (%)	*Area (%)*	*No (%)*	*Area (%)*	*No (%)*	*Area (%)*	*No (%)*	*Area (%)*
Marginal	49.0	8.5	56.0	12.8	44.0	9.7	46.0	10.0
Small	10.2	5.1	22.0	22.6	25.0	18.3	21.0	17.0
Semi-Medium	18.3	20.4	14.3	23.5	18.0	24.0	20.0	28.0
Medium	17.2	36.0	6.4	23.4	10.0	26.0	11.0	31.0
Large	5.3	30.0	1.3	17.7	3.0	22.0	2.0	14.0
Total No. of Holdings and Total Area under Holdings (in hectare)	4942	14407	19666	32936	12548	28575	13971	31088
Average Holding (in hectare)		2.9		1.7		2.3		2.2

Source: Sikkim Human Development Report, 2001.

communities. Historically too, these two communities are the representative of the landed gentry in Sikkim. A sizeable portion of the land is still used as common property. Land holding pattern in East district shows that the concentration of marginal and small farmers is highest among the districts. East district also produces highest amount rice; therefore, a conclusion may be drawn that an initiative towards the distribution of land is more necessary in East district along with West district (highest producer of food grains in Sikkim among four districts in Sikkim) for further improvement of agricultural production and productivity in the state.

Therefore, land reforms in Sikkim can still be viewed as an unfinished agenda, at least in the distributive sense. Food grain production, agricultural productivity or yield and agricultural growth have started decelerating since 2000. With increasing use of land for commercial and residential purposes, the gross sown area is also declining and it is adversely affecting the growth of yield of foodgrains.

Serious efforts are to be made to bring more land into cultivation through appropriation of surplus land possessed by big land owners and this would not only ensure distributive justice but also raise the allocative efficiency (allocative inefficiency results when, given the prices of inputs and outputs, a producer cannot optimally allocate her resources to minimize the cost of production). As a result, the state would be able to avert impending food scarcity, reduce the extent of unemployment, rise in income and fall in poverty in the rural sector of Sikkim.

References

Bagchi, Amiya (2002). "Agrarian Transformation and Human Development", in V.K. Ramchandran and Madhura Swaminathan (eds.), Agrarian Studies, Essays on agrarian Relations in Less-Developed Countries, (New Delhi: Tulika Books):156.

Banerjee, V. Abhijit, Paul J. Gretler and Maitreesh Ghatak (2002). "Empowerment and efficiency: Tenancy reform in West Bengal", *Journal of Political Economy*, 110(2): 239-280.

Bardhan P.K. (1973). "Size Productivity, and Returns to Scale: An Analysis of Farm-Level Data in Indian Agriculture," *Journal of Political Economy*, 86: 1370-1386.

Berry and Cline (1979). "*Agrarian Structure and Productivity in Developing Countries*", Johns Hopkins University Press, Baltimore, Maryland.

Boyce, James K., Peter Rosset and Elizabeth A. Stanton, (2005). "Land Reform and Sustainable Development", Working Paper Series, No 98, *Political Economy Research Institute*, (University of Massachusetts: Amherst) (http://www.umass.edu/peri/programs/development/naturalassets.htm)

Census of India (1981). Series-19, Part XIII A and B.

Census of India (1991). Series-22.

Census of India (2001). Provisional, Series-21

Chakrabarti, Anjan (2009). "*Economic Development and Employment in Sikkim*", (New Delhi : Authors Press): 19-20.

________(2010). "A Critical Review of Agrarian Reforms in Sikkim", *Economic and Political Weekly*, Vol. XLV, No. 5, February 5: 23-26.

Das, B.S., (1983). *The Sikkim Saga*, (New Delhi : Vikas Publishing House Pvt. Ltd): 5.

Deninger, Klaus (1999). "Market Negotiated Land Reform Work: Initial Experience from Colombia, Brazil and South Africa", *World Development*, Vol. 27, No. 4, April.

Deninger, Klaus, Hans Binswanger, (1999). "The Evolution of World Bank's Land Policy: Principles, Experience and Future Challenges, *World Bank Research Observer*, Vol. 14, No. 2, August.

Economic Survey: 2006-2007, Government of Sikkim.

El-Ghonemy, (1999). "The Political Economy of Market –Based Land Reform", UNRISD Discussion Paper, DP 104, Geneva, June.

Ghimire, K.B. (2001). "Regional Perspective on Land Reforms", Chapter I, *Whose Land?* IFAD UNIRSD, (Rome: The Popular Coalition): 18-19.

Government of India (2001). "*Indian Planning Experience - A Statistical Profile*", Planning Commission, Government of India, New Delhi, January 2001 and 10th Five Year Plan (2002-2007).

Government of Sikkim, *Sikkim Human Development Report*, (2001), (Delhi : Social Science Press).

Griffin Keith, A.R. Khan, A. Ickowitz, (2002). "Poverty and the Distribution of Land" in V.K. Ramchandran and Madhura Swaminathan (eds.), Agrarian Studies, Essays on agrarian Relations in Less-Developed Countries, (New Delhi: Tulika Books).

Hanstad, Tim., Jennifer Brown (2001). "Land Reform Law and Implementation in West Bengal: Lessons and Recommendations", RDI Reports on Foreign Aid and Development, 112, Seattle, Washington, USA, December.

Hilton Rodeny, ed (1976). "Transition from feudalism to Capitalism", Verso (republished by New Delhi: Aakar Books): 9-28.

Marshall, Alfred (1948). "*Principles of Economics*", 8th edn, (London: Macmillan)

Patnaik, Utsa (1994). "Tenancy and Accumulation" in Kaushik Basu (ed.) *Agrarian Questions*, (New Delhi: Oxford University Press): 156.

________ (2005). "Theorising Food Security and the Poverty in the Era of Economic Reforms" Social Scientist, Vol. 33, No. 7/8, Jul.-Aug: 50-81.

Pearce, R. (1983). "Share Cropping: Towards a Marxist View", *Journal of Peasant Studies,* Vol. 10, Nos. 2-3.

Report on Agricultural Census 1976-77, Agricultural Census Unit, Gangtok: 9, 13.

Riedinger, Jeffrey M., Wan-Ying Yang, Karen Brook, (2000). "Market Based Land Reforms: An Imperfect Solution", paper presented at an International Conference on Agrarian Reform and Rural Development, Tagaytay City, Phillipines, 5-8 December.

Risley, H.H., (1928). *Gazetter of Sikkim*, (New Delhi :D.K. Publishers Distributions P Ltd.): 74.

Sen, A.K. (1962). "An aspect of Indian agriculture", *Economics Weekly*, Annual Number: 243-66.

Singh, K.S., (1993). 'People of India', Vol XXXIX, (*Anthropological Survey of India, Seagull Books*: Calcutta): 89.

Sinha, A.C. (1975). "*Politics of Sikkim-A Sociological Study*", (New Delhi: Thomson Press (India) Limited) : 47.

________(2009). "The Politics of Identity Formation in Sikkim", *Dialogue*, Volume 10 No. 4, April-June, http://asthabharati.org/Dia_Apr%2009/a.c..htm

Smith, Adam (1776). "The Wealth of Nation", Cadel and Strahan.

Subba, Tanka Bahadur (1985). "*The Quiet Hills- A Study of Agrarian Relations in Hill Darjeeling*", ISPCK, Bangalore : 37.

__________ (1989a). "Agrarian Social structure and Change in Sikkim", *Social Change*, Vol. 19, No. 1, March: 80.

__________ (1989b). "*Dynamics of a Hill Society: The Nepalis in Darjeeling and Sikkim Himalayas*", (New Delhi: Mittal Publications): 73-79, 83.

Thapa, J.K., (1966). "Primitive Maize with the Lepchas", *Bulletin of Tibetology*, Vol. III, (1), Gangtok: 29-31.

White, J.C., (1909). *Sikkim and Bhutan: Twenty Years on the North-East Frontier* (1867-1908): 3.

*Part of the article has been published in *Economic and Political Weekly*, Vol. XLV, No. 5, January, 30, February 2010.

6

Religio-Cultural Space[1], Development and the Politics of Ecology : Evaluating the Movement of the Lepchas against the Hydro Power Project in Dzongu, Sikkim

SECTION I

Introduction

Development discourses since the Brundtland Commission Report (1987) are pregnant with catch phrases like 'sustainability', 'justice', 'equity' and 'fairness', touching every dimension of environment, natural and human. However, development research, policy and practice have typically avoided engagements with considerations of religion and spirituality (Sweetman, 1999; Selinger, 2004). This is true for major world religions and indigenous religions alike. Underlying this avoidance is the implicit assumption that religion will decline as communities modernise (Berger, 1999), and a wariness of engaging with religious issues that are frequently political and potentially socially divisive. But on the other hand, literatures on environmental preservation and protection are replete with ethical and value-laden questions, and quite often, religious roots of environmental concern and environmental stewardship are traced to religious scriptures and practices. Hence, the relevance of religion to development is arguably substantial, considered in the light of environmental concerns and needs of sustainable development. In this backdrop, this chapter makes an earnest attempt to engage with and explores the nexus between the cultural/spiritual and the material by examining the ways in which religion and development interact and pose the issues of sustainability of development processes. It juxtaposes development dynamics, religio-cultural spaces, and the politics of ecology in the context of the protest movement of the Lepchas waged against the development project in Dzongu area of Sikkim under the plea of sustainability of development on the one hand and of a community, as a response to the perceived threat of erasure of their religio-cultural spaces.

SECTION II
Religion, Environment and Development

The relationship between religion and the environment is now a well-established subject of academic discussion (White 1967; Gottleib 1996; Daedelus 2001), and has attracted formal responses from all of the major world religions (WWF 1986). Within these and other studies, three broad and over-lapping analytical approaches can be identified–(1) the exegesis of scriptures and historical texts to uncover metaphysical and philosophical teachings on the environment, as well as indications of past attitudes and behaviours, (2) ethnographic explorations of particular social and cultural practices which relate to the environment, and (3) socio-political analyses of movements and organisations that actively mobilise religious values and beliefs in pursuit of various environmental goals.

All major world religions contain environmental value and environmental prudence. Indian religio-philosophical tradition reflects upon the relationship between human beings and nature, which has been established by various categories of researched literature (Karve, 1961; Singh, 1986; Dwivedi, 1987; Lal, 1995; James ed. 1999; etc.). The Vedic philosophy came to acknowledge that the material cause of the creation happened to be the *Pancha Mahabhutas* (Five Great Elements): Earth/ Prithvi, Air/Vayu, Space/Aakash, Waters/Apah, Light-Fire/Agni. The five elements are the cosmic elements which create, nurture, and sustain all forms of life. The principle of sanctity of life is clearly ingrained in the Vedas. Unity of Man and Nature is boldly manifested in the *Prithvi Sukta* of the *Atharva Veda* (2000 BCE). An entire chapter (*Prithivi Sukta*) consisting of 63 verses has been devoted in praise of Mother Earth. Mother Earth is seen as the nourisher and provider of space for the entire family of all beings-humans and others alike. The praise is based on the cosmic vision of our planet; on the fundamental concept of *Vasudaiv Kutumbakam*: every entity and organism is a part of one large extended family which is presided over by the eternal Mother Earth, and, abuse and exploitation of nature for selfish gain is unjust and sacrilegious. The *Prithivi Sukta* also exemplifies the relevance of environmental sustenance, agriculture and bio-diversity to human beings. The Hindu philosophy of cycle of birth and rebirth, wherein a person may come back as an animal or a bird gives these species not only respect but also reverence. The Puranic philosophy teaches respect for floral species. The Hindu heritage of eco-spirituality can and perhaps has us to control our base characteristics, such as greed, exploitation, abuse, mistreatment and defilement of nature. Similarly, in Jain tradition, there is a strict observance to vegetarianism, non-possession and frugality. Additionally, the scriptures outline a continuity of life forms ranging from elemental and microbial forms to plants and animals, to humans and Gods. These beliefs and practices are akin to the fundamental tenets of deep ecology and ecophilosophy (see Singhvi, 1990 and Tobias, 1991 for details). Buddhism too emphasises the interdependence of all life forms; it contains an elaborate teaching on harmonious man-nature relationship, and concerns for sustainability (see Badiner, 1990; Schmithausen, 1991, Batchelor and Kerry, 1992, and Martin, 1997 for Buddhist teachings on environment). Bible also addresses the inseparable interrelationship and interaction of the living and non-living environment (see Abraham, 1993; Carmody, 1983; Cobb, 1992; Das, 1995; Elder, 1970; Moltman, 1985, Santamaire, 1985 among others for the understanding of the relationship between Christian values and environment). Much in the like of ecology, Bible too speaks of systemic (ecological) balance. The teachings of Islam contain environmental values (see for instance, Manzoor, 1984 and

Khalid and O'Brien, 1992 for environmental values in Islamic religious tradition). Religion, as revealed from the above discussion, has taught mankind to revere, protect and conserve nature. It has historically served as a means of protecting the environment, maintaining an ecological balance, and sustaining life on earth.

Classic example of religious modulations of ecology and environment could be found among the Bisnois of North India. The 'Bishnois' are known as the conservationists to whom the preservation of animal and vegetable life is a religion and has been so from the early 15th century. Their spiritual mentor, Jambeshwarji was a wise ecologist. He formulated *Bis* (twenty) and *noi* (nine), totalling to twenty nine tenets from which the community derives its name. The tenets were tailored to conserve bio-diversity of the area but also ensured a healthy Eco-friendly social life for the community. Out of the 29 tenets, 10 are directed towards personal hygiene and maintaining good basic health, seven for healthy social behaviour, and five tenets to worship God. Eight tenets have been prescribed to preserve bio-diversity and encourage good animal husbandry. These include a ban on killing animals and felling green trees, and providing protection to all life forms (The community is also directed to see that the firewood they use is devoid of small insects. Wearing blue cloths is prohibited because the dye for coloring them is obtained by cutting a large quantity of shrubs. The Bishnoi tribes manage sacred groves (Malhotra *et al*, 2001. This paper also details the Bishnoi life style of eco-spirituality) called *orans* in the arid and desert regions of Rajasthan, in northwest India. Despite sparse vegetation and limited water resources, the area reportedly supports a higher density of human and animal populations than any other desert region in the world because of the conservation practices of its people. The basic philosophy of the Bishnoi faith is that all living things have a right to live and share resources, and the group has a set of abiding laws including a ban on killing animals and on felling trees, especially their most sacred *khejadi* tree, which has numerous life-sustaining properties. Its dropped leaves can be used for fodder, its dropped branches for fuel and its fruit for food. *Khejadi* trees stabilise sand dunes and they are said to increase yields of crops that grow close by. The *orans* also provide a protective habitat for the Indian gaselle and blackbuck. Many tribal communities in India, although not paralleling the Bishnois with a set of well defined principles of eco-conservation, yet practice rituals maintaining a healthy balance between man and nature (See also Deshmukh *et al*, 1998 for understanding the Bishnois and their ecospiritual principles of survival).

Religion can both complement and undermine development. Religious people and institutions may be agents of advocacy, funding, innovation, empowerment, social movements, and service delivery. Equally, religious people and institutions can incite violence, model hierarchy, oppose empowerment, deflect advocacy; absorb funding. When it comes to '*spaces*' that define a religious collective, any encroachment thereto may produce resentment.

SECTION III
Lepcha Religio-cultural Space, Development and the Politics of Ecology

Lepcha: A Brief Ethnographic Note

The Lepchas are one of a number of Mongoloid tribes inhabiting the southern slopes of the Himalayas. An acknowledged fact is that the history and chronology of the Lepchas are obscure. Scholars and historians like Gorer (1938), E.C Dosey (1922), G.B. Mainwaring (1971), J. C. White (1909), Christopher Haimendorf (1982), Rahul (1970), Foning (1987), Tamsang (1983), and others point out that the Lepchas are the original inhabitants of Darjeeling and Sikkim, which the Lepchas fondly call the 'Mayel Lyang' or the Abode of the Gods. Regarding the term '*Lepcha*', there are different versions. One version says that it was the Nepalis who called them '*Lapches*' meaning vile speakers. Another version says that '*Lapche*' was a type of fish found in Nepal, having the characteristics of being submissive like the Lepchas. But the Lepchas themselves prefer to be called *Rongs* or '*Mutanchi Rongkup*' meaning '*Beloved Sons of the Mother of Creation*'. Yet some believe that the word Lepcha comes from the word '*Lep*' meaning a well of creation in '*Mayel Kyong*'. Legends have it that it is the door through which the first among the Lepchas, *Fudong Thing* (the first male) and *Nuzong Nyu* (the first female) were made to step down from paradise into this world. Lepchas regard the *Zaa Tshaong* (the family) as the most important, and fundamental unit of social organisation, where each individual member is related in kinship ties of blood and marriage (Roy, 2007). They have an elaborate clan (*moo*) system consisting of both matrilineal and patrilineal clans. However, according to Tamsang (1983), politically and geographically, the Lepchas are divided into four sections–*Renjyongmoo*[2] (Lepchas of Darjeeling, Kurseong, and Siliguri), *Illammoo* (Lepchas of Illam, the Eastern District of Nepal), *Tamsangmoo*[3] (Lepchas of Kalimpong), and *Promoo*[4] (Lepchas of Western Bhutan). The demographic structure of the Sikkim Renjyongmoo is as shown in Table 6.1:

Table 6.1: Lepcha Population in Sikkim

Year	*Lepcha Population*	*Ten Years*	*Percentage of State Total Population*
1891	5,762	-	18.92
1901	7,313	+1,551	-
1911	9,031	+1,718	11.29
1921	9021	-10	-
1931	13,060	+4,039	11.89
1941	12,523	-537	10.31
1951	13,756	+1,233	9.99
1961	-	-	-
1971	22,316	+4,280	10.63
1981	23,234	+918	7.34
1991	29,854	+6,620	7.35
2001	40,586	+10,732	7.51

Source: Roy 2008.

Since the last four decades or so, the ratio of Lepcha population to the total population of the state has remained more or less stagnant (within 7.3% to 7.5%). This small population is scattered across the four districts of Sikkim. The following Table 6.2 shows the population of the Lepchas in the four districts.

Table 6.2: Lepcha Population in the Four Districts of Sikkim

District	*Lepcha Population*	*Percentage of Total District Population*
North	14,370	37.47
East	13,126	4.89
South	7,260	5.12
West	1,845	7.87

Source: Socio-Economic Survey, 2006, DESME, Government of Sikkim.

The North District of Sikkim, where the traditional home of the Lepchas is located, houses the maximum number of Lepcha population. Yet it is only 37.47% of the total state population. This shows that the Lepchas have become a miniscule minority in their own homeland. From this it is evident that the Lepchas are vehemently opposed to any threat to their religion, culture and livelihood opportunities because it may lead to the vanishing of a vanishing tribe.

Lepchas: Environment/Ecology and the Religio-Cultural Spaces and Expressions

Gurung and Lama (2004) are of the opinion that based on the origin stories, it is acknowledged that the Lepchas are nature worshippers. They are Animists by religion, and they worshipped the spirits of the mountains, rivers, forests, a natural outcome of their surroundings (White, 1909). They believe in two types of spirits–Good and bad. *Boomthing* (priest) and *Mun* (priestess) are regarded by the Lepchas as guardians protecting them from evil spirits with their spiritual powers. Both *Boomthing* and *Mun* are categorised into sevenfold categories. Therefore, the ancient religion of the Lepchas may be referred to as *Boothingism* and *Munism,* that advocate the doctrine of one ultimate substance or principle as mind or soul or something that is neither mind nor matter, but the ground of both, the position that the reality is one (Tamsang, 1983). However, Lepchas today are divided in terms of religion, whereas, some of them have adopted Christianity as their religious faith, some are Buddhists, and yet some have still remained animists. Therefore, it may appear rather anachronistic to talk in terms of a Lepcha collective based on religious denomination. However, Lepchas culture is embedded into their origin stories which are closely tied to their animistic rituals. Despite being followers of 'new' religions, the Lepchas, in their attempt to relocate their historical origins and to preserve their cultural heritage, fall back on to their origin stories that define their sacred spaces. Tamsang (1983) also believes that Buddhist Lepchas still follow *Boomthingism* and *Munism* and even the Christian Lepchas in the interior countryside still observe their own ancestral culture, customs, manners, traditions, language, way of life and living. Moreover, bulks of the Lepchas in Sikkim, by contrast to their West Bengal counterparts, are still followers of animism as their religion. Hence, the sacred spaces defined by their origin stories have remained so even for the converted Lepchas of Sikkim and elsewhere.

Lepchas' '*Sacred*' spaces are closely related to their origin stories. According to the creation stories, the first and the foremost primogenitors of the Lepchas were *Fudongthing* and *Nuzong Nyu*. They were created by God from the pure, virgin snows of *Kingtsoomzaongboo Choo's* pinnacle and sent them down to live, prosper and spread all over the fairy land of Mayel Lyang, that lies on the lap of *Kingtsoomzaongboo Choo*, that is Mount Kanchenjunga (Tamsang, 1983). This area is what constitutes Dzongu in North Sikkim today. Lepchas everywhere consider the Dzongu to be their holy land because their race was created by Mother Nature in Dzongu. They regard Mount Kanchenjunga as their mother mountain (Tamsang, 1983; Roy, 2005 and Little, 2008). Various religious and cultural rituals of the Lepchas thank the Creator and worship the place of their origin.

Reverend Samuel Dingrongmoo Lepcha (2009) shows a complex interconnection between Lepcha religious rites and nature. A religious rite of the Lepchas, *Mukjyekding Rumfaat* is of the sacred sacrifices wherein Lepchas are said to experience their relatedness with nature. Etymologically, *Mukjyekding Rumfaat* would mean the worship of the sprouting of grass; and it could also be interpreted as the celebration of the creation of Mother Nature. It is argued that *Mukjyekding Rumfaat* is a sacred moment because it reminds them not only of the act of creation but also of their divine participation in the created world. In the prayers chanted during the *Mukjyekding Rumfaat,* Lepchas thank the creator for creating oil-giving plants, perfume and medicinal plants and grasses, and rivers, streams and the fishes therein, and animals and humans. The prayers also contain the names of several species of insects, reptiles, etc. The celebration of the *Mukjyekding Rumfaat* is regarded as Lepchas' expression of their sense of cosmic unity. They believe that all realities have life (*Aasaom*), and the prayers during the celebration of the *Mukjyekding Rumfaat* refer to every aspect of the human and non-human world, rather the entire universe, from particles (*Aajum*) to stars (*Sahaar*), to land. (*Lyang*), to rivers (*Oong-kyaong*), to mountains (*Chyoo*), and so on. Thus, through their socio-religious and cultural rituals and practices the Lepchas create a cosmic fraternity and work for the cosmic balance (which is parallel to, if not more than, the concept of ecological balance in contemporary ecophilosophical literature), both locally and trans-locally, invoking the principle of *Nung nahaan*, meaning '*guest first*'. The link between nature and society is central to the religious belief of the Lepchas. The conjunction of the natural, spiritual and social worlds can be seen in the collective performance of the most important Lepcha ritual, *Mukjyekding Rumfaat*:[5]

This reveals that Lepchas are nature worshippers with a high degree of reverence for and an intimacy with nature. In other words, Lepchas' concern for environment is modulated by religion and religious spaces.

Development as Erasure[6] of Religio-Cultural Spaces

In independent India, national development has been largely equated with economic growth and surplus. Large centralised industries, irrigation and hydropower projects have been symbols of such development, which through the process of industrialisation promised to set India on the path of modernisation and development. Padam Nepal (2009) argues that post independent India favoured western development strategies based on the 'growth' model. The growth model is the capitalist paradigm which identifies development with heavy industrialisation and market-oriented high productivity. As Paul Routledge (2003) notes "official Indian discourses of development have tended to associate a Westernised culture of progress and modernity—what Visvanathan (1985) terms a 'vision of conquest'—with development projects such as large dams. Meanwhile 'non-modern', traditional and indigenous systems of knowledge have been devalued, and portrayed as '*unscientific*' and '*irrational*'. By their very existence, such practices have been perceived by development planners as in the way of India's continued modernisation." The impact of such development projects on the tribal communities, their lifestyle and identity, socio-cultural and religious, has been simply enormous. In this context, it is pertinent to analyse the recent protests of the Lepchas against the Dzongu-Hydel project by invoking religion and religious traditions, in the light of Lepchas reverence to Dzongu as the representation of the '*Sacred*', and the hydropower project in Dzongu as the erasure of their socio-religious space.

Dzongu[7], the traditional *Fakram-Takram*[8], in the Northern District of Sikkim is located in the southern face of the Eastern Himalayas. It is bordered by the International border with Nepal in the West, China in the North, and other districts of Sikkim in the South and River Teesta in the East. It is situated 77 kilometers north of Gangtok, the capital town of Sikkim; and 15 kilometers north-west of Mangan, the headquarters of the North District. It is located between 4,000 to 7,000 feet above sea level, at the foothills of Mount Kanchenjunga, the guardian deity of the Lepchas. The total area covered under Dzongu is 15,845 hectares of a roughly triangular mountain tract and the total population of Dzongu as per 1981 census was 7,745 persons. Administratively, Dzongu today is divided into 14 revenue blocks–Sakyong Pantong, Thingbong, Lingthem, Lingdem, Lizma, Salimpakel, Lingdong, Burfock, HiGyathang, Gor Tarayang, Shipbeak, Sangtook Sangyong, Mun sangdong and Lumlimtyang. Maharaja Tashi Namgyal of Sikkim had by proclamation declared the Dzongu area as a Lepcha reserve. This area has remained ecologically rich and diverse. Dzongu, which borders Mount Kanchenjunga National Park, constitutes a part of the Himalayan Biodiversity hotspot.[9] It is a spiritual and socio-cultural homeland of the Lepchas, associated with the *Chyoo*, *Da* and *Lep* of the Lepcha clans. Kerry Little (2008) observes that Lepchas everywhere consider the Dzongu to be their holy land, and that their race was created in Dzongu by Mother Nature. He also points out the fact that Lepchas belief Dzongus sacred status is not wholly related to religion, but it predates the colonisation of the Lepchas[10] and relates to their traditional culture. Lepchas believe that their soul will go to Dzongu when they die. It is their Mayel Lyang, a hidden paradise, a place where the largest tree is never cut down, strongest deer is never hunted, and wild orchids sprout aimlessly from the top of trees, making pink and purple bursts in the sky.

The state government of Sikkim proposed to build some twenty six hydro-power projects in the state on the River Teesta. The Most contentious Hydel Project, Teesta Stage IV, was stated to be built in the Dzongu Lepcha reserve. It consisted of six projects. One more project on the border of Dzongu at Dikchhu, which is nearing completion. Development, as envisaged in the construction of hydro-power plants in the sacred place of the Lepchas, was perceived by the community as encroachment on their livelihood resources and an erasure of their religio-cultural spaces.

There was an imminent fear that the specificity of their culture that has been nurtured by being with or in proximity to Dzongu and its landscape for generations will be lost. Disturbance to Dzongu would lead to the severing of the Lepchas' affiliational and genealogical ties with the non-human world. The community feels that they belong to the land of Dzongu, and the Dzongu land inheres in them, and hence, they cannot be alienated from the land. The community and Dzongu are bound by reciprocity, whereas they sustain in their lands, they are also obligated to provide sustenance to the land through rituals and ceremonial practices. It was seen as an imminent threat to their landscape that would be devastating to their language, religion and culture. Lepchas assert, "*We don't want to lose our Mayel Lyang, if it is desecrated, then our culture becomes extinct.*"[11] To safeguard their culture and religion, Lepchas are required to sustain their lands, and amidst threats of erasure of their cultural spaces by developmental processes, the only way to sustain their Mayel Lyang was through protests and resistance. This led to the emergence of a protest movement by the Lepchas in Dzongu.

The Politics of Protest: Linking Religion/Culture and Ecology

The notion of sacred land is rooted in local history, folklore and religion of a community. Sacred landscapes merge environment, history and religion and as such, they are a key-stone in the definition of relationship between man and nature. The notion of indigenous people and their sacred landscapes is intertwined with questions concerning nature/environment. Therefore, in most of the Indian environmental movements where it involves the tribal and indigenous communities, the nature of the protest movements have been confusing, quite often overlapping in the forms of tribal movement and/or environmental movement. However, the rise of a bulk of such tribal/environmental movements trace their roots to the mistaken and ill-conceived neo liberal government development policies, which have undoubtedly sharpened and exacerbated the perceptions among India's tribals that their livelihoods, lifestyles and identities are under threat. For almost two centuries now, tribal communities in India have been witness to the collapse of their multiple relationships with the land, the forest and among themselves. The basis of their cultural ethos, their systems of meaning have faced the collective onslaught of the disruptive impact of models of economic development which have been conceived without their participation and implemented without their consent. The present environmental protest movement in Sikkim, which represents a collective action based on a complex admixture of religio-cultural values of the Lepcha tribes and the issues of environment and sustainable development too, draws its origin in the ill-conceived development policies of the government.

Lepchas protest against the encroachment of the sacred religious spaces, their fight for their homeland—the Mayel Lyang, a battle for their culture and narratives began with a meeting at the BL House in Tibet Road in Gangtok in 2006. The protest movement against the Hydel projects in Sikkim in general and Dzongu in particular was initiated by the Affected Citizens of Teesta (ACT), in coalition with the various other groups including the Concerned Lepchas of Sikkim (CLOS). The movement originated, evolved and developed through a rough terrain of divisions and dissensions,[12] however, ultimately culminating into a potential force to drive in changes in government policies affecting the Lepcha community of Sikkim. The protest movement against the hydro-electric power plants in and around Dzongu operated at multiple scales, ultimately assuming significance in terms of mobilising participants across ethnic lines.

The Lepchas protested against the project on many grounds–socio-religious, livelihood and environmental. The Lepchas are contestations against the Dam were based on many grounds.

To summarise:

1. The Lepchas are nature worshippers, and Dzongu, their land, is sacred. Dzongu being an embodiment of their religio-cultural heritage, it should not be disturbed by developmental activities. This sacred land should not be destroyed by development. The loss of Dzongu may result in their ethnocide, the disappearance of their cultural heritage that is rooted to their ancestral connections and performance of rituals connected to the land, forest, mountain, lakes and nature.[13]
2. They also argue that projects will bring thousands of workers from outside Sikkim into Dzongu for several years till the completion of the project. Thus the outsiders may outnumber the Lepcha population in Dzongu (present Lepcha population is 7000 in Dzongu), leading gradually to their extinction.
3. The presence of a large number of the workers in Dzongu with different culture, customs and beliefs may dilute and destroy Lepcha culture in course of time.
4. The Lepchas also contend that the delicate ecology of Dzongu, which is on the border of Mount Kanchenjunga National Park, and which forms a part of the Himalayan biodiversity hotspot. Dzongu is a natural paradise for birds and there are more than 200 species in the area. The sparse population with scattered houses, dense

evergreen forests with topographical extremes creates a perfect arena for avifaunal diversity. Moreover, Sikkim is seismically sensitive and is unlikely to survive Mega Hydel projects in the name of development. Hence, they have also cited environmental reasons for the protest.

5. Finally, Lepcha community of Dzongu area derives a bulk of its livelihood from the forest resources. Encroachment of forest area by developmental projects would jeopardise their livelihood opportunities.

As evident, the protest movement had to stitch-in themes of indigenous tradition and culture and ecology together to give meaning and sense to the protest, whereas, enmeshing of the former with the politics of protest makes a strong case viewed from the perspective of the constitutional and legal provisions available for the safeguard of the scheduled groups in India, the intertwining of ecological/environmental issues deriving from the notions of sacred groves not only links the idea of environmental stewardship of the tribal communities to protest politics in the context of a perceived threat to the rich biodiversity of the sacred groves, it also at the same time links itself with the national and global environmental movements, facilitating network and alliance building with various environmental groups, NGOs, etc. The protest movement of the Lepchas has waged two interrelated forms of struggle–first, it has waged a representational struggle over the meaning of such processes as democracy and development. This has involved a discursive conflict over very different imagined geographies, pitting the abstract space of the state against the lived space of the tribal folks. Second, in the cultural realm, the identities and solidarities of the communities who support the movement are grounded around issues of kinship, neighbourhood, and the social networks of everyday life. The struggle against erasure is a religio-cultural struggle, not only over material conditions and needs, but also over the practices and meanings of everyday life (Escobar, 1992). Nature or ecology/environment is central to Lepcha religio-cultural belief system. To the Lepchas, environment and religion are intertwined. The development projects have been described as a violation of sacred landscape. The protest movement is taken as the community's battle for the recovery of their land, culture and their narratives amidst erasure by developmental projects.

The movement adopted multiple types of strategies and tactics. Ŝatyagrahas, pilgrimage to Dzongu-the sacred site, rallies, demonstrations and hunger-strikes were the common forms of protests. Petitions and memoranda also formed parts of methods creating pressure on the Government. For instance, in June 2007, ACT had led two hunger strikes of 63 and 96 days under the leadership of Ren Dawa Lepcha and Ren Tenzing Gyatso Lepcha in front of the BL House in Gangtok. These two hunger-strikes were supported by similar hunger-strikes in Kalimpong, Darjeeling and Kurseong, organised across ethnic lines.

The struggle succeeded in its objectives of stalling the projects. The deputation of the organisers of the movement to the Chief Minister in 2006 obtained assurances of the government that no development project would be carried out against the interest of the local communities. Chief Minister Pawan Kumar Chamling had expressed his deep concern for the people of North Sikkim and 'culture, tradition, and identity would never be compromised for the sake of development alone'. Consequently in 2008, the Government of Sikkim declared the stalling of four projects in and around Dzongu as a response to the local protests. The four projects that were cancelled as a result of the agitation are Ringpi (90 MW), Rukel (33 MW), Rangyong (117 MW) and Lingza (120 MW). The cancellation of these projects was announced by the Government of Sikkim in a letter addressed to Shri Athup Lepcha.[14] To commemorate the scraping of the Projects by the Government, the 96 days hunger-strike was called off by the ACT on 15 June 2008. However, the organisation continued its mobilisation against the two other Mega Projects-one in Panang and the other-Teesta IV in Dzongu.

SECTION IV:
Analysis and Concluding Observations

Narratives, text, discourse, metaphor, rituals, actors, and performances, the key themes of contemporary cultural analysis have not been widely employed to explain how social movements come into being and develop. The present chapter has illustrated the complexity of the interactions between these elements of the cultural complex including religion (an aspect of the complex of culture), development and the environment, and some of the ways in which this nexus is relevant to development policy and practice. Viewing the state-directed development process as inimical to local socio-religious tradition and livelihood, many social movements actively affirm local identity, culture and systems of knowledge as an integral part of their resistance. In doing so, these movements articulate locally-based terrains of resistance to the dominating discourse of development, expressing their own counter-hegemonic and/or anti-development discourses and practices. For instance, morally and spiritually, the Lepcha community owes responsibility for maintaining the power of the sacred site of Dzongu, through observance of rituals and ceremonies. The present movement has emerged in Lepchas attempt to sustain and maintain the power of the sacred site of Dzongu amidst threats of encroachments by the process of development that would disturb the serenity and purity of the place. The kind of sustainable nature-society relation envisioned by the present movement required the development of decentralised, democratic control over natural resources, and, even more fundamentally, the decommodification of nature as such for its realisation, simultaneously protecting and preserving the religion and culture of the community in question, in keeping with Spicer's (1952) observation that changing peoples' customs is more delicate responsibility than surgery, which the protest movement consciously and deliberately attempts to avoid. Lepchas' collective action transcended a simple struggle for land, and that what did in fact animate their participation in the protest movement amidst inherent dissensions and divisions was the wish to defend a way of life that was valuable to them in multiple tangible and intangible ways. It was the *value* of maintaining the community as much as the *interest* in maintaining their land that propelled them to resist.

The protest movement has successfully contributed, although incrementally, to sustainable development experience in Sikkim. Various reports had already started pointing out the ill-effects of mega dams in Sikkim. There was glacial break at Zemu, the source of River Teesta, and occasional flash floods had started taking place, Sikkim experienced cut off from rest of the country because of landslides and resultant road blocks. The timely stalling of a few projects in response to the protest movement has at least contributed to reducing such impacts, and thereby, contributing to sustainability. Moreover, the movement, grounded in their religio-cultural belief system, helped the Lepcha-folks to rediscover their history, culture, language and narratives, and mobilise them to actively participate in politics, thereby bringing about political and cultural consciousness among the Lepchas. The preservation of tribal culture within the context of a development process taking place within that culture's own environment and under its control provides opportunities for cultural sustainability Alongwith environmental sustainability. In a nutshell, the movement contributed to the sustainability of both natural and social systems (and social institutions of the Lepchas), thereby bringing in the concept of inclusive developmental policy and sustainable development experience in Sikkim.

Notes

1. Tong Chee Kiong and Lily Kong (2000) in their Religion and Modernity: Ritual Transformations and the Reconstruction of Space and Time explore the meaning of the concept the sacred/ space. According to them, the concept of religious space can be understood in a variety of ways, focusing on what is conceived to be sacred. They argue that research on the investment of religious meanings in places has been multi-disciplinary. One is the examination of macro-and microcosmic parallelism which involves the symbolic religious meanings invested in cities, kingdoms, palaces and temples, particularly in their physical layout, particularly in terms of how the world of humans is patterned after the domain of gods (Kong, 1990). The second is the exploration of the symbolism of religious buildings, architecture and objects (Tillich, 1966; Dillistone, 1966). The third is the analysis of how places and objects become imbued with religious meanings, that is, the *process* of sanctification (Eliade, 1957). The fourth is the examination of people's experience of sacred places (James, 1902; Otto, 1917; Kong, 1992).
2. The Renjyongmoo Lepchas are the Lepchas of Sikkim, Darjeeling, Kureong and Siliguri. Tamsang (1983) says that the inclusion of these three categories of Lepchas into one *moo* owes to the fact

that this geographical area was once a part and parcel of Sikkim until 13 January, 1835, since when these territories were annexed to British India. *Renjyong* here means Sikkim and *moo* as a suffix means *'belong to'*, hence referring to Lepchas of Sikkim.

3. Tamsang (1983) points out that Kalimpong was once an independent state ruled by a Lepcha King named Gaeboo Achok Pano. King Gaeboo Achok Pano and his forefathers, according to Tamsang, belonged to belonged to the Lepcha Clan called Tamsang, and they were also called Tamsang Pano by the Lepchas. Hence, owing to their history of being ruled by Tamsangs, they are called Tamsangmoo. He further argues that this kingdom came to an end with Gaeboo Achok Pano being killed at Daling Fort, after which it became a part of Bhutan and, eventually Kalimpong became a part of British India in 1865 when Bhutan was defeated at Daling by the British under the command of Brigadier General Dunsford CB (see Tamsang, 1983, p. 44 for details).
4. '*Pro*' in Lepcha refers to the country of Bhutan. According to Tamsang (op.cit), after the Daling War, the Lepchas in the Terai region were uprooted by British Tea Planters who moved eastward and settled in a place called by the Lepchas as Zaongsaw in the Western part of Bhutan. This group of Lepchas in Western Bhutan are called the *Promoo* Lepchas.
5. The link between nature and society is central to the religious beliefs of almost all adivasis. The parallel of Mukjyekding Rumfaat of the Lepchas is found in case of the Bhilala Tribes of the Narmada Valley. For Bhilalas, affecting nature's cycle is intrinsic to a cosmology that imbues *all* natural phenomena with spiritual life, so that the hills, trees, stones and crops actively intervene in people's daily life. The conjunction of the natural, spiritual and social worlds can be seen in the collective performance of the most important Bhilala ritual—*indal pooja* (the worship of the union of the rain and earth which brings forth grain. This has been referred to in Routledge (2003).
6. The concept of 'Erasure' used here is borrowed from Paul Routledge (2003) Voices of the Dammed–Discursive Resistance amidst Erasure in the Narmada Valley, India.
7. Ren Lyangsong Tamsang of the Indigenous Lepcha Tribal Association based at Kalimpong, in his letter addressed to Shri Pawan Kumar Chamling, the Hon'ble Chief Minister of Sikkim, clarifies the meaning of Dzongu. According to Tamsang, the current usage 'Dzongu' is a mispronunciation of the correct

'*Dzongbu*, which means the land of plenty, of abundance, of prosperity. Explanations on Dzongu-the Mayel Lyang could also be obtained from D. T. Tamlong (2008) The Mayel Lyang and the Lepchas About Sikkim and Darjeeling), Mani Printing House Darjeeling.

8. The concept has been explained by Roy (2007) thus: Dzongu was originally called *Faokram-Takram* by the Lepchas. *Faokram* in Lepcha means a ladder and *Takram* refers to a standing tree which is cut at different places to act as a ladder so that the climber can climb up. The physical-topographical structure of Dzongu is said to look like a staircase. However, according to Tamsang in his letter addressed to the Chief Minister of Sikkim, the meaning of *Faokram Takram* is the "Source of Lepchas' Origin and Life'.
9. The area has been recognised as a part of the Himalayan Biodiversity hot spot, details of which has been provided at http://www.biodiversityhotspots.org/xp/Hotspots/himalaya/Pages/default.aspx and has also been referred to by Kerry Little (2008) p. 231.
10. Lepchas today believe that the Lepchas were colonised by the Tibetans following the Blood Treaty signed between the Lepchas and the Tibetans *at Kabi Longtshok*, nearly 20 kms. north-west of Gangtok. It is regarded as the beginning of the end of the self rule of the Lepchas. The exact date of the agreement is not available as there are contending versions on the period of the treaty. However, according to Tamsang (1983), the Blood Treaty was signed sometimes in the 13th century.
11. Athup Lepcha's communication with Vibha Arora quoted in Arora (2007), p. 3451.
12. See article entitled "AILSDO Not to Participate in ACT's December 12 Rally", Sikkim Express of December 11, 2006, p. 1 and 'Concerned Lepchas of Sikkim Backs ACT", NE News Bureau, Sikkim Express, December 12, 2006, p. 1 for the details on the initial dissentions and divisions within the protest movement organisers and the participants.
13. Arora, *op.cit.* p. 3453.
14. See the letter issued by Shri P Wangchen, PCE cum Secretary, Government of Sikkim, addressed to Shri Athup Lepcha, vide Ref DO No. 102/GOS/EDP/05-06/1391 dated 12 June 2008. This letter has also been reproduced in Aachulay, Vol. 12, No. 2, July 2008, p. 15.

References

Abraham, K.C. (1993). *Eco-Justice: New Agenda for Church's Mission*, Bombay: Bombay Publishing.

Arora, Vibha (2007). "Unheard Voices of Protest in Sikkim", *Economic and Political Weekly*, August 25.

Badiner, A.H. (1990). *Dharma Gala: A Harvest of Essays in Buddhism and Ecology*, Berkeley, California: Parallax Press.

Banerji, A.K. and Others (1980). *West Bengal District Gazetteer, Darjeeling.*

Banerji, G.C. (1977). *The Problem of the Lepchas in Darjeeling Himalayas*, Man in India, 57(3).

Batchelor, M. and Kerry Brown (1992). *Buddhism and Ecology*, London: Cassell Publishers.

Berger, Peter L. (1999), *The Desecularisation of the World: Resurgent Religion and World Politics*. Michigan: William B. Eerdmans.

Carmody, J. (1983). *Ecology and Religion: Toward a New Christian Theology of Nature*, New York: Paulist Press.

Christoph, von Furer-Haimendorf (1982). *Tribes of India*, Berkeley: University of California Press (Indian Reprint: Oxford India Paperbacks).

Cobb, John B. (1992). Post-Modern Christianity in Quest of Eco-Justice", After Nature's Revolt: D Hessel edited *Ecojustice and Theology*, Pa, VSA: Fortress Press.

Census, 1971, Series 22, *West Bengal District Handbook, Darjeeling*, 1981 Census Report.

Daedelus (2001). Journal of the American Academy of Arts and Sciences Special Issue: *Religion and Ecology: Can the Climate Change*? Fall 2001.

Das, A.K. and S.K. Banerjee (1961). The Lepchas of Darjeeling District, Bulletin of Cultural Research Institute.

Deshmukh, S., Gogate, M.G. and A.K. Gupta (1998). "Sacred Groves and Biological Diversity: Providing new dimensions to conservation Issue", Ramakrishnan et al eds*Conserving, the Sacred for Biodiversity Management* , New Delhi: Oxford and IBH Publishing Co.

Dozey, E.C. (1922). *A Concise History of Darjeeling District since 1835 with a complete Itinerary of Tours in Sikkim and the District* (2nd edn) Calcutta: Art Press.

Dwivedi, O.P. and B.N. Tiwari (1987). *Environmental Crisis and Hindu Religion,* New Delhi, Gitanjali Publishing House.

Elder, F. (1970). *Crisis in Eden: A Religious Study of Man and Environment*, Ambingdon.

Escobar, A. (1992). "Culture, economics, and politics in Latin American social movements theory and research". A. Escobar, and S. E. Alvarez (Eds.), *The making of social movements in Latin America* (Boulder: Westview Press.

Foning, Authur, R. (1987). *Lepcha: My Vanishing Tribe,* New Delhi: Sterling Publishers Pvt. Ltd.

Gorer, G. (1938). *Himalayan Village: An Account of the Lepchas of Sikkim*. London: Thomas, Nelson & Sons Ltd.

Gottleib, R. (ed.) (1996). *This Sacred Earth: Religion, Nature, Environment*, Routledge: London.

Lal, S.K. (1995). "Pancamahabhutas: Origin and Myths in Vedic Literature", in Sampat Narayan Edited *Prkakriti: A Integral Vision* (Vol. 2), New Delhi, Indira Gandhi National Centre for Arts.

Little, Kerry (2008). "Lepcha Narratives of their Threatened Sacred Landscapes", *Transforming Cultures Journal,* Vol. 3, No. 1.

Little, Kerry (2010). "democracy Reigns Supreme in Sikkim? A Long March and a Short Visit Strains Democracy for Lepcha Marchers in Sikkim", *Australian Humanities Review*, Issue No. 48.

Lepcha, Dingrongmoo Samuel (2009). "Mukjyekding Rumfaat of the Lepcha Tribe: Tribals outlook on Nature: Through Nature to God", *Aachulay*- A Quarterly Bilingual News Magazine, Kalimpong, Vol. 13, No.1, April.

Mainwarning, G.B. (1971). *A Grammer of the Lepcha Language*. New Delhi. Manjushree Publishing House.

Malhotra, K.C., Y. Gokhle, S. Chatterjee, and S. Srivastava (2001).*Cultural and Ecological Dimensions of Sacred Groves in India*, New Delhi: INSA.

Martin, Julia (1997). *Ecological Responsibility: A Dialogue with Buddhism*, New Delhi: Tibet House.

Moltmann, J. (1985). God in Creation: An Ecological Doctrine of Creation (SCM Press).

Morris, G. (1938). *Living with Lepchas*, London: William Heineman Ltd.

Nepal, Padam (2009). *Environmental Movements in India: Politics of Dynamism and Transformations*, New Delhi: Authorspress.

O'Malley, L.S.S. (1907). *Bengal District Gazetters, Darjeeling*, New Delhi: Logos Press.

Rahul, Ram (1970). *The Himalayan Borderland*, New Delhi: Vikas Publishing.

Routledge, P. (2003). "Voices of the Dammed: Discursive Resistance amidst Erasure in the Narmada Valley, India", *Political Geography* 22 (2003) 243-270.

Roy, Dulal Chandra (2007). "Demographic Profile of the Lepchas in the World: A Case of India, Nepal and Bhutan," *Aachulay*-A Quarterly Bilingual News Magazine, Kalimpong, Vol. 12, No. 1, April.

Roy, Dulal Chandra (2008). "Women Among the Lepchas: A Socio-Economic Study ," *Aachulay*-A Quarterly Bilingual News Magazine, Kalimpong, Vol. 11, No. 2, July.

Schmithauser, Lambert (1991). *Buddhism and Nature*, Tokyo: The International Institute of Buddhist Studies.

Selinger, L. (2004) "The Forgotten Factor: The Uneasy Relationship between Religion and Development", *Social Compass* 51 (4): 523–543.

Singh, Karan (1986). *The Hindu Declaration in Nature*, Declaration on Religion and Nature made at Assisi, Italy, Gland, Switzerland, WWF.

Sweetman, C. (1999). "Editorial", *Gender and Development* 7 (1): 2–6.

Tamsang, K.P. (1983). *The Unknown and Untold Reality About the Lepchas*, Hongkong: Luen Sun Offset Printing Co. Ltd.

Tobias, M (1991). *Life Force: The World of Jainism*, Berkeley, California, Asian Humanities Press.

Visvanathan, S. (1985). From the Annals of the Laboratory State. Lokayan Bulletin, 3(4/5), 23-46.

White, J.C. (1909). *Sikkim and Bhutan: 21 Years on the North East Frontier (1887-1908),* London, 1909.

White, L. (1967). "The Roots of our Ecological Crisis" *Science* 155: 48-56.

World Commission on Environment and Development (1987). *Our Common Future* (Bruntland Report), Oxford: Oxford University Press.

WWF, (1986). *The Assisi Declaration: Messages on Man and Nature from Buddhism, Christianity, Hinduism, Islam and Judaism*, London: WWF.

7

Empowerment, Development and the Status of Women in Sikkim

Introduction

The empowerment of women is recognised globally as a key element to achieve progress in all areas. It is one of the eight Millennium Development Goals adopted by 189 nations and signed by 147 heads of states and governments during UN Millennium Summit held in 2000. Today the empowerment of women has emerged as an important issue in our society. The empowerment and autonomy of women and the improvement of women's social, economic and political status is essential for the achievement of both transparent and accountable government and administration and sustainable development in all areas of life (Pargunan 2007). In India, women constitute half of the country's total population– 623.7 million male and 586.5 million female (Census 2011). The development of women thus, have a direct link with nation's development because it is not possible for the nation to develop without the development of this vast segment. In other words, the real progress of a country can only be made if women are made partners in the process of development. Women plays direct role in agriculture, animal husbandry, horticulture, forestry and so on for sustainable development. Therefore, both developed and developing nations across the world focused their policies on the need for development of women and their active participation in the mainstream of development. Development, be it social, economic or humane is not possible without the active participation of women. And it is a well-known fact that women empowerment is essential both to attain the gender equality and to treat all women at par with men by removing all sorts of discrimination, humiliation, disgrace, and dishonour of women by men. The concern of gender development is therefore unquestionable and imperative. Thus, in a gender issue, improvement of women's position and empowerment of women is inextricately linked with human development and one cannot go without other (Sanyal 2001).

Understanding Empowerment

The idea of empowerment has taken a hold over the minds of increasing number of persons in the last few years. It is now widely employed in the press, on television, and in political, academic and even legal circles (Beteille 1999). Empowerment, today has became a buzz word among the scholars, academicians, political scientists and social activists and the 'women empowerment' has become a new phrase in the vocabulary of gender literature. The gender equality and empowerment of women has been recognised as a central issue in determining the status of women.

The term 'empowerment' has much in common with other concepts used by development practitioners and planners, such as 'participation', 'capacity building', 'sustainability', or 'institutional development' (Rowlands 2006). There is no common and universally accepted definition of the term empowerment and therefore we found various definitions by different scholars. Empowerment, in its broadest term, refers to an institutional environment that enables women to take 'control over material assets, intellectual resources and ideology' (Batliwala 1994). According to Koko U (1992) empowerment is a process which helps people to assert their control over the factors which affect their lives. McWhirter (1991) defines empowerment as 'the process by which people, organisations or groups who are powerless (a) become aware of power dynamics at work in their life contexts, (b) develop the skills and capacity of gaining some reasonable control over their lives, (c) exercise this control without infringing upon the rights of others, and (d) support the empowerment of others in the community'. The above definitions on empowerment reflects that empowerment is a process through which people gain control over the variables that hinder their choices and holds them back from exercising their choices towards enhancing the quality of their life (Ravillion and Chen 2001; Rowlands 1995; Nussbaum 2000; Sen 1999). Empowerment of women means developing them as more aware individuals, who are politically active, economically productive and independent and are able to make intelligent decisions in matters that affect them (Pamecha and Khatik 2005).

Women and Constitution of India

In India, the upliftment of women both socially and economically was initiated with the adoption of the Constitution in 1950. In an attempt to make a radical departure from the age old poor social status of women, the framers of the Indian Constitution has made a several provisions for the advancement of women in India. This grant of constitutional gender equality in the spheres of social, economic and political in independent India has attained a legal support in the process of empowerment through a series of legislation. The original Constitution of India has incorporated some special provisions for women of the country in regard to gender equality under the chapter of Fundamental Rights and Duties and the Directive Principle of State Policy. Most important among them are equality before law and equal protection of law (Article14), prohibition of discrimination on sex (Article 15(1)), empowering the state to make special provision for women and child (Article 15(3)), prohibition of trafficking in human being (Article 23), equal pay for equal work for both men and women (Article 39), to secure just and human condition of work and maternity relief (Article 42) and a constitutional duty of every citizens of country to renounce practices derogatory to the dignity of women (Article 51A(e)). Above provisions clearly shows the country's concern in safeguarding the rights and privileges of women in the Constitution of India.

Women and National Plans

Empowerment of women is the prime objectives of all national plans right from the very beginning. The First Five Year Plan (1951-56) envisaged a concept of women's development, and therefore, adopted measures mainly of welfare oriented. The establishment of Central Social Welfare Board in 1953, organisation of *Mahila Mandals* and other welfare programmes under Community Development Programmes and National Extension Services were the few steps taken in this direction. The Second, Third, Fourth and Fifth Plans continued to reflect the very same welfare approach adopted in First Plan. All plans accorded high priority to education and health of women.

The Sixth Plan (1980-85) was regarded as landmark in the history women's development. The plan saw a shift in the approach from 'welfare' to 'development'. The plan adopted the multi-disciplinary approach with a special thrust on the three core sectors of health, education and employment. For the first time, separate chapter on women and development was included in the plan document.

The Seventh Five Year Plan (1985-90) continued the developmental programmes for women with the major objectives of raising the economic and social status and bringing women into the mainstream of national development. A significant step in this direction was to identify and promote the 'Beneficiary-Oriented Schemes' in various developmental sectors which extended direct benefits to women. The Eighth Plan (1992-97) saw the shift of approach from development to empowerment. The plan promised to ensure that the benefits of development from different sectors do not bypass women and special programmes will be implemented to complement the general development programmes. This plan focused on empowering women, especially at the grass roots level, through reservation of seats in the local bodies.

The Ninth Plan (1997-2002) adopted a strategy of Women's Component Plan. Under this component plan, not less than 30 per cent of funds/benefits flow to women from all the general development sectors. The plan also suggested to keeps special vigil on the flow of the earmarked funds or benefits through an effective mechanism to ensure that proposed strategy brings forth a holistic approach towards empowering women.

The Tenth Plan (2002-2007), based on the recommendation of National Policy on the Empowerment of Women of 2001, has suggested the three-fold strategy for empowering women through social empowerment, economic empowerment and gender justice.

Objective of the Study

Given this background, an attempt has been made to study the present status of women's empowerment in Sikkim. The principal thrust of the study has been to assess the socio-economic and political conditions of women, to evaluate and measure the extent of women's empowerment and to suggest some remedial measures to improve the women's status in the state.

Methodology

The present study is a combination of both descriptive and diagnostic. It is descriptive as it seeks to describe precisely and accurately the state of empowerment in general and women empowerment in particular in Sikkim. The study is diagnostic in the sense that it seeks to diagnose as to what are the forces and factors that tend to contribute/hinder the process of development and empowerment of women in Sikkim. Both the primary and the secondary data were collected from various relevant sources. Primary data were collected through discussion, observation and interview. Besides, the census reports, NFHS reports, official records, statistical publications and the Gazetteers of the Government etc. were used as secondary data for the study. Statistical tools, such as ratios, percentages, tables, charts, etc. were used for the analysis and interpretation of data.

Sikkim, an erstwhile Himalayan kingdom became a twenty-second state of Indian republic in 1975. It is situated in the western part of the Eastern Himalaya region. The total geographical area of Sikkim is 7,096 sq.km that is 0.22 per cent of the total geographical area of India. About 83 per cent of total area of the state is covered by forest. High peaks, deep valleys, hilly terrain and a wide variation in altitude and vegetation characterise the topography of the state. The state at present comprised of North, East, South and West districts.

According to the 2011 Census, the population of the state is 6,07,688 persons. The decadal growth rate of population during 2001-2011 is recorded at 12.36%, which is lesser than in earlier decade (33.07%). The state is sparsely populated having a density of 86 person per sq.km as compared to 382 person for the country as a whole.

Sikkim, with a women population of 2,86,027 (i.e., 45.42%) (Census 2011), has a sound track record of maintaining gender equality. The state government has consciously worked to consolidate this tradition of not discriminating on the basis of gender and giving due respect to both genders (Lama 2001). The Gender related Development Index (GDI) in the state has steady improvement from 0.499 in 1995 to 0.528 in 1998. Moreover, women in the state, unlike in other parts of the country, are not secluded and practice of dowry, sati and female infanticide are absent. However, the sex ratio in the state (889/1000) is the lowest in relation to other north-east states. In contrast to the unfavourable sex ratio, the numbers of women in government jobs are fairly good, and comparatively, the women in the state enjoy better position than the women of some other states of Indian union. Still the women here are victims of domestic violence, gender inequality and social taboos. Alcoholism, wife-beating bigamy, etc. are the common features in Sikkimese society.

Social Empowerment

Empowering women contribute to social development. Economic progress in any country, whether developed or underdeveloped, could be achieved through social development (Singh and Kumari 2007). According to Tenth Plan Document, social empowerment means to create an enabling environment through various affirmative developmental policies and programmes for development of women besides providing them easy and equal access to all the basic minimum services so as to enable them to realise their full potentials.

Education

Education is a key to development and empowering women. It is in fact a dynamic force in the life of every individual influencing his physical, mental, emotional, racial and ethical development. Education is one of the most important means of empowering women and of giving knowledge, skills and the self-confidence necessary to be full partner in the development process. Education to females greatly improves the ability of household to manage basic child care, increases the nutritional content of diets, ensure more effective diagnosis of diseases, acceptance of family planning and their empowerment. Moreover, education enhances a woman's position through decision-making autonomy, control over resources, knowledge, exposure to the modern world and husband-wife closeness (Jejeebhoy 1995; Kishor and Gupta 2004). According to UNICEF (1999), educating the girls would bring broad social benefits– (i) the more educated a mother is, the more infant and child mortality is reduced, (ii) children of more educated mothers tend to be better nourished and suffer less from illness, (iii) educated women are less likely to die in child birth, and (iv) educated women are more likely to play a role in political and economical decision-making at community regional and national levels. There is thus a close link between education and better health care. Amartya Sen, Nobel Laureate, in the book 'India: Economic Development and Social Opportunity' observes that women empowerment can positively influence the lives not only of women themselves but also of men and children. Mahatma Gandhi had also said, "If you educate a man, you will educate but one. But if you educate a woman, you will educate a nation." The educational level of women has an inevitable impact on the entire family in creating a healthy, educated and disciplined nation (Immanuel 1998).

According to Census of 2011, the female literacy rate in Sikkim is 76.43 per cent far below the male literacy, that is, 87.30 per cent but higher than the all-India female literacy of 65.46 per cent. Yet, 23.57 per cent of the female in the state are illiterate and unaware of various factors of life to improve its quality. The literacy rate of male increased from about 11.19 per cent in 1951 to nearly 87.30 per cent in 2011. The corresponding change in female literacy rate has been from around 1.2 per cent to 76.43 per cent. Table 7..1 shows the literacy rate of male and female in Sikkim from 1951 to 2011.

Table 7.1: Female Literacy Rate in Sikkim (1951-2011)

Year	*Male*	*Female*	*Total*
1951	11.19	1.2	6.59
1961	19.5	4.2	12.3
1971	25.37	8.9	17.74
1981	43.85	22.2	34.05
1991	65.7	46.76	56.94
2001	76.73	61.46	69.68
2011	87.30	76.43	82.20

It is clear that female literacy rate is much less as compared to male. The prevalence of poverty, existence of few educational institutions and the monarchial system of government where only affluent class of people had access to schools in Sikkim have been the major causes of low literacy among both the men and female. The merger of Sikkim to India in 1975 led to the formation of democratic government and this democratically elected government initiated various welfare programmes including the establishment of schools in different part of the state. This change in the political system has also brought improvement in the rate of literacy in Sikkim. Besides, the implementation of the national programmes for education like National Literacy Mission, Operation Black Board, Sarva Siksha Abhiyan and other non-formal education schemes, have greatly improved the literacy rate in general and female literacy in particular. The state at present has 739 pre-primary schools, 183 lower primary, 313 primary schools, 127 junior high schools, 80 secondary schools and 36 senior secondary schools.

Despite all these efforts on the part of the government and comparatively good performances of the state in Gender Development Index (GDI), the enrolment of girls is lower than that of boys at all levels, except in the middle schools. The enrolment position of boys and girls aged 15-24 indicates that there is a considerable difference between the boys and girls enrolment at higher secondary and higher levels and proportion of male enrolment (13.05) is much higher than the female enrolment (9.15 per cent) at the state level. Their dropout rate

Table 7.2: Female Literacy and Gender Gap in Literacy Rate: Sikkim and North-East States

State	*FLIT 2011*	*GDLR 2011*
Sikkim	76.43	10.86
Arunachal Pradesh	59.57	14.12
Manipur	73.17	13.32
Meghalaya	73.78	3.39
Mizoram	89.40	4.32
Nagaland	76.69	6.6
Assam	67.27	11.54
Tripura	83.15	9.03
India	65.46	16.68

Sources: Census of India, 2011.
Note: FLIT – Female literacy.
GDLR – Gender difference in literacy rate.

is also higher due to relatively early age of marriage. Over 60 per cent of rural women and 70 per cent of urban women get married before they are 20 years old (HDR 2001). The Parliamentary Committee on Empowerment of Women in its report on Educational Programmes for Women (2000-2001) also ascribed low Gross Enrolment Ratio (GER) and high dropout rates to gender inequality, social discrimination and economic exploitation coupled with low enrolment of girls in school, low retention and high drop-out rates.

Health

Health is another important component in the process of women's empowerment. Health, according to the definition of WHO (1948), is a state of complete physical, mental, and social well-being and not merely an absence of disease or infirmity. The attainment of the highest possible levels of health by all peoples is one of the fundamental rights of every human being. The health and nutrition problem of women and children is a matter of great concern on both national and state level. The health of these segments of population has profound implications for the socio-economic well-being of any country. In an endeavour to provide good quality health care for all, the central government has launched the National Rural Health Mission (April 2005) which seek to improve the health care infrastructure in village level not only by integrating ongoing health programme and providing additional medicine and facilities, but also creating a dedicated health worker in every village. In the first phase, focus will be on 18 states from the northern and central India, the North-East and Jammu and Kashmir. Among the 18 selected states, Sikkim is one of them. The main goals of NRHM are to reduce infant and maternal mortality rates, prevention and control of communicable disease etc. It also calls for creation of one health worker ASHA or Accredited Social Health Activist, at every village. In the financial year 2011-12, Rs. 18,172 crore was allocated for NRHM. For both the objectives and increased allocation of resource for health is the necessary step.

In Sikkim, the health standard has improved significantly over the last 20 years. The improvement in health and medical facilities helped to reduce both maternal and infant mortality rate in the state. The state today has 24 primary health centres (PHCs), 147 primary health sub-centres (PHSCs), and 4 community health centres besides the central referral hospital

Table 7.3: Estimate of Infant Mortality Rate (no./000): Sikkim and India

Year	*Sikkim*			*India*		
	Rural	*Urban*	*Total*	*Rural*	*Urban*	*Total*
1995	47	27	47	NA	NA	NA
1996	47	32	47	77	46	72
1997	51	41	51	77	45	71
1998	52	44	52	77	45	72
1999	50	33	49	75	44	70
2001	49	36	49	74	43	68

Source: Sikkim: A Statistical Profile, 2005-06.
Note: Total= (R+U); NA=Not Available.

at Gangtok. Along with this expansion of the public health infrastructure, the government has also increases the budgetary allocation of resources from Rs. 759 lakhs in 1997-98 to Rs. 1600 lakhs in 2002-03.

These developments in the health sector have helped to some extent in reducing the maternal and infant mortality rates in the state. The infant mortality rate (IMR) in 2001 was 49 per thousand which is lower than the all-India average of 68 per thousand (Census 2001). IMR is always high in rural areas as compared to that in urban areas. The rural IMR (49) was much higher than IMR of 36 reported in urban areas. The poor delivery of health care services, low nutritional level, low rates of women's literacy etc. in the rural areas are some of the reasons for this high mortality rate. The low literacy among the females has a great impact on infant mortality. The deprivation of education not only affects the advancement of women in life but also influence nutrition, health and disease burdens. Lower literacy and education levels of mothers have an impact on the infant mortality and child mortality. States with lower female literacy generally have higher infant mortality (India Vision 2020). The malnutrition and under-nutrition continue to be a cause of concern. A 1989 survey of the record age, weight and height and calculation of nutritional index indicated that: 29 per cent of the mothers were under nourished, 14.8 per cent were stunted (height less than 145 cms) and over 40 per cent of children under 5 years of age were suffering from various degrees of malnutrition (Lama 2001). Though there was little improvement in the figures mentioned above during the later course of time, the challenge of nutrition security before the state is still formidable.

Anemia among the women is another major concern for the government. According to NFHS-II, every second women in India suffers from some degree of anemia. Severe anaemia is reported by 2 per cent of women, while mild and moderate anaemia levels affect 95 per cent and 15 per cent respectively. Anaemia is defined as mild when hemoglobin concentrations are less than 10g/dl but less than cut off value, moderate when concentration is between 7g/dl and 10g/dl and severe when the figure is below 7g/dl (Dutta and Ashrit 2006) The National Commission for Women in its document entitled Status of

Women in India-2001 brought out in 2002 also said that anaemia continues to be a greater villain that increases gynecological morbidity of women. Anemia in a pregnant women leads to adverse pregnancy outcomes such as high maternal and neonatal mortality, low birth weight, obstetrical risks, increased morbidities, serious impairment of the physical and mental development of the child, etc. (Dutta and Ashrit 2006). Sikkim stands seventh in all India rank of women suffering from anaemia. It has 60.0 per cent of women with one or other type of anaemia which are higher than national average of 55.3 per cent (NHFS 3). Among the north-eastern state, Sikkim has very high incidence of anaemia and stand only after the state of Assam (69.5 per cent) and Tripura (65.1 per cent) (Table 7.4).

Table 7.4: Women Suffering from Anaemia: Sikkim and Other North Eastern States

States	*Percentage of women with any type anaemia*	*Mild anaemia*	*Moderate anaemia*	*Severe anaemia*
Sikkim	60.0	42.1	16.2	1.7
Arunachal Pradesh	50.6	36.6	12.5	1.6
Manipur	35.7	30.1	5.1	0.5
Meghalaya	47.2	32.8	12.6	1.8
Nagaland	38.4	27.8	9.6	1.0
Mizoram	38.6	29.1	8.8	0.7
Assam	69.5	44.8	21.2	3.4
Tripura	65.1	49.0	14.8	1.3
India	55.3	38.6	15.0	1.8

Sources: NHFS-3(2005-6)

Sex Ratio

The sex ratio in India was 1000 males to 972 female in 1901 which came down to 1000 male to 940 females in 2011. The situation in Sikkim is no exception. The comparative figure shown in the Fig. 7.1 below gives the clear picture of sex ratio in Sikkim and India. Except in Census years of 1921 and 1931, the sex ratio in Sikkim is always much below the national average both in pre-merger and post-merger of Sikkim into the mainstream. In 2001 Census, the female/male ratio was 875 for Sikkim whereas the figure increases to 889 in 2011 Census. The sex ratio in Sikkim is deteriorating steadily between the age of 30 and 59. It may be mentioned here that sex ratio in Sikkim is lowest in relation to other north-eastern states.

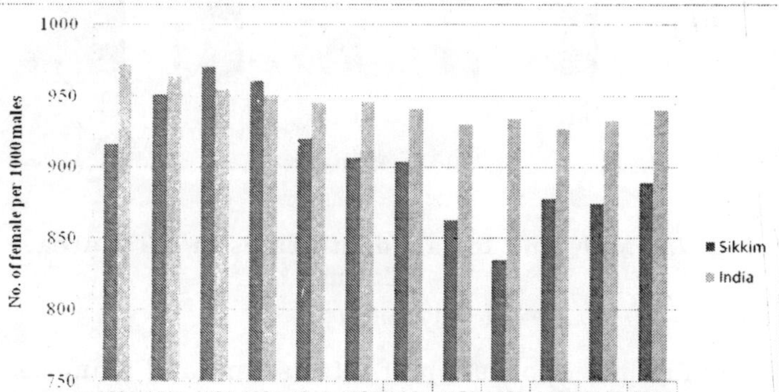

	1901	1911	1921	1931	1941	1951	1961	1971	1981	1991	2001	2011
Sikkim	916	951	970	961	920	907	904	863	835	878	875	889
India	972	964	955	950	945	946	941	930	934	927	933	940

Year

Fig. 7.1: Decennial sex ratio (1901-2011) of Sikkim and India
Sources: Bureau of Economics and Statistics 1999, Census 2001 and Census 2011.

In some districts of Sikkim, the ratio is much lower than the state average. For example, north district recorded the lowest sex ratio of 769 followed by 872 for east. The highest decline in the ratio was recorded in 1971 and 1981 census. The adverse decline of ratio in the state is due to many factors. In some of them, firstly, the death rate for rural women aged from 15 to 50 years is extremely high (43.85 per cent) (Fig. 7.2). Secondly, there is high maternal mortality rate. Most of the deliveries take place outside the health centres and is undertaken by untrained persons. Around 53 per cent of the deliveries in the rural areas are carried out by relatives or untrained midwives. Further, 41.24 per cent of the rural women and 22.91 per cent of the urban women do not receive any antenatal care (Sikkim People's Vision 2001).

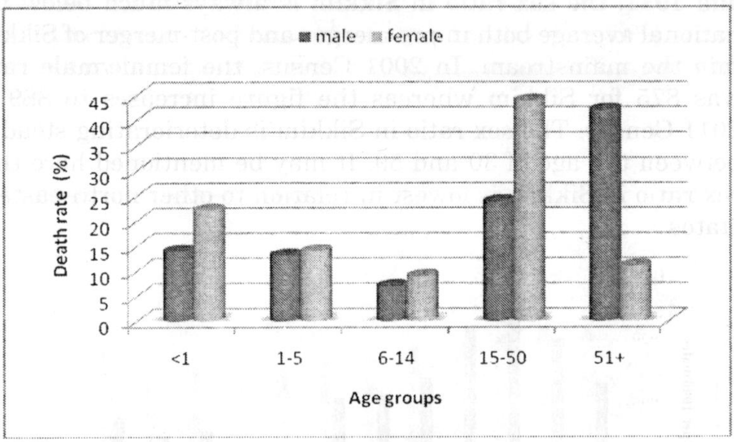

Fig. 7.2: Male and female death rates in rural areas of Sikkim

Source: Sikkim: The People's Vision 2001.

Finally, the application of ultra-sound and amniocentesis to detect the sex of the foetus followed by female foeticide is the main cause for the decreased number of females in the population.

Economic Empowerment

Another best course to empower women is to make them economically more independent. The social and political empowerment of women would be meaningless until and unless they were economically empower. Thus, to widen their role beyond reproduction and child caring, women should be encouraged and favoured for economically productive role. In fact, the social status of women is greatly influenced by the extent of their active participation in income earning activities outside the household. Women's gainful employment outside home exposes her to the outside world; delays age at marriage,

Table 7.5: Distribution of Male and Female Work Forces in Sikkim

	North	*West*	*South*	*East*	*Total*
Total workers (main + marginal)	23,634	53,131	69,753	1,16,802	2,63,320
Male	15,173	33,250	40,250	77,284	1,65,957
Female	8,461	19,881	29,503	39,518	97,363
Main workers	17,572	45,169	57,272	92,465	2,12,478
Male	13,050	30,298	36,015	67,303	1,46,666
Female	4,522	14,871	21,257	25,162	65,812
Marginal workers	6,062	7,962	12,481	24,337	50,842
Males	2,123	2,952	4,235	9,981	19,291
Females	3,939	5,010	8,246	14,356	31,551
Cultivators	9,174	35,757	48,527	37,964	1,31,422
Males	4,815	20,612	24,982	19,745	70,754
Females	4,359	15,145	23,545	18,219	61,268
Agricultural labourer	2,097	4,187	2,675	8,080	16,939
Males	1,067	2,355	1,212	3,980	8,614
Females	1,030	1,732	1,463	4,100	8,325
Household industry	285	913	530	1,522	3,250
Males	176	788	344	979	2,287
Females	109	125	186	543	963
Other workers	12,078	12,374	18,021	69,236	1,11,709
Males	9,115	9,495	13,712	52,580	84,902
Females	2,963	2,879	4,309	16,656	26,807

Sources: Census 2001 and Sikkim: A Statistical Profile 2002.

provide a sense of financial independence and increase her bargaining power and autonomy within the household and society (Dixon-Mueller 1993).

The women in Sikkim are relatively in better position than the women in the rest of the country. The government in the state has reserved 30 per cent of seats for women in public employment. In most of the government departments, the 50 per cent of employee are women and in some department they outnumber the male counterpart. Thus despite the unfavourable sex ratio, the number of women in some government services is greater than that of men and the number is perhaps highest as compare to other states of India. The reservation, therefore, provides an opportunity for employment in the higher echelon of government in the state civil services as doctors, engineers, administrators, teachers etc. So far as distribution of workers in Sikkim is concerned, 57.58 per cent are male workers and 39.59 per cent are female workers (Table 7.5).

The total workers here comprise both the main and marginal workers. In case of male worker, the total percentage

Table 7.6: Female Work Participation Rate (FWPR) and Gender Gap in Participation

States/India	*FWPR All India rank*	*FWPR*	*WGAP All India Rank*	*WGAP*
Sikkim	24	45.5	20	21.0
Arunachal Pradesh	23	45.0	22	17
Manipur	25	46.2	27	10.5
Meghalaya	21	43.7	23	15.9
Nagaland	22	44.8	28	9.4
Mizoram	28	56.8	26	11.3
Assam	08	24.9	07	34.5
Tripura	06	24.3	08	34.2
India		30.3		31.0

Source: Census of India 2001.

is high (57.58) than the non-workers (42.42 per cent). However, in regard to females, the situation is just the reverse. The percentage of total female workers is much lower (39.59 per cent) than the non-workers (61.41 per cent). This has an effect in work participation rate and also in gender gap in work participation. The female work participation rate (FWPR) in Sikkim is 45.5 per cent and gender gap in work participation (WGAP) is 21 per cent (Table 7.6).

There is need to encourage women of the state to take active participation in both public and private sectors. Female work participation in non-agricultural sector and level of wage are also considered as determinants of empowerment (Srinivasan 1990; Kulkarni and Chitanand 1990). Females' work participation not only increases their family income but also brings economic independence of women in household. This helps them to participate more effectively in intra-household decision-making and have better access to information (Chattopadhayay 2005). The total percentage of women (married) employed in the professional, technical and managerial jobs which are traditionally male-dominated are 5.9 per cent in the state which is much higher than the national figure.

Table 7.7: Percentage of Married Women Employed: Sikkim and North-East States

States / India	*Employed*	*Employed for cash*	*In professional, technical or managerial jobs*
Sikkim	22.1	21.0	5.9
Arunachal Pradesh	59.5	17.3	2.4
Assam	20.2	1.8	18.1
Manipur	69.9	48.7	6.7
Meghalaya	47.6	32.5	3.8
Mizoram	49.9	38.3	6.8
Nagaland	63.8	25.4	4.7
Tripura	22.6	4.1	18.7
India	39.1	26.2	2.0

Source: NFHS-2 .

There are only a few states viz., Mizoram (6.8), Manipur (6.7), Sikkim (5.9), Delhi (5.3), Goa (5.2), where the proportion of women working in these occupations rises to 5-7 per cent. Among the North-eastern states, Mizoram with 6.8 per cent of women (married) stand first in all India rank in professional, technical and managerial jobs. In India as whole, only 2 per cent of married women aged 15-49 are in such occupations (Table 7.7).

Women's control and access to various resources like money, land, credit, marketing, etc. are key to their economic empowerment. But traditionally, in our country, the women, have enjoyed less control and access to these resources. They have been discriminated in providing inherited property or possessing productive assets. In Sikkim, both men and women however, have co-equal power and enjoy equality in the use and control of resources. The state government recently enacted Inheritance Right Act under which both son and daughter is the equal beneficiary of parental property. So far as access to money is concern, 36.9 per cent women of Sikkim can decide alone how to use them. This percentage is infact highest among the north-eastern states. Similarly, the women's bank account holder in the state is also high (20.9 per cent) as compare to other north east states (Table 7.8). Further it is very interesting to note that as per the survey of NFHS III, 94.6 per cent of currently married women in the state said that they alone or jointly with their husband decide how their own earnings are used (Table 7.9). The ownership and control over resources/ assets not only create a sense of belonging and owning but also helps women to enhance their self esteem and confidence.

As far as knowledge and use of micro credit programme is concerned, the women in Sikkim have comparatively less idea on the programme. Micro-credit programmes normally extend small loans to poor people for self employment projects. It provides a combination of services and resources to their clients in addition to credit for self employment. In Sikkim, only 18.3 per cent of women have knowledge of this programme and of this, only 0.8 per cent of women have taken a loan from the micro-credit programme (Table 7.8).

Table 7.8: Women's Access to Money and Credit

States	*Women's access to money*		*Women's knowledge and use of microcredit programme*	
	% who have money that they can decide how to use	*% who have a bank or saving account that they themselves use*	*% who know of microcredit programme*	*% who have taken a loan from a microcredit programme*
Sikkim	36.9	20.9	18.3	0.8
Arunachal Pradesh	38.7	19.0	31.4	2.5
Assam	26.9	11.7	41.7	1.4
Manipur	32.0	8.0	65.1	4.2
Meghalaya	35.3	16.9	22.8	1.5
Mizoram	19.5	8.1	7.8	0.7
Nagaland	36.5	7.4	23.8	1.3
Tripura	26.9	18.7	38.7	2.3
India	44.6	15.0	38.6	4.0

Source: NFHS 3 (2005-06).

Table 7.9: Control Over Cash Earning

States	*Percentage of currently married women who report that they:*		
	alone or jointly with their husband decide how their own earnings are used[1]	*alone or jointly with their husband decide how their husband's earning are used*[2]	*earn more or about the same as their husband*[3]
Sikkim	94.8	82.5	29.9
Arunachal Pradesh	91.7	85.3	32.7
Assam	90.3	74.7	32.6
Manipur	95.7	91.6	25.5
Meghalaya	87.9	80.0	27.7
Mizoram	91.5	89.1	46.9
Nagaland	95.2	93.6	34.2
Tripura	75.3	50.3	23.7
India	80.9	68.2	21.0

Source: NHFS 3(2005-06).

Notes: 1. Women who are employed for cash.

2. Women whose husbands earn cash.

3. Women who earn cash and whose husbands earn cash.

Political Empowerment

The objective of the democracy will fail if the women lack equal opportunity to participate in the governmental decision-making process. The political participation of all people irrespective of caste, class, sex, etc. is the hallmark of any given democratic set-up. Keeping this in mind, the framers of our Constitution made a provision, and guaranteed equal political and civil rights to both men and women under which, both have equal access to participate in any decision-making process at any level, national, state or local. The representation of women in the political sphere is, however, not adequate. Both in parliament and in state legislature, the majority of members are male. The representation of women in Lok Sabha had never been more than 10 per cent. In Sikkim also the representation of women in the state assembly are not up to the mark. In the last assembly election of 2009, only four women candidates got elected in the 32 assembly seats. Of these, only two candidates have been accommodated in the 12 members' council of ministers. Till date, only one woman was elected to the Lok Sabha and women in Sikkim yet to get a chance to represent the state in Rajya Sabha. The state has one seat each in Lok Sabha and Rajya Sabha. The low representation of women in the decision-making organisations

Table 7.10: Representation of Women in the Sikkim State Legislature

Assembly Election	*Year*	*Total Number of seats*	*No. of Women Members*
First	1974	32	01
Second	1979	32	Nil
Third	1985	32	Nil
Fourth	1989	32	01
Fifth	1994	32	01
Sixth	1999	32	01
Seventh	2004	32	03
Eighth	2009	32	04

Source: Chhetri 2010.

Table 7.11 Category-wise distribution of Women Elected Representatives (WER) of Panchayats (as on April 2010)

Panchayat Level	*No.*	*Total Member*	*WER (Total)*	*SC*	*ST*	*OBC*	*MBC*
Gram Panchayat	163	891	356	22	161	87	80
Zilla Panchayat	4	95	38	2	20	8	8
Total	167	986	394	24	181	95	88

Source: Chhetri 2010.

is due to the political parties that harbour very conservative view about women. Different parties through champion the cause of women in their manifesto, but during election time, they give tickets mostly to men (Singh, 2000).

In panchayat, the representation of women is comparatively better than the representation in assembly. The 73rd and 74th Amendment Act (1992) ensures the one-third of total number of seats for women in all levels of local self-government. This has been hailed as hallmark achievement in the political empowerment of women. The reservation for women in local bodies' election has made a significant beginning. At present, there are 356 women members in panchayats of Sikkim. Of these, 256 are the members of Gram Panchayats and 38 members are from Zilla Panchayats. Out of this, 24 are SC women members, 181 are ST women members, 95 are OBC women, and 88 MBC women representatives. In Zilla Panchayats, there is one woman Adhakshya and two Up-Adhakshya. Though the one-third reservation of seats in the panchayat had led to the participation of maximum rural women in the decision-making processes, but this sharp increase in the number of women members is mainly due to the increase in the percentage of seats reservation from 33 to 40 per cent by State Government in 2007. In municipality also, the state government provides 40 per cent seats reservation for women.

The women in Sikkim enjoy the autonomy in taking decision in number of matters, for example, in cooking food, health care, buying ornaments and the likes (Table 7.12). Only 2.7 per cent of women in the state are not involved in any decision-making. Among the north-eastern states, the women in Nagaland enjoy maximum autonomy in every aspect, and

Table 7.12: Decision making authority enjoyed by women in Sikkim and North-Eastern states of India

States	*Decision making authority enjoyed by women (%)*						
	Women not involved in any decision making	*Cooking food*	*Own health care*	*Purchasing jewelers*	*Staying with parent/ sibling*	*Go to marketing*	*Visiting friends/ relatives*
Sikkim	2.7	92.1	79.5	57.9	56.7	38.2	83.7
Arunachal Pradesh	1.4	93.6	70.0	76.5	74.8	46.8	53.7
Manipur	3.3	87.4	43.3	66.3	63.2	28.6	28.3
Meghalaya	2.6	91.7	78.9	70.6	78.4	46.5	48.5
Nagaland	0.4	97.4	69.4	77.3	80.0	17.3	20.1
Mizoram	5.8	88.2	73.2	77.8	77.0	64.2	59.5
Assam	4.6	88.4	65.1	54.3	45.4	13.2	13.9
Tripura	NA	NA	51.2	50.5	48.1	27.4	24.4
India	9.4	85.1	51.6	52.6	48.1	31.6	24.4

Source: *IIPS 2000.*

Note: NA= Not Available.

the percentage of women who are not involved in any activities is in fact very insignificant i.e. 0.4 per cent.

Conclusion

Women in the state though enjoy relatively better position than their counterpart in the other states of India but they are still deprived of many benefits of development. An analysis of most of the social and economic data reveals that women in the state continue to be relatively disadvantaged in matters of education, health, nutrition, etc. The deprivations are the biggest hurdles in their empowerment. To achieve the holistic change in the overall social, economic and political conditions of women, a more integrated approach is required encompassing inter-alia advocacy, access to resources and information, capacity-building and organisational issues. To raise the status of women in the state and to empower them fully in every respect, the following may be suggested:

- To raise the economic condition of women, the state government should make plan for women of the state on the line of sub plans for STs and SCs. This will ensure allocation of funds directly for women.
- Women should be considered as an active participant in the welfare programmes rather than beneficiaries.
- For achieving higher literacy, a provision of primary education for all with greater emphasis on the girl child is to be made compulsory. The government should also fix the date and year for eradicating the women illiteracy in the state.
- Reorient health services in order to reduce infant mortality and maternal mortality at zero level in the state.
- State should promote research on women and increase fund for women's health issues and services.
- To ensure equal wage for both male and female for the same work, Government should enact laws.
- Provide equal access to all women in employment, markets resources utilisation and trade, as well as in information and technology.

- Eliminate sexual harassment and other forms of discrimination in the work place.
- Women development should be given top priority as an indispensable part of human resource development by recognising their needs and potential as partners in development.
- The government should establish at least one Women Study Centre at the state capital so that more research can be done in the areas of women's development.
- Government, political parties and other organisations should encourage women's participation in politics and in the exercise of political responsibilities.
- Government should encourage the women to organise Self Help Groups under various poverty alleviation programmes and offer them a range of economic options along with necessary support to enhance their capabilities.

References

Beteille, A. (1999). Empowerment, *Economic and Political Weekly*, 6(3), March, 6-13.

Census of India 2001: Registrar General and Census Commissioner, India.

Census of India 2011: Provisional Population Totals Paper 1 of 2011, Sikkim Series 12, Director of Census Operations.

Chattopadhyay, A. (2005). Women and Entrepreneurship, *Yojana,* Vol. 49.

Dixon-Mueller, Ruth (1993). Population Policies and Women's Rights: Transforming Reproductive Choice, Westport, Connecticut: Praeger.

Dutta, R. and Ashrit, R.R. (2006). Anaemia-A Silent Emergency, *Yojana,* Vol. 50.

Friere, Paul (1991). The Pedagogy of Development, cited in S.C. Dubey *Modernisation: The New Paradigm*, New Delhi, Sage.

Government of Sikkim: Sikkim- A Statistical Profile 2004-05, DESME.

Immanuel, M. (1998). *Women and Development*, Ahmedabad, Karnavati Publications.

Jejeebhoy, S.J. (1995). Women's Education. Autonomy and Reproductive Behaviour: Assessing what we have Learnt, Program on Population East-West Centre.

Kishor, S. and Gupta, K. (2004). "Women's Empowerment in India" in Irudaya Rajan and K.S. James (eds) *Demographic Change Health Inequality and Human Development in India*, Hyderabad CESS.

Kulkarni, S. and Chitanand, R. (1990). 'Status of Women in India: Concept, Indicators and Determinants: Some Issues', All India Seminar on Status of Women and Demographic Changes in India, IIPS, Mumbai.

Lama, M.P. (2001). Sikkim Human Development Report, Delhi, Social Science Press.

National Commission for Women (2002). Status of Women in India 2001.

Pargunan, M. (2007). "Political Empowerment of Women-An Illusion" *A Journal of Rural Development,* Vol. 55 No. 5, March 2007.

Planning Commission: *Tenth Five Year Plan 2002-2007 Vol. II.*

Planning Commission: *India Vision 2020,* New Delhi, Academic Foundation.

Presser, H. B. and Sen, G. (eds) (2000). *Women's Empowerment and Demographic Processes*, Oxford, Oxford University Press.

Sanyal, B.M. (2001). *India: Decentralised Planning: Themes and Issues,* New Delhi, Concept.

Sen, A. and Dreze, J. (1995). *India: Economic Development and Social Opportunity*, New Delhi, Oxford University Press.

Sikkim: Human Development Report, 2001, Delhi, Social Science Press.

Sikkim: The People's Vision, 2001, Government of Sikkim.

Singh, J.P. (2000). Indian Democracy and Empowerment of Women, *Indian Journal of Public Administration*, Oct.-Dec.

Singh, Indrabhusan and Kumari, U. (2007). Rural Development and Women Empowerment, *Kurukshetra,* Vol. 55 (5), March.

Srinivasan, K. (1990). 'Demographic and Socio-economic Consequences of Low Status of Female in Indian society', IIPS, Mumbai.

World Bank (2001). World Development Report 2001, Oxford, Oxford University Press.

8

Sikkim: A Historical Perspective on the Politics of Merger

Birth of Democracy and Its Continuity

The emergence of the political parties in Sikkim can be traced back to the 1940s. The birth of an organised political party in the form of Sikkim State Congress was directly the impact of the Indian National Congress. The then popular leaders in Sikkim such as Tashi Tshering, Kazi Lhendup Dorjee Khangsarpa, D.B. Gurung, C.D. Rai, Captain Dimik Singh Lepcha, Sonam Tshering, B.B. Gooroong, L.B. Basnet and many others were inspired by democratic struggle waged by the Indian National Congress for the Independence of India. The Congress programme of broadening of democratic base and liquidation of feudalism deeply impressed these leaders.

Graced with special rights and privileges from the *Maharaja* of Sikkim, the Sikkimese *Kazis* and *Thikadars* (contractors) exploited and suppressed the common people. Thus, the voice of the people began to rise against their exploitation, suppression and cruelty. It sought to eradicate Sikkim from the evil of the *Zamindari* system, the practices of *Kalobhari*, *Jharlangi*, *Kuruwa*, *Theki-bethi* and *Dhurikar*. However, the suppression and exploitation of the feudal lords and *Kazis* gradually came down. As a result, in the beginning of 1946, sequentially there arose three more political parties. They were the 'Praja Sammelan' at 'Temi Tarku], the Praja Mandal at Chakhung and the Praja Sudhar Samaj in Gangtok. On the 7th of December 1947, the similarities among the three Parties regarding their aims and objectives brought them together at Polo Ground (present Palzor Stadium). There a meeting was held followed by a long deliberation. In it the representatives of the Parties coming from every nook and corner of Sikkim decided to dissolve all the three Parties. Thus, in lieu of the three Parties, they decided to form one political party. Thus, under the Presidentship of Tashi Tshering, the Sikkim State Congress came into being. As a result, the Sikkim State Congress started striving for– (i) abolition of landlordism, (ii) formation of a responsible and popular interim Government, and (iii) Sikkim's merger with India. Later on, a number of political parties emerged to support, interact with and counter these moves in Sikkim.

Once again, SSC leaders requested to the Government for the eradication of the *Zamindari* system, the establishment of a responsible government and the merger of Sikkim with India. However, these issues went unattended. Against these failures of the Government, SSC under the leadership of Tashi Tshering held the 2nd Congress meet from 4-6 February 1949, to launch 'No Tax' movement. The movement began and its result was the imprisonment of eleven of its party workers– C.D. Rai, Namgyal Tshering, Chuk-Chuk Sangderpa, Rashmi Prasad Alley, Changchup Bhutia, Abhichandra Kharel, J Ratna Bahadur Khatri, J. Buddhiman Rai, Katuk Lama, Brihaspati Parsai, and Ongdi Bhutia. Soon after gaining the popularity of the party, the government realised the potential of the movement. So, it released all the prisoners unconditionally as per the advice of the Political Officer, Harishwar Dayal. However, all these events could not make the government active. The demands of the party remained unfulfilled; the party decided to continue its movement. In due course, the movement adopted the Gandhian Principle. It was *Satyagraha* launched from 29 April 1949 to 1 May 1949. Thus, the movement was unprecedented in the history of Sikkim. Finally, intimidated by the growing popularity of the movement, the Palace invited the party to form its ministry.

On 9 May 1949, under the Chief Ministership of Tashi Tshering, a five member Ministry consisting of Tashi Tshering, Chandra Das Rai, Captain Dimik Singh Lepcha, Dorjee Dadul, Rashmi Prasad Alley was formed. Soon after the formation of the ministry, a tug of war between the government and the ministry over the issue of power began. Taking advantage of this power struggle, the Indian Political Advisor, stationed at Gangtok, Hariswar Dayal, under the threat of using the Indian Army and the Deputy Foreign Minister of India B.V. Keshkar decided to dissolve the 29th days' old ministry and transfer the powers into the hands of the Political Officer on 6 June 1949. Thus, from 11 August 1949, Dewan Rule began in Sikkim, and J.S. Lall, who belonged to the Indian Civil Service took over the administration on the seventeen month after Dewan's rule in Sikkim, Pandit Jawaharlal Nehru, the Prime Minister of India and Sir Tashi Namgyal, the *Chogyal* of Sikkim, came up with a tentative unilateral agreement. On the basis of this agreement, the Congress demanded for merger with India, but turned Sikkim into a Protectorate of India. It was finally formalised on 5 December 1950 with the signatures of Tashi Namgyal representing Sikkim and Harishwar Dayal, representing India, in a small ceremony held at the Palace Chapel, Gangtok.

Amidst these events, Sikkim underwent a flurry of electoral activities. Different political parties framed their Political programmes and the two major political parties of Sikkim *viz.*, Sikkim State Congress and the Sikkim National Party participated with the Government of Sikkim in a tripartite discussion. This discussion in 1951, ended in a 'Tripartite Agreement'. It was signed by Captain Dimik Singh Lepcha and Kashi Raj Pradhan (SSC) and Sonam Tshering (National Party) and by the representatives of Government of India. It envisaged a system of seat allocation on the basis of *parity*, among the three communities *viz.*, the Nepalis, the Lepchas and the Bhutias of Sikkim. According to L.B. Basnet *parity* formula was protested by the leaders of the State Congress (SSC) but was of no avail. For the first time, election was declared in Sikkim. It was to be held in two stages–Primary and General. The Lepcha/Bhutia candidates were supposed to fight twice, both at the Primary and General stages. To be declared elected, they had to win of both the stages. For election, the Declaration divided the whole of Sikkim into four Provinces. They were Pemayantse, Namchi, North-Central and Gangtok. Each of these provinces was to elect members to the Council (Table 8.1).

Table 8.1: Distribution of Constituency and Seats

Constituency	*Seats*
1. Pemayantse Constituency	1 Lepcha-Bhutia and 2 Nepali
2. Namchi Constituency	1 Lepcha-Bhutia and 2 Nepali
3. North-Central Constituency	2 Lepcha-Bhutia and 1 Nepali
4. Gangtok Constituency	2 Lepcha-Bhutia and 1 Nepali

Source : Sikkim : History of Democratic Movement 2002.

Besides these, the declaration provided His Highness, the *Maharaja* of Sikkim the power to nominate 5 members to the Council. The total strength of the Council was therefore 17. It was also to function for a period of 3 years. But as times rolled on, a fresh declaration, was issued on 23 March 1953. The important point to be noted here is that it clarified the powers and positions of the Councillors. Accordingly, it was made clear that the Councillors could only recommend policies without exercising authority to work for the welfare of the public. The major departments remained in the hands of the Government, and the insignificant ones were in the hands of the Councillors. In the meantime, the party got a hint that a third declaration, which wished to take away the powers of the Councillors and weaken the edifice of democracy, was spread round the corner. So, the party felt the necessity to address two questions–(a) Should it take part in the election? (b) In the event of its victory, should it join the Government? To consider these, on 23 February 1953, the party assembled at Gangtok. After a long deliberation, the meeting unanimously decided in favour of participating in the election.

On the question of joining the government, it decided that even if it were victorious, it would not join the government, if it were not provided with the authority to work for the welfare of the people. With these decisions in the background, the party took part in the election. The Congress fielded 6 Lepchas and 6 Nepalis candidates, and the National Party fielded 6 Lepchas and 6 Nepalis. From both sides, the campaign was vigorous and when the results came, the Congress won all the 6 Nepalis seats contested by Kashi Raj Pradhan and 5 others and the National Party all the Lepcha-Bhutia seats contested by Sonam Tshering and 5 others. It was very historical that not even one Bhutia-Lepcha of the Congress and not even one Nepali of the National Party were elected.

After the result, there was a discussion within the Congress on the question of forming the Government. In the discussion, the majority of the party members expressed their negative views because they felt that their view was in accordance with the party decision of 23 February 1953. But, the views of the elected candidates were against the majority view. Thus, there was, however, a clear difference of opinion within the party. Consequently, the elected candidates persuaded the government to declare the date for the oath taking ceremony. The elected candidates along with 17 others, held a secret meeting at Gangtok. It was held under the leadership of Kashi Raj Pradhan under the pretext of emergency. At mid-night, the meeting passed a vote of no confidence against the existing Congress President, Tashi Tshering and elected Kazi Lhendup Dorjee Khangsarpa as the new President. But, the whole process of removing the President, Tashi Tshering contravened the provisions of the Constitution of the party.

As per the constitution of the party, the removal could have been effected only with the concurrence of 2/3rd members present and voting in the Executive Body of the party. After violating the party Constitution, the elected members of the Congress, along with 17 others reached the Palace to take part in the oath-taking ceremony. The elected members of National Party were there. On the basis of the *Parity Formula*, Tashi Namgyal, the then *Maharaja* of Sikkim appointed the Executive Councillors. Sonam Tshering and Kashi Raj Pradhan. The former represented the Lepcha-Bhutia community and the later, the Nepalis. Subsequently, Sonam Tshering was given the responsibility of Health, Agriculture, Veterinary and

Forest Departments. The departments of Trade and Commerce, Education, Excise and Transport came under the charge of Kashi Raj Pradhan. One month after the oath taking ceremony, Tashi Tshering, having tested the treachery of his own party colleagues, breathed his last on 10 May 1954, and with him, the vision of a prosperous Sikkim was lost for ever.

In 1954, soon after N.K. Rustomji assumed the Office of the *Dewan*, the Seven-Year Plan of Sikkim, the first of its type in the history of Sikkim, was launched with an outlay of Rs. 32.369 million (4.315 million dollars), wholly contributed by India. The accent of development was on roads and bridges, education, medical services, fostering of cottage industries and the building of some micro-hydel projects.

The Council, according to the Provisions of the Constitutional Proclamation, had been elected for a period of three years. In 1956, the term of the Council was extended to December 1957, by a Proclamation issued by the *Maharaja*. Further, the composition of the Council was changed by the *Maharaja*'s Proclamation, dated 17 March 1958. It means, the member of Councillors was raised from 17 to 20. The addition of one more nominated seat further tilted the balance in favour of the *Maharaja* and the National Party.

The Second General Elections of Sikkim were held soon after the issue of the Proclamation of 17 March 1958, the formation of the Executive Council in the wake of 1958 elections had some peculiar features. The State Congress had won a clear majority – 8 out of 14 elected seats and had two Bhutia-Lepcha members among its elected Councillors apart from the one Bhutia-Lepcha seat that the Congress had won, its victorious candidate in the General seat contest was also a Bhutia. Thus, admirably fulfilled all the conditions needed to form a one-party Executive Council. Yet, no voice was raised in this behalf. But other voices were also active. Kashi Raj Pradhan, Sonam Tshering and Nakul Pradhan were all involved in an election petition that alleged corrupt practices had been adopted in the election. The *Maharaja* issued a notification on 27 December 1958, and published as a Gazette in January 1959, that the election petitions would be decided by the Tribunal and accordingly delivered its judgement on 25 May

1959, declaring election of Sonam Tshering, Kashi Raj Pradhan and Nakul Pradhan void. In addition, all the three of them were disqualified for membership of the Sikkim State Council for a period of 6 years. With effect from the date that the finding of the Election Tribunal takes effect. However, later on, the Sikkim *Darbar* reduced the disqualification of Kashi Raj Pradhan and Nakul Pradhan for seeking the membership of the Sikkim Council for a period of six months with effect from 15 May 1959, and Sonam Tshering for a period of three years with effect from 28 May 1959.

The Real Politics Begins

The Gazette greatly tempered the zeal of Kashi Raj and Nakul Pradhan in continuing the parleys. A joint convention was held in September 1959 and on 22 October 1959 at Rangpo and Singtam respectively, the parties represented were the Swatantra Dal, the Sikkim National party (Sonam Tshering-faction), the State Congress and the Sikkim Scheduled Castes Leagues. Among the participants, the most prominent were Kazi Lhendup Dorjee Khangsarpa, the Congress President, who had fought the elections on Swatantra Dal ticket and lost; Sonam Tshering, who had been ousted from the Presidentship of the National Party and was now leading a faction within it, nursing grievances against the Sikkim *Darbar* for the gross discrimination displayed by it.

The Joint Convention

It reiterated the old Congress demand for a responsible Government, introduced a new element *viz.*, the drafting of a democratic Constitution for Sikkim, should incorporate 'Fundamental Rights' and Directive Principles as inspired by the Indian Constitution. But, the resolutions were contemptuously disregarded by the Sikkim *Darbar*. By now N.K. Rustomji had left Sikkim, having admirably fulfilled the task of consolidating the powers of the Sikkim *Darbar*, and throwing the political parties in disarray by means of the unfettered and unprincipled exercise of authority by him and the *Maharaj Kumar*. The new incumbent though allowed to retain the title of Dewan, was a comparatively a junior member of the Indian Administrative Service, one Baleshwar Prasad, admirably suited to serve the Sikkim *Darbar* as its obedient administrative Officer.

Dates for holding by-elections for the seats vacated by three Executive Councillors were announced. Hectic political activities began. It also happened soon after the Tribunal's award had been punished. Political parties and party candidates had begun to warm up for the inevitable bye elections. The Congress had lost two stalwarts, and both of them E.Cs. As there seemed none among the party members, who could replace Kashi Raj Pradhan, but the party's choice had fallen on Chandra Das Rai, the young firebrand of 1947-49, who had post-graduated in history from the Benaras Hindu University and joined the Sikkim Government as a Magistrate. Urged by his former Political colleagues, Congress President Kashi Raj Pradhan foremost among them, Chandra Das Rai had resigned from service.

Further, that the Sikkim *Darbar* had reduced the period of disqualification of Kashi Raj Pradhan, which made him eligible to contest the bye-election for the seat, he himself had vacated, Kashi Raj forgot all his promises to Chandra Das Rai and placed himself as the State Congress candidate from Namchi Constituency. As for the candidature of Nakul Pradhan, the party consensus was in his favour. Chandra Das Rai, who had given up his secured job just to fight the bye-election, could not yield to the demand of Kashi Raj Pradhan, and there were many who preferred him to Kashi Raj. Kashi Raj finally exercised the powers of the President of the State Congress by refusing to allow Chandra Das Rai to use the election symbol of the Congress. Chandra Das Rai chose a fresh election symbol, while Kashi Raj retained to party symbol, and the two Congress candidates fought for the Namchi seat.

The Namchi election became a focal point of struggle. The fight was not only between Kashi Raj Pradhan and Chandra Das Rai, but also between the Congress policies of subservience to the Sikkim *Darbar*, shaped and followed by Kashi Raj, the disgruntled votaries of democracy in and out of the State Congress. Namchi had the reputation of being the most politically conscious of all constituencies, Chandra Das Rai hailed from his constituency, which had been the field of his political activities in 1947-49. Kashi Raj was staking his all 10 years' political career, the prestige of the Congress President and his record as an Executive Committee for 5 years.

Kashi Raj Pradhan lost the fight, and lost it so badly as to forfeit his deposit. He polled 634 votes to the 3013 polled by Chandra Das Rai. Nakul Pradhan also won his fight. He was promptly appointed as an Executive Councillor, but Chandra Das was not. The chair vacated by Kashi Raj should have gone to Chandra Das, who despite a separate election symbol was very much a State Congress Councillor. The post had obviously been meant for Kashi Raj, the individual, rather than for the State Congress.

Chandra Das Rai's past marked him as a staunch democrat and the Sikkim *Darbar* did not trust him to meekly tread on the foot prints of Kashi Raj. The Sikkim *Darbar*, by ignoring Chandra Das Rai's claim to the Executive Councillorship, exposed its own policies as clearly as it exposed what Kashi Raj's real role in Sikkim politics had been. The mantle of Kashi Raj Pradhan fell on his nephew, Nakul Pradhan. The other Executive Councillor with Nakul Pradhan was Martam Topden. Two Bhutias and one Nepali were appointed as Deputy Executive Councillors.

However, at this time, there were many politicians in the field, politicians who had reasons to be aggrieved by the Sikkim *Darbar*'s policies of discrimination, by the want of justice and fair play in its dealings, and by its open defiance of all democratic norms. They could not remain idle, passively witnessing to erosion of whatever little democratic process there was, without seriously jeopardising their very careers in politics.

Birth of a New Political Party: Sikkim National Congress

In May 1960 at a sizeable rally held at Singtam, the three leaders formed a new party, the Sikkim National Congress, wherein were merged the Swatantra Dal, the Praja Sammelan, the dissenting wing of the State Congress, and the Sonam Tshering faction of the National Party. The Sikkim National Congress, later developed into a full blooded opposition party and posed a tough challenge to the Sikkim *Darbar*. At the meeting, they recommended the legitimate demands of the people of Sikkim, such as the establishment of a responsible

Government, a written Constitution, Universal Adult Franchise based on joint electorate etc. They also realised for the unity and integrity of the people so as to fulfil the genuine demands. Further, they also felt the need of amalgamating more Parties so as to give the shape of large political organisation from one platform. Hence, Kazi Lhendup Dorjee Khangsarpa was elected President, Sonam Tshering and D.B. Tiwari were elected Vice-Presidents, and Bhim Bahadur Gooroong was elected the General Secretary.

Even though the Sikkim National Congress had yet to fight election, it had 4 Councillors in the Sikkim State Council as a result of the merger of the four groups. The party position in the Council is shown in Table 8.2.

Table 8.2: Party Position in the Council

Constituency	*Seats*
1. The National Party	06 (with 01 *Sangha* Seat)
2. Sikkim National Congress	04
3. Sikkim State Congress	03
4. Vacant	01

Source : Basnet 1974.

The formation of the Sikkim Nation Congress did not however, affect the National Party with the exception of Sonam Tshering's permanent rupture with it. It rather gained for while formerly, as a result of the 1958 elections, it had been an unimpressive second to the State Congress, it now occupied the top position in the Council. On the other hand, the Sikkim State Congress was pulled down from the top to the very bottom among the political parties. Apparently, the influence of Kashi Raj Pradhan and his relatives was on the wane. The National Party appealed to the section of population which cared little for democracy and much more for the maintenance of the old order and as such, its following, largely composed of vested interests and illiterate Bhutia-Lepcha electorate, was immune from the call of democracy given by the Sikkim National Congress making any appeal to them. Since, the State Congress swore by democracy, and almost ritualistically passed the old Congress resolutions every year, the real battle was between the Sikkim National Congress and the State Congress, for they both addressed themselves to the same electorate. Without the slightest effort other than organising a rally and bringing together some leaders, the Sikkim National Congress had already dealt a crippling blow to the State Congress. The Sikkim National Congress was naturally critical of the whole system of elections, the powers and functions of the Executive Council, and the working of the State Council, among other things. Having learnt from experiences that merely passing resolutions and submitting them to the Sikkim *Darbar* as the State Congress had been doing with great consistency was unlikely to bring about the basic changes the party sought in the body-politic, the party threatened to launch a *Satyagraha* with a view to compelling the Sikkim *Darbar* to yield to its demands. The leaders were, however, advised by the Political Officer that Prime Minister Nehru was prepared to meet them and hear their grievances and that, therefore, there was no point in launching a *Satyagraha*.

Accordingly on 20 August 1960, the leaders of the Sikkim National Congress represented a delegation to Delhi and submitted a Memorandum of their grievances and demands to the then Prime Minister, Pandit Jawaharlal Nehru and Subimal Datta, Foreign Secretary of India. After a series of talks with Nehru and other leaders, the Sikkim National Congress leaders returned to Sikkim. Where as no visible changes were introduced in the framework of Sikkim Government in the wake of the Delhi talks, *Satyagraha* was dropped from the party programme, and the Sikkim National Congress settled down to the role of a 'Paper-Opposition' party by launching a relentless propaganda campaign in the Press by means of pamphlets and party resolutions against the Sikkim *Darbar*'s actions and policies.

The Growth of Dissent and Nationalism

The struggle of the Sikkim National Congress towards the achievement of the lofty aims enshrined in the party constitution was carried out, not in the field among masses, but at Kazi Lhendup Dorjee Khangsarpa's cozy *bungala* at Kalimpong, where the publicity wing of the Sikkim National Congress functioned with efficiency, and an enviable measure of success in the person of the Kazi's second wife, Kazini Elisa Maria Dorji of Chakung, an indomitable personality.

Fresh impetus for political activity came in July 1961, the Sikkim *Darbar* published the Sikkim Subjects' Regulation, laying down conditions that governed the Subject-hood of Sikkim Nationals. It was highly discriminatory and unfavourable to the Nepalis. The SSC and SNC, both of whom relied on the Nepalis for their support, found in this sufficient grounds to become active, and raise a clamour for changes in the Regulations. The Government of India had finally to intervene and bring about reconciliation in the form of a much more reasonable Subjects' Regulations.

In 1959, the Dalai Lama had fled from Lhasa followed by some 60,000 Tibetan Refugees, some of whom the Sikkim ruler volunteered to rehabilitate in Sikkim. Sikkim was in far from a sound economic position to take any effective measures to promote the welfare of its own people, and relied heavily on India even for small things. The *Maharaja*'s high sounding understanding to rehabilitate 5,000 or so Tibetan refugees in Sikkim had come on the promise of adequate financial assistance from India. Besides, being of Tibetan origin, the ruling party saw in this a nice opportunity of strengthening the Bhutia-Lepcha population, even though the indigenous Bhutia-Lepcha Population was far from sympathetic to the rehabilitation programme.

On 18 December 1969, a new political party was born in Sikkim founded by Lal Bahadur Basnet, former General Secretary of the Sikkim National Party for many years known as the Sikkim Janata Party. Towards the middle of June 1970, the President of India was scheduled to visit Sikkim. According to Shukla there were secret meetings of the Study Forum, which wanted a show-down with India by staging a 'Black Flag' demonstration on the occasion of the President's visit. The visit was postponed owing to 'inclement weather'. The Indian authorities succeeded in averting an unpleasant situation, which would have created a stir in India and caused raised-eye brows, abroad though for different reasons. In Sikkim, anti-Indian elements having ganged the moral weakness of India, began to devise more effective methods to bully the wallowing giant.

The Sikkim United Front was launched in September 1970. It heralded its birth by issuing a leaflet in which it criticised India for having foisted the 1950 Treaty on Sikkim, and demanded its revision as precursor to Sikkim's total Independence. The most strident voice among the members of the United Front was that of Krishna Chandra Pradhan, the erstwhile General Secretary of the Janata Party, who had found his new affiliation highly lucrative.

If the brains behind the United Front had just wanted to probe the reactions of the Indian Government, this limited objective was more than achieved by a single demonstration that followed propaganda tour of the United Front leaders all over Sikkim. One Sunday in October 1970, the United Front held an open meeting at Gangtok Bazaar. Prominent leaders were displayed all over, asking Indians to quit Sikkim and grant full Independence to her. The leaders spat venom on India and the Indian Government. Indians in Sikkim, soldiers, businessmen, diplomats and Officials were greatly perturbed by increasing anti-Indian sentiment of the United Front and other Sikkimese.

Alarmed by the Political Officer's report, T.N. Kaul, the Foreign Secretary, Government of India flew from Delhi to Bagdogra and hopped by helicopter from there to Gangtok to take over things with the *Chogyal*. Unlike his visit following the 1968 Children's Demonstration, this time the Foreign Secretary was cold shouldered and had to beat a hasty treat within 24 hours. Asked by the press about his sudden and short visit, Kaul assured that he had just come to pay his compliments to the *Chogyal* and the *Gyalmo*. Many people read in Kaul's remarks the plain message that the birds of the policy makers in Delhi had come home to roost.

In May 1971, a high powered delegation of Sikkimese went to Delhi for talks over Sikkim's Fourth-Five Year Plan. The *Chogyal* also visited Delhi from time to time to guide the Sikkimese delegation. However, eventually the outlay rose steeply and stopped a trifle short of the original Rs. 26 crore and the Sikkimese had expressed their satisfaction.

I.S. Chopra, a retired Indian diplomat, had joined the Sikkim Administration with the high sounding title of *Sidlon* on 4 June 1969. He enjoyed very high perks and other privileges not enjoyed by any other previous head of the administration. In addition, the unofficial title of 'His Excellency' was appended to his name and freely bandied in Sikkim. Chopra, gradually emerged and had given convincing assurances to the *Chogyal* that if he were appointed the head of the Sikkim-Administration, he had sufficient pull in the External Affairs Ministry to the Government of India to bring about the revision of 1950 Indo-Sikkim Treaty to be followed up by the *Chogyal*'s elevation to the status enjoyed by the Ruler of Bhutan, a vertical jump from His Highness to His Majesty, and all the concomitant benefits and Sikkim's entry into the United Nations Organisation. Such was the confidence inspired by the *Sidlon* that the *Chogyal* went all out to humour every passing whim of the dignitary and loaded him and his wife with costly gifts, including an expensive foreign car, of course, out of public funds.

Towards the middle of 1971, the *Sidlon* had already completed two years in Sikkim, yet the opportune moment for him to take up the issue of the Treaty revision did not seem to have arrived. At about this time, the Himalayan Observer, an English language weekly published from Kalimpong, exposed through a series of articles, rank corruption in the Sikkim Administration, supported by irrefutable facts and figures, evidently furnished by persons working in the departments concerned. Since all of the high Officials concerned were the confidants of the *Chogyal* and members of the Study Forum into the bargain, the administration failed to institute any enquiry or take any other action despite the hue and cry raised, including questions and resolutions in the Sikkim Council. It was emphasised by L. B. Basnet that while the public mind was still agitated over the scandals, the Himalayan Observer came out with a real scoop divulging that the *Sidlon* had been granted a 'loan' of Rs. 2 lakhs by the *Chogyal* for constructing a house in Delhi. Though the Government of Sikkim tried to draw a red herring across the trail, the harm had been done sufficiently; the Indian Intelligence Agencies carried out secret investigations and found the allegations to be true. During the course of the investigations, some more skeletons in Chopra's cupboard were discovered. It came to light that Chopra, who had been entrusted with the task of ordering expensive foreign fittings and furnishings for the Sikkim House in Delhi, had been ordering extra quantities of these items for his own house too – of course the Government of Sikkim or the people of Sikkim were footing the Bill. Chopra's name had begun to stink in the corridors of the Foreign Ministry in Delhi, of which the old man seems to have been wholly oblivious.[1]

The Sikkim National Party submitted for discussion and adoption in the Sikkim Council, September 1971 session, a resolution demanding the removal of Clause 15 (ii) from the 1953 Proclamation, which debarred the Sikkim Council from "discussing, asking questions about and dealing in any manner with, the external relations of the State, including relations with the Government of India and any commitments entered into by the *Maharaja* with the Government of India." According to L. B. Basnet where as even fairly well informed Political leaders had believed that the 1953 Proclamation had been issued by the *Darbar* with the consent of the Government of India, it was now revealed that the Proclamation had been drafted by Indians, approved by the Government of India and the *Chogyal* had merely been asked to sign it. However, it also came to limelight that even the more, the slightest change in the Proclamation had to have the prior sanction of the Government of India. In keeping with this clause on the advice of the *Sidlon*, the resolution was withdrawn and in its place, a petition was prepared requesting the Government of India to accord their sanction so that the resolution could be introduced in the Council. The signatures of all the Councillors except, Kazi Lhendup Dorjee Khangsarpa of the Sikkim National Congress, who bluntly refused to have anything to do with a matter that sought to undermine, in any degree, the Indians hold in Sikkim, were obtained.

At this stage, the *Sidlon* could no longer avoid discharging the obligation he had undertaken at the time of being appointed to this highly remunerative job in Sikkim. Armed with the petition bearing the signatures of the Councillors of Sikkim, Chopra went to Delhi to find that the other side was more than ready to meet him. Chopra not only failed in his mission, but came back with the threat that if the 1953 Proclamation had to be changed at all, it had to be changed thoroughly in consonance with the times, and the people should have a proper say in this regard, clearly implying thereby that the Councillors elected under the existing system were not the true representatives of the people. This was enough to throw the *Chogyal* and the leaders of Sikkim National Party into total disarray, and the matter rested there for the time being.

After the *Sidlon*'s fruitless mission to Delhi, even the leaders of the National Party began to comment on the waste of Public money in the maintenance of a white elephant as the *Sidlon* of Sikkim. Since, the Government of India had insisted upon the recovery of loan from Chopra, there was no choice for the *Chogyal*, but to let the *Sidlon* continue in Office so that the money could be recovered from his emoluments. Such, however, was the force of Public clamour than Chopra was relieved of his Executive Functions on 27 July 1972; but he went on receiving his full emoluments for the simple reason that a substantial portion of the 'loan' of Rs. 2 lakhs remained yet to be recovered from him. According to Shukla S.R., the Chogyal had bulled the false hopes of I.S. Chopra and was only too glad to propitiate him with costly presents now and then. He was given a loan of Rs. 2 lakh for constructing a House in Delhi. It was later recovered that Chopra had to build his house in Delhi when 'Sikkim House' was also being built there. It enabled him to buy costly furniture and fittings from foreign countries in the name of 'Sikkim House' on Government account, and use the same for his own house. Chopra's activities when became known to the public in Sikkim that only helped increase feelings against India which was sending such 'corrupt officers'. The Chogyal was disillusioned and not long before the *Sidlon* was relieved of his duties on 27 July 1972, although he continued receiving his full emoluments including Rs. 3000 p.m., entertainment allowance Rs. 48,000 per annum and a host of other perks and priviliges until the time loan was fully adjusted. Chopra's *sidlonship* will go down in the history of Sikkim as the period during which, corruption, nepotism and communalism reigned supreme. The rate of interest charged for the loan is not available.

Around that time, the internal situation in Sikkim had been steadily deteriorating. Corruption, nepotism, favouritism and rank communalism had begun to grow at the very vitals of the Administration. As even the 'Paper-opposition party' of Kazi Lhendup Dorjee Khangsarpa had become a part of the administration. On 26 January 1972, SNC issued its Bulletin No. 2, which carried a scathing criticism of the *Chogyal* and the Administration. In connection with the Bulletin No. 2, Kazi Lhendup Dorjee Khangsarpa was summoned by the *Chogyal* and asked to explain his conduct in the presence of witnesses. The Kazi pleaded that the Bulletin was issued by the majority vote of party delegates, and as such, he was helpless. Kazi apologised to the *Chogyal*, he was asked to submit an apology in writing, but he did not do so because such a step would irrepairably damage his image and ruin his future political career. Later on, as a sequel to the resolution adopted by the Sikkim Council, the Sikkim Government filed a complaint against the Publicity Secretary of the Sikkim National Congress, D.B. Gurung, under whose signature the Bulletin had been published, charging him with sedition under section 124A of the Indian Penal Code (IPC). Before the warrant of arrest could be extended against D.B. Gurung, Kazi Lhendup Dorjee Khangsarpa whisked him away to Kalimpong.

On 28 May 1972, Kazi Lhendup Dorjee Khangsarpa was dismissed from the Executive Council. The next day he set out for a visit to Europe with his wife, leaving D.B. Gurung under the watchful eye of Nar Bahadur Khatiwada, a young college student who, apart from functioning as the Assistant Publicity Secretary of the Sikkim National Congress was a factotum in the Kazi's household.

The Sikkim Intelligence was fully informed of D.B. Gurung's plight, aggravated by the mounting tyranny of Nar Bahadur Khatiwada according to L.B. Basnet. Cautious approaches were made to D.B. Gurung assuring him that if he came to Sikkim, surrendered himself, and made a clear statement, he would earn the *Chogyal*'s clemency and eventual pardon. Gurung escaped one evening in June and the following morning, surrendered himself in the Chief Magistrate's Court, where he pleaded that he did not know English language, in which original Bulletin had been published, and that he had been used as the cat's paw by the Kazi, his foreign wife and Nar Bahadur Khatiwada. Following a Government complaint, the Chief

Magistrate issued non-bailable warrants of arrest against Kazi Lhendup Dorjee Khangsarpa and Nar Bahadur Khatiwada under section 124 A of the Indian Penal Code and Rule 12 of the Sikkim Public Security Rules, ordering the two accused to be produced before him on 27 July 1972. While in Delhi, Kazi Lhendup Dorjee Khangsarpa just after back to Europe tour met Nirmal Sinha, a former Director of Sikkim Research Institute of Tibetology (Namgyal Institute of Tibetology), Government of Sikkim, who was removed from his post unceremoniously. Both of them have had detailed discussions over the deteriorating situation and administrative problem of the State of Sikkim under the ruling of the *Chogyal*. Further, they planned and decided to meet the former Prime Minister, Indira Gandhi so as to apprise the *Chogyal*'s activities after obtaining appointment through P.N. Haque, Principal Secretary to the then Prime Minister Indira Gandhi, however, she had already gathered the facts about the overall activities of the *Chogyal* and some immediate measures were made effective.

With the departure of I.S. Chopra, the first and the last *Sidlon* of Sikkim, the *Chogyal*, thereafter, took upon himself the direct control and supervision of the administration from June 1972, thus, setting aside the intermediary rung between himself and the Chief Secretary. To make himself more approachable by the officers and the public alike, he duly shifted his office from the Palace to the main Secretariat Building for convenience to all concerned.

The Ambitiously Waiting to Poll the Election

In September 1972, the Government of Sikkim issued an Extra Ordinary Gazette Notification announcing the holding of the Fifth General Elections of Sikkim in January 1973. It was closely followed by a Press release of the Government. Cautioning the people not to fall victim to the tenacles of the disgruntled and short-sighted political leaders, who were trying to show the dragon's teeth with a sinister purpose of fostering communalism and discord. Further, the Government warned the people that the liberal and accommodative policies pursued by the Sikkim *Darbar*, should not be construed as a weakness, but, in all matters affecting peace, tranquillity and security of the country as a whole, the Sikkim *Darbar* would not hesitate in taking strongest measures against such anti-national elements, who were found bent upon disturbing the peace and tranquillity of the country as a whole. Owing to inner dissension, prevailing among the leaders of the Sikkim State Congress and the Janata Party, a new organisation known as the Sikkim Janata Congress had already come into being during August 1972. SJC was again a combination of the break-away group of the two parties, mainly composed of such aspirants and opportunists, who were stampeding for seats in the forthcoming elections.

Broadly speaking, the birth of the Sikkim Janata Congress, thus, acted like a booster to the leaders of the State Congress and the National Party, who felt fully satisfied on account of the dent caused on the overall strength of the Sikkim National Congress, which was their main opponent. There were no untoward incidents worth mentioning, and polling in all the polling stations were satisfactory. A fresh poll was ordered for Bigmat Constituency of South Sikkim for some reasons. On 29 January 1973, the counting of the votes started in the White Memorial Hall at Gangtok, while in the said process of counting a major incident developed involving the ballot boxes of the two Nepalis candidates fielded by the Sikkim National Party, polled at the Rabang Polling Station of South Sikkim Constituency. Prominent leaders of the Sikkim National Congress detected some kind of rigging in the two boxes where ballot papers were found to have been manipulated by the Presiding Officer. Vehement protests and written complaints were lodged on the spot to the Election Committee requesting the investigation of the anomaly in regard to the alleged rigging of the two boxes of the Nepalis candidates of the National Party and to order for a fresh election. The complaining parties approached to the Election Tribunal for the redress of their grievances. It was at this point, the Rubicon was crossed, which was to blow off an unprecedented uprising of the Sikkimese people against the feudal regime of the *Chogyal* that led Sikkim to ultimately go for a merger with India.

The Election results for the Fifth General Election of the Sikkim State Council of 1973 were declared (Table 8.3).

Deriving an analysis from the above table, the Sikkim National Party had come out with an absolute majority, while

Table 8.3: Result of the 5th Election of State Council

Party	*Bhutia-Lepcha*	*Nepali*	*TSong*	*Scheduled Castes*	*Sangha*	*General*	*Total*
Sikkim National Party	7	2	-	1	1	-	11
Sikkim National Congress	-	3	1	-	-	1	5
Sikkim Janata Congress	-	2	-	-	-	-	2
Total	7	7	1	1	1	1	18

Source: Basnet 1974.

the Sikkim National Congress and the Sikkim Janata Congress trailed far behind, even their combined strength being poor second to the Sikkim National Party's brilliant first. On 8 March 1973, the new Councillors including 6 members nominated by the Sikkim *Darbar*, were sworn-in. The Sikkim National Congress and Sikkim Janata Congress Councillors, despite earlier pledges before the people to boycott the oath taking ceremony also took the oath.

However, the Sikkim National Congress and Sikkim Janata Congress leaders decried the election results as the product of rigging and a conspiracy between the SNP and the Sikkim Administration, and heightened their criticism of the Government. The propaganda became so serious that the Government arrested K.C. Pradhan, the former General Secretary of the Janata Party, who after flirting with the Sikkim United Front, had managed to become the President of the Sikkim Janata Congress. Pradhan's arrest was a signal to the impatient young men, who were already straining, as it were, at the leash, to break all restrictive bounds. Processions were taken out at Namchi and Gyalzing, where the Nepali Population was preponderant. Under the direction of the youth leaders, people began to pour into Gangtok, the Capital, for holding a demonstration.

About 2,000 people squatted on the Palace lawns for a couple of days. The new Council was inaugurated on 28 March 1973, by the *Chogyal*. The Sikkim Janata Congress and Sikkim National Congress Councillors boycotted it. The *Chogyal*, once again, refused to take any immediate steps to meet the demands of the two parties.

The youth leader like R.C. Poudyal went on an indefinite hunger strike on the palace lounge. He was later accompanied by the other members N.K.Subedi, Karma Peda and K.N. Upreti. The hunger strike was stopped on the intervention of senior leaders of the party.

Even though, under such an unfavourable atmosphere, the *Chogyal* appointed six Executive Councillors, four from the Sikkim National Party and one each from the Sikkim National Congress and the Sikkim Janata Congress diplomatically, so as to further strengthen the Sikkim National Party in the

Council and the government and also at the same time to cripple the Sikkim National Congress and the Sikkim Janata Congress on the foot print of the *Chogyal* and the Sikkim National Party reflected as their United Front. The two Executive Councillors – designate from the Sikkim National Congress and the Sikkim Janata Congress had secretly consented to join the Executive Council against the express mandate of their parties, and party volunteers, including irate ladies, had to use physical force to restrain the two turn coats from attending the oath taking ceremony.

People Marching to Polling Booths: To Exercise Adult Franchise

4 April 1973 was the 50th birthday of the *Chogyal*. Lavish preparations were being made by the Sikkim Government to celebrate the *Golden Jubilee* in a befitting manner. The Sikkim Janata Congress and the Sikkim National Congress formed a Joint Action Committee (JAC), with Kazi Lhendup Dorjee Khangsarpa, as its Chairman so as to fight for their joint demands. Finding the *Chogyal*'s attitude unbending, the Joint Action Committee (JAC) issued an ultimatum that if their demands were not fulfilled before 4th April, they would prevent the Birthday Celebrations. The oil was put in the fire. On the 3 April 1973 the people of Sikkim had already begun to converge at Gangtok in groups, carrying Sikkim National Congress and Sikkim Janata Congress flags with shouting slogans. Despite the Government's determination to march ahead with the preparations for the celebrations had spilled over the second day, i.e., 5 April 1973, it began to appear that unlike the previous threats of Political leaders, which had invariably failed to materialise as this time the people seemed to be resolute on a show down with the government. A last minute bid by Sonam Tshering, the Chairman of the Birthday Celebrations Committee, to thrash out the matter across the table led to talks in the evening of 3 April 1973 between Government Representatives and the (Joint Action Committee) JAC leaders, which lasted till late night. Unfortunately, they could not reach on the consensus.

The following morning, 4 April 1973, the 50th birthday of the *Chogyal* of Sikkim began with early morning prayers in all the Monasteries of Sikkim and the one Church and one Mosque at Gangtok.

At about the same time, just outside the mosque at Gangtok, a full-throated chorus of 5,000 or more voices echoed the morning atmosphere with anti-*Chogyal* slogans. The confrontation between the ruler and his subjects was about to begin in right earnest. About a hundred yards below the road crossing that marked the starting point of the town proper, the police had raised a barrier beyond which the demonstrators were to be prevented from advancing. A strong contingent of the police, some armed with 303 rifles, some with *lathis* (wooden sticks) and some with tear-gas shells had taken their position.

At 6:30 a.m. the demonstrators, after some pep talk from their leaders advanced towards the barrier. Tear gas shells exploded. Undeterred, the demonstrators surged forward. The police *lathi*-charged, the mob still pressed forward. The barrier gave way. A young Deputy Superintendent of Police lost his nerve and shot two shots from his revolver. It was a signal for some trigger happy policemen who discharged a burst of revolver fire. Dozens of demonstrators were wounded mercilessly, the mob ran helter-skelter.

Once again, the leaders rallied the demonstration. A second wave of demonstrators prepared to advance once again. In the meanwhile, the number of the demonstrators continued to swell owing to the arrival of a constant stream of marchers.

In Gangtok town some policemen ran amok, beating innocent people just because they happened to be wearing the Nepalis traditional dress. A number of milkmen were the victims of police brutality.

Anyone finding wearing the Nepalis dress, or just the Nepali cap or just carrying a *khukuri* (a Nepali traditional cutting tool) was beaten up and hauled off to a camp prepared for detaining demonstrators.

Some 500 Tibetan refugees were hastily issued with *lathis* and asked to help the police. The refugees took their task seriously and joined their forces with the police in the *lathi*-charges. However, wave after wave of demonstrators advanced towards the town only to be dispersed by *lathi*-charge and rifle-fire.

While this mob was going on in the capital town, up at the Palace Chapel, the functions/events was pretended as if nothing had happened to mar the event. At 11:00 a.m., the *Chogyal* took the salute at the march past of the girl guides, boy scouts and a small contingent of the Sikkim Guards.

The march past was followed by the award of 'Birthday Honours' inside the Chapel. Thereafter, the rest of the celebrations were called off at noon. At 1:30 p.m., the weather suddenly adversed. A gale blew, followed by a heavy down pour. The police and the demonstrators ran for shelter and everything was forgotten, for the time being, except the thought of protecting oneself from the fury of elements. Towards evening, the ardour of the demonstrators flagged, and they retreated to Ranipul, 12 km below Gangtok, for food and rest for the night. The day's toll had some 60 injured and wounded. The same evening the crown prince, Tenzing Namgyal, drove to Ranipul, accompanied by a Security Officer. With the rashness of youth, and perhaps flushed by a premature sense of victory over the demonstrators, he crashed through the barrier erected by the latter. A shout was raised and the young man, the security officer fired revolver shots at random, wounding three by-standers, two of them were women. This further exacerbated the people's feelings towards the ruling family and perhaps, accounts for the mounting resentment shown by the people says L. B. Basnet in his work, Sikkim : Short Political History.

More specifically, there is another version according to Sunanda K. Dutta Ray, who had in fact described in his work, *Smash and Grab – Annexation of Sikkim* (1984). "*The rising might have fizzled out then but for a piece of foolishness by Crown Prince Tenzing, who decided to venture out in his Jonga, Mrs Gandhi's gift in happier times, to see what was happening. His companions, Captain Roland Chettri, Rinchen Wangdi, and Drojee Dadul, a youth in the Sikkim Intelligence, were all in their early twenties, and none of them noted for prudence. They were four high spirited young men out for adventure.*

The drive to Singtam, just an hour away, was uneventful. Knots of people stood about along the road, but they seemed to bear no ill will to the handsome young prince. Most stared, some folded their hands in greeting, a few even smiled and waved. Singtam was peacefully deserted. But the mood changed when Tenzing and his companions were returning. A barricade had been flung across the road at Ranipul, eight miles south of Gangtok, and Tenzing, who was driving, had to pull up as smooth faced young Nepalese boys wearing scarlet armbands and waving the JAC tricolour, swarmed into the road. Not only was the crowd bigger, but it was surely, and some volunteers began pounding the Jonga's sides. Captain, Chettri lost his nerve and fired into the air; he feared for the prince's safety and hoped to frighten the mob into scattering. Simultaneously, Tenzing pressed hard on the accelerator, crashed the barrier and the Jonga was soon lost in a speeding cloud of dust." (Datta Ray 1984: 181-182)

Datta Ray goes on to elaborate the claims of JAC that the Crown Prince had fired at and killed some people eventually got exposed as the blatant lies they were.

"From pulpit and forum, Kazi denounced the Chögyal's son's murderous activities which had resulted in three deaths: the JAC even identified one of the 'victims' as Miss Kamal Tsong of Assam Lingsey village in east Sikkim. But Miss Tsong, said to have been gunned down in Ranipul on 4 April, proclaimed on 18 May: 'I am very much alive and request you to consider this grave defamation that they have tried to bring on me'. Ram Chandra Poudyal, by then encamped in the Paljor stadium, also denied Kazi's charge that the crown prince had made an attempt on his life." (Datta Ray 1984 : 182).

A motorcar accident on Nam Nam road cruelly snuffed out Crown Prince Tenzing's life in 1978.

> Captain Roland Christopher Chettri, loyal to the last, is passed away.
>
> Kazi is no more.
>
> R.C. Poudyal decamped from Paljor Stadium long ago and now lives in East Sikkim.
>
> "Miss Tsong is still alive" quotes Tenzing C. Tashi..

We have lost our country and king long back and earned ourselves a democracy. Events of some thirty years later bear out a procrastinated truth-that kingdoms are an anachronism in today's modern world. Nepal's unpopular monarchy has been forced to step down and Bhutan's enlightened monarchy has opted to give her people democracy.

Democracy is a powerful tool. But democracy does not give anyone the right, in whatsoever garb, academic or otherwise, to present a one-sided version of events and try to wrongly influence the future in what it will believe about the past (Tashi, 2008).

The other version in the book '*History of Democratic Movement*' described : *on that day, more than twenty thousand Sikkimese walked out of the villages and the bazaars. They were reacting against the nonfulfillment of their demands for a written Constitution and a system of one man one vote, the effects of which were that the representatives of the majority community failed to represent their people. The mass of humanity moved towards Gangtok accompanied even by the merchants and the government employees. The event coincided with the period, when the Government had imprisoned the leader of the Janata Congress, K.C. Pradhan. Under the leadership of Kazi Lhendup Dorjee, the procession, with fervour, moved towards the palace, but their movement was halted by gunfires. Many succumbed to death. Teargas splintered them yet they moved on. When the Sikkim guard persisted in the use of teargas and guns, the crowd began losing its control. Amidst these, the news of three casualities at Ranipool owing to the use of revolver by the escort of the Crown Prince, stoked the fire of the revolution. The police surrendered before the agitated crowd, state power passed into the hand of the people, law and order broke down in Sikkim. The people burnt the police booths, destroyed telephone line and mutilated Government documents. A group of people from Ranipool moved towards Gangtok shouting slogans, "We want people's rule", "Down with the king" "Down with the Chogyal".* With black flags in their hand they also burnt the effigy of the king [IPR (G.O.S.), 2002].

The next day, 5 April 1973, around 8,000 people once again face the police personnel. The top leaders were called by the Political Officer for amicable talks, who had been deputed soas to tackle the situation. Knowing the fact that the warrants of arrest had been issued against Kazi Lhendup Dorjee Khangsarpa and some other leaders, took the advantage of their presence in the India House Sanctuary, requested the

Political Officer for asylum and accordingly blessed it. At the current stage, the demonstrators abandoned by their influential leaders were completely ignorant of the latest developments. The ignorant demonstrators were mercilessly beaten up by the police and the Tibetans, who had by now been joined by some Sikkimese-Bhutia volunteers. Such was the on slaught that the demonstrators, who had throughout remained non-violent, fled for safety in all directions, eventually reaching their camp at Ranipul. It was projected that more than a hundred demonstrators were injured and badly wounded on 4 and 5 April and later six according to L.B. Basnet were succumbed. The saddest scene in the Capital was an apparent failure of demonstration. Hence, the demonstrators were regrouping at Ranipul under second echelon leaders, a history was being created in other towns and district head quarters. On 4th, in all district head quarters and towns of Sikkim, except Mangan in the north, the people led by the budding youth leaders, had held black flag demonstrations.

The Sikkimese flags flown on roof tops had been pulled down, ripped and trampled under foot. The feeble attempt made by some loyal officials, supported by a handful of police had further inflamed the anger of the youths, who, ignorant of the developments in Gangtok, and without the counsels of cautious and timid leaders to temper their zeal, had taken possession of all official buildings and police stations and proclaimed the 'People's Rule'. With little local variation, almost everywhere this pattern had been repeated. While the authorities at Gangtok were heaving a sigh of relief in the evening because a major part of Sikkim had passed under the *Janata* or *People's Rule* that all was not well in other parts of Sikkim, impinged on the authorities at Gangtok, when a detachment of the Sikkim Guards under Lieut. Col. K.S. Gurung of the Indian Army and the District Magistrate of Gangtok deputed to relieve the pressure at Namchi, reached Singtam, found that they could penetrate farther, and returned beyond Singtam, the *Chogyal*'s writ no longer ran. Hardly this shock had the time to register when Avatar Singh, accompanied by the Political Officer and the Major General commanding the Indian troops in Sikkim, called on the *Chogyal* and apprised him of the worsening the law and order situation and the total collapse of the Sikkim – Administration in Namchi (South), Gyalshing (West) and Gangtok (East), except Mangan (North). The *Chogyal* was persuaded to bow before the storm and his signature on a prepared draft, purporting to be a request from him to the Government of India to intervene and restore law and order, was obtained. A similar request had already been received from Kazi Lhendup Dorjee Khangsarpa and others, who, having abandoned the people to their fate, had sought Political asylum at the India House. The talks to bring about normalcy started the same evening. K.C. Pradhan, who had been brought from jail to take part in the talks, refused to go back to jail, and thus, secured his freedom.

It is a historical fact that the Indian Army, which had maintained at least a fighting division in Sikkim since the Sino-Indian war of 1962, came forward to take over from the rebel's hands all the police stations and administrative head quarters already captured earlier. Further, it was a pathetic scene that the Sikkim Police at Gangtok was confined to barracks; while Indian troops took over police functions in the capital as well as elsewhere until they were relieved by CRPF.

The evening of 7 April 1973 was another significant historical day and date that the *Chogyal* was sent a fresh 'draft' by the Political Officer whereby the *Chogyal* was to request the Government of India to take over the administration of Sikkim till the period some workable formula was developed, which led to the enactment of a force in the Palace and that throws light on the working of the minds of some Bhutia Officials, who even at that crucial hour failed to realise the gravity of the situation. However, some Bhutia Senior Officers and host of Nepalis Officers were hastily collected to study the 'draft' and help the *Chogyal* so as to conclude a decision. There in the presence of Nepalis officers, some Bhutia officers were still advising the *Chogyal* to use force and wipe out the demonstrators and anybody who dared to raise his voice against the government. However, the counselling prevailed that these Buddhists, the followers of the Prophet of non-violence, were reconciled to adopting less violent methods to cope with the revolt. It appeared they did not fully grasp the fact that the effective control over the instruments of violence had already passed from their hands.

Despite the fact, therefore, a statement was drawn up where in the officers present undertook to share the blame for the administrative failure leading to the revolt and subsequently handing over the administration to the Government of India. Around mid-night the 'draft' sent by the Political Officer was signed and returned by a special courier to the concerned officer. During this particular period, the revolt was practically over when the Government of India intervened.

At present, the Indian Army was in firm control, permitting the 'rebels' to stage noisy, but peaceful demonstrations. These demonstrations continued for many days. People from all over Sikkim continued to pour into Gangtok, under the safety ensured by the presence and active control of the Indian Army lending zest and vigour to the daily round of demonstrations. Anti-*Chogyal* sentiments gained with each passing day. During one of these demonstrations, the effigies of the *Chogyal*, the *Gyalmo*, and the Crown Prince were burnt and demand for the *Chogyal*'s abdication began to be shouted around. The Government of India, very closely observing the deteriorating situation in the State of Sikkim, appointed B.S. Das as the Chief Administrator, and accordingly, he took over the charge on 9 April 1973. Kewal Singh, the Foreign Secretary of India, held talks with the *Chogyal*, the leaders of the Joint Action Committee (JAC) and representatives of the Sikkim National Party. The JAC had presented a list of 14 demands with original five demands–a written Constitution, fundamental rights, a full-fledged democracy, *one man, one vote* and the abolition of *Parity* formula, as the main issues. At first, the abdication of the *Chogyal* was also included, but later on it was dropped on the advice of Kewal Singh, the then Foreign Secretary, Government of India.

However, the Indian Press continued to flash that the agitation was escalating completely, and had the Indian Army taken control over the situation. In the scene more than 20,000 or so demonstrators who had gathered in the Capital, after letting out steam in the shape of slogan – shouting – processions where any number of anti-*Chogyal* slogans were shouted, were being fed and generally cared for, by the Indian Army. The Foreign Press was kept out of Sikkim first by the 'Inner-Line Permit (I.L.P.) restrictions that were operative even before the beginning of the agitation and later by Government of India fiat, which came when the Chairman of JAC. who had completely placed himself at the beck and call of the Political Officer and the Foreign Secretary, requested the Government of India to keep out 'Non-Indian Foreigners', who were 'out to create fissures in the friendly relations between the Indian authorities and the Sikkimese people'. As a result, the talks held by Kewal Singh, Foreign Secretary of India with the *Chogyal*, and the Joint Action Committee and the Sikkim National Party, an agreement was signed at Gangtok on 8 May 1973. This historical tripartite agreement purported to be the basis of a future Constitution for Sikkim as well as that of the future of 'Indo-Sikkim Treaty'. Further, the agreement called for 'the establishment of a fully responsible Government of Sikkim with a more democratic Constitution, the guarantee of fundamental rights, the rule of law, an Independent Judiciary and greater legislative and Executive Power for the elected representatives of the people'. It also called for the election based on Adult Suffrage, equitable representation to all sections of the people and the voting to be based on the principle of 'one man, one vote'.

On the basis of the above said agreement, the *Chogyal* and the people of Sikkim had requested to the Government of India to provide immediately the Head of the Administration, and the Government of India had agreed to do so at its earliest. Moreover, the agreement also provided for an 'Assembly' in Sikkim. The election to this Assembly 'shall be held every four years'. The Assembly shall have power to propose laws and adopt resolutions for the welfare of the people of Sikkim on any of the matters enumerated below:

(i) Education
(ii) Public Health
(iii) Excise
(iv) Press and Publicity
(v) Transport
(vi) Bazars
(vii) Forest
(viii) Public Works

(ix) Agriculture

(x) Food Supplies

(xi) Economic and Social Planning, including State Enterprises

(xii) Home and Establishment

(xiii) Finance

(xiv) Land Revenue.

The Assembly, 'shall not discuss or ask questions on", among other things as per the following : (*For details, see Government of India (Amendment) Act, 1974*)

"T*he Chogyal and the members of the ruling family ...'*

"Any matter which concerns the responsibilities of the Government of India, under the agreement or under any other agreement between India and Sikkim." (For details, see – May 8th Agreement 1973).

Furthermore, the agreement provided for an Executive Council, 'which shall consist of the elected members of the Assembly who shall be appointed to the Executive Council by the *Chogyal* on the aid and advice of the Chief Executive. The Chief Executive shall preside over the meetings of the Executive Council'. Any difference of opinion between the *Chogyal* and the Chief Executive 'shall be referred to the Political Officer in Sikkim, who shall obtain the advice of the Government of India, which shall be binding'. The agreement also leaves many questions unanswered. On many matters, it is vague and equivocal. Only when it takes more concrete shape in the form of a 'written Constitution', will this vagueness be removed. There is no indication when the promises contained in the agreement are to be translated into action.

Finally, however, some conclusions can be derived from the agreement. Firstly, the Powers of the *Chogyal*, even though he remains the 'Head of the State', had been drastically reduced. Secondly, the preponderant ascendancy of the Bhutias in every field had been rudely shaken. Thirdly, the Nepalis of Sikkimese origin, which had risen in revolt, had been assured of a fairer deal. Ultimately, the Government of India had gained enormously. The Indian hold over Sikkim became more firmer.

The internal administration of Sikkim had, to all intents and purposes, been taken over by the Government of India with an objective exercising a greater power with her neighbouring Countries in the cradle of the Indian Sub-Continent.

The Political turmoil that rocked the State ultimately led to the signing of the 'Tripartite Agreement' on 8 May 1973, postulated the formation of a responsible Government, wider legislative and Executive Powers for the elected representatives of the People, a system of election based on, 'Adult Suffrage', which would give an equitable representation to all the sections of the people on the basis of the principle of one man one vote. It was also agreed that there should be an Assembly in Sikkim. The Assembly would be elected every four years. Elections would be conducted under the supervision of a representative of the Election Commission of India, who would be appointed for the purpose, by the Government of Sikkim.

The Election to the New Sikkim Legislative Assembly: 1974

Accordingly, the Proclamation of Representation of Sikkim Subjects Act, 1974 was issued by the *Chogyal* in the month of February, 1974. In accordance to this Act, the Assembly was to be composed of 32 members and Sikkim was divided into thirty one Territorial Constituencies and one *Sangha* Constituency. The *Sangha* Constituency was to compromise the *Sanghas* belonging to Monasteries recognised by the *Chogyal*. This Constituency was to elect one member through an electoral college of the *Sanghas* whose members were not eligible to vote for any other Constituency. Out of the 32 seats, 15 seats were reserved for the Bhutia-Lepcha and 15 for the Nepalis community. One was reserved for the *Sangha*, the other was reserved for the Scheduled Castes. Election to the 31 Territorial Constituencies of the Assembly would be held on the basis of Adult Suffrage. A candidate, in order to be a member of the Assembly, must be a subject of Sikkim and of above 25 years of age. The Government of Sikkim was to form rules for the conduct of Election in consultation with the Government of India. R.N. Sengupta, I.A.S. representative of the Election Commission of India, was appointed Commissioner for the New Sikkim Assembly Elections, 1974.

At the moment, the political parties were busy in setting up their machineries for the ensuing elections. The Sikkim Janata Congress and the Sikkim National Congress were by this time merged together in the name of Sikkim Congress. The party started its election propaganda. The categorical pledges of the party, which definitely influenced the people, as was evident from the election results, covered a wide range including the development of agriculture and allied fields, industry, power, administrative reforms, land reforms, safeguard for the minorities and backward classes, promotion of education, construction of roads and bridges, etc. Beside these, the party sought in the sphere of Indo-Sikkim relations, closer ties with the Government and People of India. A record number of candidates who filed their nomination papers from the 31 Territorial Constituencies were 120. The number of accepted *validly* nominated candidates of the *Sangha* Constituency was 6. However, ultimately, the number of contesting Candidates from the Territorial Constituencies, to whom symbols were allotted for the first time on the ballot papers, became eighty one, fighting for the election battle.

It was on 16 March 1974, the *Chogyal* Promulgated the Sikkim Election Offences and Corrupt Practices Act, 1974. This Act enumerated the rules prohibiting public meetings on the day and preceding day of the poll; penalty for disorderly conduct in or near the polling stations, offences relating the disturbances at the election meetings, offences for generating enmity between classes in the context of election, etc. In another notification, the Election Commission issued directions prescribing the manner for the conduct of elections. It contained that there would be a common ballot box for all the contesting candidates, only one ballot would be placed to receive the ballot papers at any point of time. No symbol would be pasted on the ballot box. Every ballot paper was to contain the names of all respective Constituencies in English, Nepali and Tibetan/Bhutia, the symbols allotted to them. Further, it also contained procedures to be followed for maintaining secrecy of voting, for issuing ballot papers to the voters, keeping of records of spoilt and returned ballot papers, including unused materials, etc. In another notification, the Election Commissioner issued directions/guidelines relating to counting of votes and other related matters and the number of Polling Stations this was 103 including the *Sangha* Constituency, while in 1953, the total number of Polling Stations were only 69 installed for.

Table 8.4: Sikkim Legislative Assembly Results: 1974

Sl. No.	*Name of the Party*	*No. of Elected Members*
1.	Sikkim Congress	31 (including 03 unopposed)
2.	Sikkim National Party	01
3.	Independent Candidates	00

Total Number of Seats = 32.

Source : Sikkim Darbar Gazette, Ex. Gazette No. 55, dated 30.04. 1974 and Ex. Gazette 29, dated 05.03. 1974.

Merger and After

The results of the Elections to Sikkim Legislative Assembly, held under a new system based on the Principle of *ONE MAN – ONE VOTE*, showed that the Sikkim Congress made a landslide victory by capturing 27 seats out of 28 contested seats, one seat went to the National Party which in the previous election captured half of the elective seats. Karma Gampo Lama, who won the *Sangha* seat was also a Sikkim Congress candidate. Three of the Sikkim Congress candidates including its President Kazi Lhendup Dorjee Khangsarpa were declared as elected unopposed. Bhawani Prasad Khanel was elected unopposed from Ratey-Pani West Pendam, B.B. Gooroong from Chakung and Kazi Lhendup Dorjee Khangsarpa from Tashiding. As such, the Sikkim Congress won all the Assembly seats except one.

The above table shows the total numbers of electorate including 2,004 of Sangha voters and a total of 10,740 voters of the three Constituencies where from candidates were returned unopposed. The figure of the invalid votes was insignificant. The systems of election were quite new in comparison to those of the earlier elections. The voters were not conversant with the system of single ballot, the system of only one ballot box with no symbol pasted on the ballot box and the system of casting only one vote. Even then, only 1,498 votes were found invalid. The electorate, it might be suggested, had a quick grasp of the system. By 1974, they had participated in a number of elections of varied systems and this had gained their experiences, understanding and farsightedness.

Table 8.5: The Number of Votes Polled in Favour of Different Political Parties

Sl. No.	*Name of the Party*	*No. of Votes Polled*
1.	Sikkim Congress	26,767
2.	Sikkim National Party	1,040
3.	Independent Candidates	7,189

Source :IPR 1974..

An interesting fact, during this election the system of voting and counting of votes which had changed and a contrast to early elections became conspicuous. For instance, Nar Bahadur Khatiwada was declared elected, simply because he secured the highest number of votes without any consideration of the votes of his own community or other communities. However, an extraordinary system of election followed upto 1973 in the *Chogyal*'s regime in Sikkim.

From Table 8.6, a change in Election procedure and system since 1974 can be drawn in Sikkim.

It was the prelude to a change that the Sikkim National Party members contested only 5 seats and a number of erstwhile National Party members contested the elections as independent candidates. Ultimately, the verdict of the people, as reflected through voting could be taken as a clear mandate in favour of democracy, social and economic justice for which the Sikkim Congress stood. It was a historical day that on 10 May 1974, the newly constituted Sikkim Assembly was inaugurated by the *Chogyal*. Later, a Constitution, called the Government of Sikkim Bill, 1974 was adopted by the Sikkim Assembly. The Government of Sikkim Bill having been assented to by the *Chogyal*, a Council of Ministers had to be formed. Accordingly, the *Chogyal* appointed a 4-member Council of Ministers in July 1974 with Kazi Lhendup Dorjee Khangsarpa

Table 8.6: Result of Election in Dentam

Name of the Constituency	*Total No. of Electorate*	*Name of the Candidates*	*No. of Valid Votes Secured*
Dentam	3,236	1. C.B. Chhetri	13
		2. D.S. Gurung	108
		3. I.B. Gurung	102
		4. N. Pradhan (Newar)	35
		5. N.B. Khatiwada	**758** (Winner)
		6. Padam S. Subba	147

Source : Sikkim : Results of Elections : 1974.

as the Chief Minister – designate. However, the Ministry, in no time, came in conflict with the *Chogyal*. The conflict of ideology mingled with the conflict of power assumed such a dimension that by 16 May 1975, the tiny Himalayan State lost its identity as a Protectorate, first by being an Associate State of India by 35th Amendment Act, 1974, and later by completely merging with and becoming a full fledged Constituent State of India by 36th Amendment Act, 1975. The Sikkim Assembly, formed through the elections of 1974 with 32 members, became the Legislative Assembly of the State of Sikkim duly elected under the Constitution enacted for. Further, Sikkim was allotted one seat in the Lok Sabha and the whole of Sikkim constituted one Parliamentary Constituency. A long journey of democrats ultimately achieved their goals so as to establish a democratic institution with good will and strong faith under the umbrella of Mother India. After a long dark night, a sunny morning was born in the face of Mother Sikkim facing the Mount *Khang-chen-dzonga* (the guardian deity of Sikkim). Thus, the dawn of democracy depicts the birth of democracy in Sikkim doing away with more than 333 and more years of Namgyal Dynastic rule. It is, therefore, the duty of the people, political parties and leaders to safeguard this hard-won freedom to make Sikkim more and more prosperous and not only a model State but one of the best States of India.

We express our gratitude to Shri Pema Wangchuk for having given permission for re-production of the above article which was already published in "Now" (English) daily from Tadong, East Sikkim.

Notes and References

1. Author's interview with C.D. Rai, Ex. Councillor, Govt. of Sikkim, Retd. Secretary, Govt. of Sikkim dated 26.06. 2007, B.B. Gooroong, Ex. Chief Minister of Sikkim and now Advisor to the Hon'ble Chief Minister of Sikkim, Pawan Chamling (Gangtok), dated 11.08. 2007.
2. Basnet, L.B. (1974). Sikkim: A Short Political History, New Delhi, S. Chand & Co. Pvt. Ltd., pp. 71-188.
3. Government of Sikkim (2002). Sikkim, History of Democratic Movement, Gangtok, IPR Publication, pp. 7-27.
4. Sengupta, N. (1985). Sikkim: State Government and Politics, New Delhi, Sterling Publishers Pvt. Ltd., p. 239.
5. Shukla R. Satyendra (1976). Sikkim: The Study of Integration, New Delhi, S. Chand & Co., Pvt. Ltd., p. 217.
6. Grover, B.S.K. (1974). Sikkim and India: Storm and Consolidation, New Delhi, Jain Brothers Publication, pp. 235-36.
7. Sinha, A.C. (1975). Politics of Sikkim: A Sociological Study, Faridabad, Thompson Press, (India) Ltd., p. 110.

9

Agriculture in the Sikkim Himalaya: A Geographical Note[1]

Introduction

Taking into account its geological character and the geomorphic processes operating therein 'the Himalayan arc extends between latitudes 26°20´ and 35°40´ North, and between longitudes 74°50´ and 95°40´ East' (Ives and Messerli 1989, Ives 2004). It extends from the Indus Trench below Nanga Parbat (8,125 m) in the west to the Yarlungtsangpo-Brahmaputra gorge below Namche Barwa (7,756 m) in the east, a west-northwest to east-southeast distance of about 2,500 km and a width of 200-300 km (ibid). Tentatively, such a definition[2] includes, politically, the independent kingdoms of Nepal, Bhutan and Indian states of Jammu and Kashmir, Himachal Pradesh, Uttaranchal, Sikkim, Darjeeling region of West Bengal, Arunachal Pradesh and some hill districts of northern Assam. The region directly provides life-support base for over 65 million mountain people. Furthermore, Himalayan environment indirectly affects the densely populated Indo-Gangetic and Brahmaputra plains.

Regional Setting of the Sikkim Himalaya

Sikkim shares the same geological history of the larger Himalayan Arc and hence forms an important unit of the Himalayan geology. It is located on the western end of Eastern Himalaya. It lies between latitudes 27° 5' north to 20° 9' north

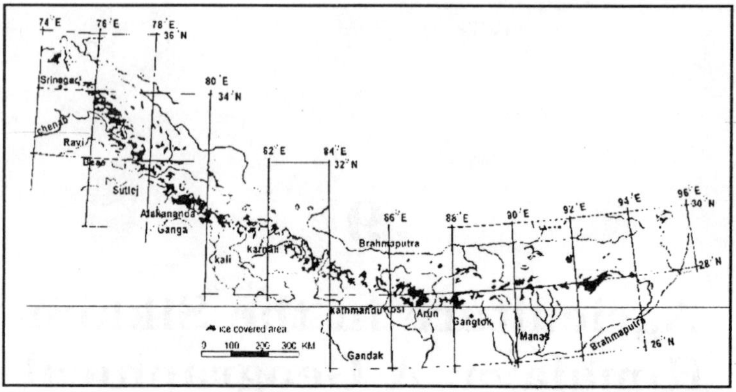

Source: WWF 2005

Fig. 9.1 Geographical location of the Himalaya

Table 9.1: Regional Divisions of the Himalaya

Regional Division	*Sub-Division*	*Geographical Extent*	*Area*
Western Himalaya	Kashmir Himalaya	32º17' and 36º58' north and 37º26' to 80 º30' east	222,800
	Himachal Himalaya	30º 22' 40" to 33º 12 40" north and 75º 45' 55" to 79º 04' 20" east	55,673
Central Himalaya	Uttaranchal Himalaya	28º 53' 24" to 31º 27' 50" north and 77º 34' 27" to 81º 02' 22" east	51,125
	Nepal Himalaya	26º 12' to 30º 27' north and 80º 4' to 88º 12' east	147,181
Eastern Himalaya	Sikkim Himalaya	27° 5' to 28° 9' north and 87° 59' to 88° 56' east.	7,096
	Darjeeling Himalaya	26° 31' to 27°13' north and 87° 59' to 88° 53' east	3,149
	Bhutan Himalaya	26°45' and 28°10' north and 88°45' to 92° 25' east.	47,000
	Arunachal Himalaya	26°30' and 29°30' north and 91°30' to 97° 30' east.	83,743

Source: Compiled by the author

and longitudes 87° 59' east to 88° 56' east. It is wedged between Nepal in the West and Bhutan in the East and China in the North and North-East. In the South it shares its Indian border with Darjeeling Himalaya of the state of West Bengal. It has a total geographical area of 7,096 sq. km.

Sikkim forms a part of both Lesser and Greater Himalayan ranges and geographically it shares an important portion of the Eastern Himalaya. Covering just 0.2 percent of the country Sikkim Himalaya is characterised by formidable physical features. It presents a compound landscape because the complexity of geomorphic evolution has played an important role in the development of the existing topography. Starting at the foot with a meager elevation of less than 300 m it stretches up to as high as 8,550 m above the mean sea level. The hills rise abruptly and the elevation increases northward and northwestward. The third highest mountain ridge Mt. Kanchenjunga (8,598 m) and other high elevations are located in the northwestern part of the Sikkim Himalaya.

Sikkimese Society

Different social, religious, linguistic and ethnic groups co-exist in the Sikkim Himalaya practicing different types of agriculture and pastoral activities. The present population of Sikkim primarily consists of Lepcha, Bhutia, Nepali[3] and plainsmen. The records of the Gazetteer of *Sikhim* (1891) throws us the light that in the late 19th Century Nepalis with 56 per cent constituted a majority of the population followed by the Lepchas with 19 per cent and Bhutias constituting 16 per cent. There were also other groups like the Khambus and slaves. A little over century later, the share of Lepcha population has gone down to 14 per cent whereas that of the Nepalis climbed to almost 70 per cent with the Bhutias constituting more or less the same share (Sikkim Human Development Report 2001). These ethnic groups traditionally have their own language, culture and social practices although homogenisation of such practices has gradually been taking place in recent times.

All the ethnic groups are characterised by specific ecological adaptations as well as by the social organisation of the region where they live (Bhasin and Bhasin 1996: 270). Majority of the social groups are found throughout Sikkim Himalaya although some areas are dominated by Lepchas and Bhutias. The Dzongu and Lacheng/Lachung regions of North Sikkim are the strongholds of Lepchas and Bhutias respectively. Lepchas, traditionally nature worshipers, are now mainly Buddhist or Christian by religion. Bhutias are also Buddhist and follow a form of Lamaism while majority of Nepali speakers are Hindus. Geographically, the northern Sikkim is very scarcely populated while the eastern part is densely populated followed by southern and western region.

Sikkimese Economy

Sikkim is primarily a rural and agricultural economy where over 60 per cent of its population are directly engaged in agriculture and allied activities while 85 per cent of the population is in one way or the other linked with agriculture and allied activities including livestock. The state has limited industrial potential due to its geologic and geomorphic constraints. More recently small and medium scale industrial units like fruit processing, pickle making, jewels, distillery etc are, however, gradually penetrating in the region. Sikkim is also a well-known producer of alcoholic beverages (Bhasin and Bhasin 1996: 279). Notably, the contribution of agriculture and allied activities on GDP of Sikkim has drastically reduced over the years while that of secondary and tertiary sector has increased. Conversely, however, the proportion of Sikkimese dependant on agriculture and allied activities has remained constant or decreased negligibly during the same period.

Table 9.2 Structural Change in the Gross Domestic Product of Sikkim (%)

Sectors	*1980-81*	*1985-86*	*1990-91*	*1995-96*	*1999-00*	*2004-02**
Primary	51.59	50.96	46.49	39.41	25.52	20.54
Secondary	18.11	16.46	12.97	18.80	19.73	30.22
Tertiary	30.30	32.58	40.54	41.79	54.75	49.24

**Quick Estimate, Source: Lama 2007:3.*

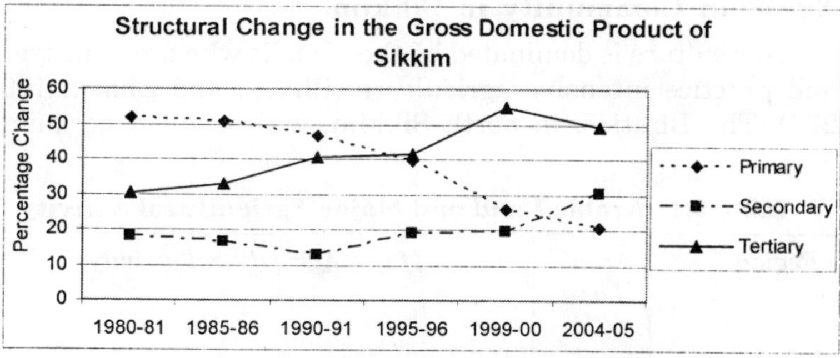

Fig. 9.2: Structural Change in GDP of Sikkim.

Table 9.3 Economic Arrangement in the Himalaya

Region	*Major Economic Activity*	*Other Sources of Economy*
Jammu & Kashmir	Agriculture and allied activity (about 70%)	Household industry, Manufacturing, Tourism
Himachal Pradesh	Agriculture and allied activity (about 90%)	Forest, Hydropower, Tourism
Uttaranchal	Agriculture and allied activity (more than 80%)	Forest, Hydropower, Tea, Tourism, Small scale & cottage industry,
Darjeeling	Agriculture and allied activity (about 26%)	Tea, Tourism, Forest
Sikkim	Agriculture and allied activity (more than 85%)	Hydropower, Tea, Tourism, Forest,
Arunachal Pradesh	Agriculture and allied activity (more than 90%)	Forest, Hydropower, Tourism, Cottage industry & handicrafts
Nepal	Agriculture and allied activity (more than 91%)	Forest, Hydropower, Tourism, Manufacturing, Household Industry.
Bhutan	Agriculture & allied activity (93%)	Forest, Hydropower, Tourism

Source: Compiled by the author

Agrarian Community in Sikkim

Agriculture is dominated by the Nepalis who are industrious and practice intensive agriculture (Bhasin and Bhasin 1996: 276). The Bhutias, in north Sikkim, with their large animal

Table 9.4 : Arable Land and Major Agricultural Activity

Region	*Arable Land (%)*	*Major Agricultural activity*
Jammu & Kashmir	5.0	Rice, Maize, Wheat, Millet, Pulses, Fruits, Vegetable, Saffron, animal husbandry
Himachal Pradesh	10.0	Wheat, Maize, Rice, barley, pulses, millet, gram, potato, fruits, ginger, vegetables, kuth, sugarcane, medicinal herbs, animal husbandry, Poultry, Fish culture
Uttaranchal	14.4	Millet, Wheat, Rice, Ginger, Sugarcane, Fruits, Vegetables, Animal Husbandry
Darjeeling	25.0	Rice, Maize, Wheat, Barley, Millet, Potato, Fruit, Vegetable, Flowers, Medicinal herbs, Ginger, Cardamom, Livestock.
Sikkim	11.0	Rice, Maize, Cardamom, Wheat, Barley, Millet, Potato, Fruits, Vegetables, Medicinal herbs, Ginger, Livestock.
Arunachal Pradesh	2.5	Barley, Wheat, Maize, Soybean, Paddy, Potato, Millet, oilseeds, Fruits, Vegetables, Spices, Sugarcane
Nepal	20.2	Rice, Maize, Wheat, Barley, Millet, Oilseed, Potato, Jute, Tobacco, Cotton, Indigo, Opium, Vegetable, Fruits, Medicinal herbs, Livestock.
Bhutan	3.4	Rice, Maize, Buck-wheat, Root crops, Citrus fruits, Cardamom, Spices, Animal husbandry, Poultry.

Source: Compiled by the author

herds practice pastoral economy on high altitudes, while Lepchas practice subsistence agriculture.

The original inhabitants of Sikkim were not agriculturists. They led a very primitive life. Gathering of wild roots, fruits, hunting and fishing were their means of livelihood. When Bhutia people migrated to Sikkim they started semi-pastoral economy and sedentary farming. They ploughed only the flat pieces of land available here and there. Settled agriculture stepped into Sikkim only with the arrival of Nepali immigrants. These sturdy, hardy, energetic and innovative people cleared large tracts of forestlands and made the land fit for agriculture (Bhatt and Bhargava 2005).

Major Agricultural crops

Principal food crops cultured in the region include maize, paddy, barley, millet, wheat, buck wheat, beans, etc. Important cash crops are cardamom, ginger, potato, soyabean, fruit crops and vegetables, etc. Horticulture crops like cardamom, ginger, orange and are raised on commercial basis and are exported within and outside the country. Sikkim has the largest area and the highest production of large cardamom in India (Bhatt and Bhargava 2005: 126). It is a foreign exchange earner crop of Sikkim. Therefore, special steps are being taken to augment the production of cardamom. A special kind of tea much valued by the connoisseur for its taste and quality is also produced in Sikkim. A government tea estate is being developed in Temi in the southern part of Sikkim. The estate extends over an area of 400 acres. Further, livestock and animal husbandry engage a measurable proportion of rural folks in the area. In short, agriculture, horticulture and animal husbandry constitute a mainstay of the largest segment of Sikkim's population.

Geography of Agriculture

Sikkimese agriculture has to be seen in the context of larger Himalayan geography and environmental specificities therein. Physiography of the region has made agricultural conditions extremely diverse. Agriculture is greatly impacted by altitude and slope aspect. Agricultural fields are invariably terraced all over Sikkim Himalaya. The nature of terrain and varied micro climatic conditions influence agriculture in Sikkim to a great extent.

Table 9.5: Physical Geography of the Sikkim Himalaya

Type of Land	*Level of Elevation (meter)*
Lower hills	270 -1,500
Middle Hills	1,500-2,000
Higher Hills	2,000-3,000
Alpine Zone	3,000-3,900 (with vegetation)
Snow Bound Land	Up to 8,580 (very high mountains without vegetation and with perpetual snow cover)

Source: Sikkim-A Statistical Profile 2002; 2003: 62.

Table 9.6: District-wise Area Under Major Crops % Share

Crops/Districts	*North*	*East*	*South*	*West*
Maize	7.8	24.3	33.8	34.1
Rice	9.1	42.0	33.9	15.0
Wheat	12.6	33.5	23.4	30.5
Barley	12.3	28.3	18.9	40.6
Pulses	0.0	25.5	35.5	38.9
Potato	8.0	23.2	13.4	55.4
Cardamom	31.6	29.8	19.6	19.0

Source: Computed from Bhatt and Bhargava 2005: 128.

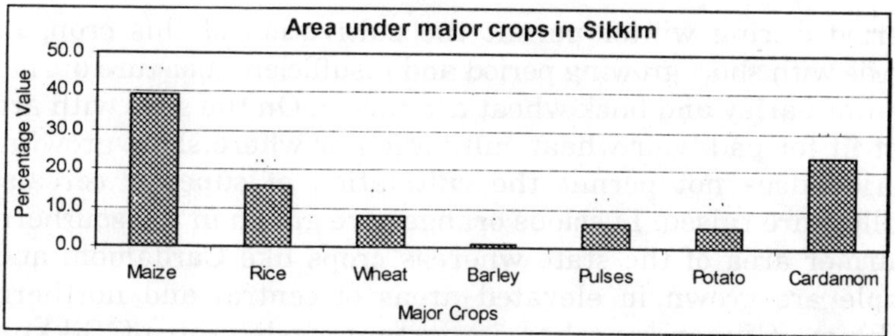

Fig. 9.3

Usually, agriculture is practiced on irrigated terraces called *Khet* or rain fed terraces called *Bari*. *Khets* are mostly seen on the lower altitudes and is meant mainly for paddy cultivation although winter or dry season crops are also grown in addition to paddy at many instances. *Bari* on the other hand are prevalent both at lower and higher altitudes. With the increase in altitudes, the proportion of *Bari* to *Khet* increases as a result of cooler dry season conditions, increasing slop gradient and inaccessibility of water. Livestock supply draught power and serve as the primary and perhaps the most important source of fertiliser. The villagers use the pairs of oxen to cultivate the terraced fields. Animal manure is indispensable for field fertilisation as chemical fertilisers are hardly used.

The humid tropical zone of southern Sikkim constitutes the maize cultivation belt. Needing high temperature and good amount of rainfall, maize is sown in early summer and harvested in September-October. Maize is an exacting crop and requires a good amount of human labour for thinning and weeding process.

Paddy is a crop mainly of river valleys. Along river beds the crop is raised with the help of irrigation. Small channels taken out of the rivers irrigate the surrounding land. On higher areas where temperature and rainfall conditions permit the cultivation of paddy the crop is grown on terraced fields. Paddy is a summer crop and it is grown everywhere in the state except in very high areas. Because of copious water requirement during its growth period paddy is raised on irrigated fields.

Wheat and barley are winter crops. They are mainly raised in southern and central Sikkim where temperature and growing period during winter permit the cultivation of this crop. In areas with short growing period and insufficient moisture during winter barley and buck wheat are raised. On the soils with are not fit for paddy or wheat cultivation or where short growing period does not permit the cultivation of superior cereals, millets are raised. Luscious oranges are grown in the southern warmer area of the state whereas crops like Cardamom and apple are grown in elevated areas of central and northern Sikkim. Ginger, another important cash crop of Sikkim Himalaya, is a feature of lower elevations in the region.

Sikkim has only 13 per cent of its reported area under net sown area while the gross cropped area comes to around 18 per cent. Further, the intensity of agriculture on the land resource of Sikkim is alarming given its geo-environmental location. The figures available with us highlight that the intensity of agriculture on land comes to over 133, which is higher than the national average in this respect. Such high

Table 9.7: Intensity of Agriculture on Land Resource

	Net sown Area (%)	*Gross Cropped Area (%)*	*Intensity of agriculture on land resource*
Sikkim	13.4	17.9	133.7
Arunachal Pradesh	2.7	4.7	172.0
Assam	34.5	48.6	141.1
Manipur	6.3	9.0	142.1
Meghalaya	9.4	11.1	118.1
Mizoram	3.1	5.1	164.6
Nagaland	12.3	14.1	114.8
Tripura	26.4	43.9	166.1
Northeast	16.5	23.4	141.8
India	46.6	61.1	131.2

Source: Computed from Khullar, 2000.

intensity of agriculture on land resource can be explained by the fact that Sikkim has relatively higher percentage of its land under forest and other uses. Hence, the small amount of land available for agriculture is intensively utilised, often beyond the carrying capacity of the resource base.

BOX 9.1: A TYPICAL VILLAGE ECONOMY: SULDUNG-KAMLING, WEST SIKKIM

Suldung Kamling is a Gram Panchayat unit in West Sikkim district under Chakung constituency. Due to rain shadow of the Darjeeling hills the area receives scant rainfall with a long lean season of 3-4 months. The terrain is very steep with the average slope being about 45 degrees, with some areas being still steeper. The soil in the area is of two types: lateritic with better soil depth and sandy shallow soil. The villagers have made a sustainable use of the limited resources they have. The steepest part of the fields are planted with useful trees, moderately steep areas are planted with pulses and less steep and terraced fields are used for cultivating maize and ginger. The main challenges provided by nature are geographic wherein steep lands combined with scant rainfall reduce productivity.

Culturally, Rais, Lepchas, Chettri and Mangers dominate the landscape. The economy is largely agrarian with ginger and pulses providing the main source of income. The total absence of irrigation facility is the main bottleneck for sustainable farming. Incomes from ginger have gone down drastically over the years due to reduced productivity. The productivity has fallen from 4-5 times to 2-3 times now. The main source of cash incomes is from sale of ginger, pulses and from wage labour amounting to about Rs. 1500 per month. About 50 per cent of the income is used for buying rice while the remaining is used for purchasing grocery, clothes, etc. Amongst livestock poultry, goatery and cattle are reared in limited numbers. Cattle are reared for manure, milk and for ploughing while chicken and goat function as rural household banks, to be liquidated during times of need.

Based on field survey conducted by officials[4] of the Government of Sikkim[5] led by Vimal Khawas, 5 July 2007.

Conclusion

Agriculture, horticulture and animal husbandry constitute a mainstay of the largest segment of Sikkim's population engaging large chunk of them in this sector. Agriculture is the primary driver of the economy. Over 85 per cent of the population is directly or indirectly dependent on agriculture and allied activities for its livelihood. The varied topographic and agro-climatic conditions permit the cultivation of a wide variety of crops and fruits ranging from sub-tropical to cool temperate. The cropping pattern of the region reflects the varying conditions of altitude, climate and soil on the one hand and on other the various agronomic and cultural practices and traditions evolved over the centuries such as elaborative terracing, crop rotation and very efficient traditional irrigation system[6].

Agriculture is concentrated mainly in the lower hills and in the valleys of Sikkim Himalaya. At some cases, however, patches of agricultural land have also been carved out in the high mountain areas. Rice is the principal crop in the well-watered valleys while maize is an important rain-fed crop on the hillsides. Other cereal crops are wheat, millet and barley. Cardamom, potatoes, fruits and vegetables are major cash crops.

Food production in the Sikkim Himalaya has, however, not kept up with the population growth. Agriculture is handicapped by steep and hilly terrain, climatic hazards, small and scattered holdings, thin stony soils, limited irrigation and small cultivated area. The scope for increasing cultivated/ cultivable area is not much. Physical environment restricts the cultivated land to a large extent in the area hence exhibiting acute shortage of arable land. It has further infused a high degree of adaptive skill and uncommon physical vigour among the people to cope with the inhospitality of the environment. To secure agricultural land, rugged terrains are arduously terraced even on such steep slopes where the land should be left under pasture or forest. Since alternative sources of livelihood other than agriculture are limited, the peasantry has to eke out its existence under difficult conditions where nature is a stern mother.

Notes

1. de Roover (2002) raises an important question: "How to explain the persistence of the idea of secularism, while this idea is not intelligible in the first place?"
2. "We have come to equate secularity, the disengagement and differentiation of the public sphere from religion, with modernity. In fact, the emergence and form of the western secular nation-state have everything do with Christianity, and Protestantism in particular" (Friedland 1999: 315).
3. Discriminatory treatment towards the Nepali groups brewed acute discontent and contributed to political instability in Sikkim during the ninety-seventies, thereby justifying Indian government's intervention to stabilise the region after Tibet was annexed by China.
4. Democracy comprises more than an institutional context for decision-making by a majority but emerges as a site of tug between competing forces and ethnic groups to ultimately facilitate accommodation, opposition, and reconciliation of demands and interests.
5. In 1984, the judged concurred that that the matter was not for the courts to decide as it was of a political nature and they were wary of an Assam like situation developing in Sikkim. So the issue was kept pending until 1993.
6. Padmasambhava (8th century) is credited with spreading Buddhism in Tibet.
7. It is associated with the Karma Kargyu school of Mahayana Buddhism that was founded in the 12th century by Dagpo Lharje Gampopa based on the teachings of Naropa and Milarepa. There is much controversy around the Karmapa legacy. H.H. the Dalai Lama recognises the Karmapa claimant H.H. XVII Gyalwa Karmapa Orgyen Drodul Trinley Dorje. However, the government of India is not permitting him to enter Sikkim.
8. *'Brasmo ljongs gnas yig* or the guidebook to the sacred places by Lhatsun Jigmed Pawo (1682-1717) is the most commonly referred version and is available as a block print text at the Namgyal Institute of Tibetology, Gangtok, Sikkim.
9. For detailed analysis of the Rathongchu movement refer to Arora (2004, 2006b).
10. Sonam Gyatso and N. Dorjee of the Ecclesiastical Department, Government of Sikkim during an interview in April 2002 in Gangtok.

11. Paper presented at the International Expert Meeting 'Conserving Agricultural Heritage System in Mountainous Landscape' organised by United Nations University, Sikkim University and Kyoto University, November 4-6, 2007, Gangtok, Sikkim, India.
12. Mention should, however, be made here that the Himalayan environment supports and affects a much larger geographical area, covering India, Pakistan, Afghanistan, Nepal, Bhutan, Bangladesh and Burma, than its actual geographical stretch.
13. The term Nepali does not connote social group in the technical sense but a nationality of Nepal. It is also that all the Nepali language speakers residing in different parts of the world are called Nepali. There are, however, several social groups within the larger Nepali community.
14. Sandeep Tambe, D.K. Pradhan, Nakul Rai, Sangam Rai, Sonam Rinchen Lepcha, Karma Gurmey Bhutia, Abhina Thapa.
15. This exercise was primarily a part of Monitoring and Evaluation Training imparted by the Council for Social Development, New Delhi to the Officers of the Government of Sikkim. It was a field exposure to the trainees to supplement classroom lectures on Monitoring and Evaluation delivered by relevant experts.
16. Such irrigation system is called *Kuhl* in Himachal, *Gul* in Uttaranchal and *Kulo* in Darjeeling-Sikkim. Further, in regions like Uttaranchal and Himachal Pradesh it also provides water for small water mills.

References

Bhasin, Veena and M.K. Bhasin (1996). Sikkim Himalayas: Ecology and Resource Development. *Journal of Human Ecology*, 7(4): 265-299.

Bhatt S.C and Gopal K. Bhargava (2005). *Land and People of Indian States and Union Territories: Sikkim,* Vol. 34, Delhi: Kalpaz Publications.

Ives, J. D. (2004). *Himalayan perception: Environmental change and the well being of mountain peoples.* London: Rutledge (Rprint 2006).

Ives, J. D. and B. Messerli (1989). *The Himalayan dilemma: Reconciling development and conservation*. London and New York: Routledge.

Khawas, Vimal. 2003. Environment and Rural Development in Darjeeling Himalaya: Issues and Concerns. *Spatio-Economic Development Record*, 10 (2): 27-33.

Khawas, Vimal (2005). Conservation and Management of Water Resource in Sikkim Himalaya: some suggestions. *Spatio-Economic Development Record*, 12 (4): 27-31.

Khawas, Vimal (2007). Environmental Challenges and Human Security in the Himalaya. Paper Presented at National Seminar *Himalayas in the New Millennium: Environment, Society, Economy and Polity*, January 11-12, 2007, Centre for Himalayan Studies, North Bengal University, Darjeeling.

Khullar, D.R. (2000). *India-A Comprehensive Geography*, New Delhi: Kalyani Publishers.

Lama, M.P. (2007). *Sikkim Economic Survey*, Gangtok: Government of Sikkim.

Lama, M.P. (2001). *Sikkim Human Development Report,* Government of Sikkim.

10

Food Security in Sikkim: A Critical Review

Introduction

Availability of and access to food are the two essential determinants of food security. Availability however does not ensure access. It has been observed that even though food may be available globally, a considerable difference in distribution or access to food is visible within countries, households within countries, or individuals within households.

Food security policies aim specifically at ensuring that households have an adequate dietary intake and that the possibility of food deficiency among the households should get minimised. The reduction of poverty and hunger has been identified as two most important aspects in the development agenda in the new millennium and it was also clearly reaffirmed in the Rome Declaration of the World Food Summit in 1996 as well as in World Food Summit in 2001.

In the Indian context, according to Acharya's (1998) observations, the policy package consisting of introduction of high-yielding varieties of wheat and rice, strengthening agricultural research and extension services, measures to increase the supply of agricultural inputs such as chemical fertilisers and pesticides, expansion of major and minor irrigation facilities, announcement of minimum support prices for major crops, government procurement of cereals to maintain a buffer stocks and to meet food grains demand to sustain public distribution system and the provision of agricultural credit on a priority basis, had raised the rate of growth of productivity in India per hectare of all crops taken together from 2.07 per cent in the decade ending 1985-1986 to 2.51 per cent per annum during the decade ending 1994-1995. Similar evidence of an increase in yields, a partial measure of productivity gains given by output per unit of land area has also been observed.

From the last decade or so, a reversal of trend has been observed. According to observation of Planning Commission, Government of India (2001) during the Tenth Plan, agricultural GDP grew at an annual rate of mere 2.1 percent against the targeted growth rate of 4 percent, and this may be the result of stagnation or decline in productivity during the last decade. Agriculture Strategy for Eleventh Plan (2007) has categorically mentioned that a particular area of concern is foodgrains, whose production during Tenth plan was less than during Ninth plan. Per capita annual production of cereals has declined from 192 kg in 1991-95 to only 174 kg in 2004-07 and of pulses from 15 kg to 12 kg.

Since a large section of the rural poor are either subsistence farmers or landless labourers and as they derive their livelihood either by acting as a producer or by selling their human labour, therefore, inadequate food grain production is bound to add misery among these sections of rural populace. In addition to that, urban food insecurity is also on the rise.

SECTION I
STATUS OF AGRICULTURE IN SIKKIM

In Sikkim, almost 70 per cent of the total working force is engaged in agriculture and allied activities, and they cultivate around 16 per cent of the total land area. Unlike the plain areas, the agricultural lands are crescent shaped (4.5 m to 7.5 m long and 2.5 m to 3.5 m wide) and terraced, (Dasgupta, 1992) and have a varied elevation of 300 metres to 3,000 meters. Diversity in ecological condition along with the varied elevation has brought considerable variation in agricultural practices in the state, and a vast area has become unsuitable for traditional agricultural practice.

Out of the total land area of 7,096 km^2, 44.09 per cent area is under forest; another 40.02 per cent area is under permanent snow or alpine pasture. Thus, only 15.69 per cent of total land area is presently under cultivation.

Trend in Agricultural Production, Productivity and Agricultural Growth in Sikkim (1975-2002)

Total food grain production in the state has registered a healthy increase in absolute term and a rising trend is witnessed both in productivity as well as in the area of cultivation, however, since 2000-01 the production, and from 1990-91 onwards yield and area under cultivation of all the major crops have started falling (Tables 10.1, 10.2 and 10.3). Food grain production has increased from 31.15 thousand tonnes in 1975-76 to 104.81 thousand tonnes in 1997-98, and then declined to 76.9 thousand tonnes in 2001-02 (Table-10.1). Simultaneously, the productivity has gone up from 669 kg/ hectare (1975-76) to 1423 kg/hectare in 1990-91, and then deceleration started and reduced to 1234.6 kg/hectare in 2001-02 (Table 10.2). Though maize has never been a staple food in Sikkim, its production has steadily increased over the periods, and it contributes half of the food grain production in the State. Maize production has increased from 16.5 thousand

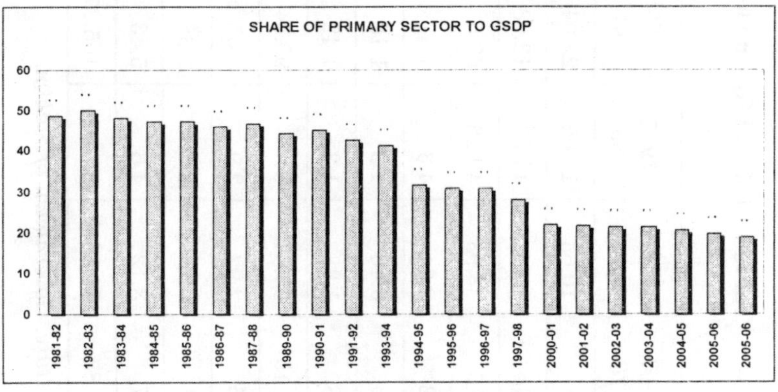

Fig. 10.1: Share of Primary Sector to GSDP (1981-82 to 2005-06)

Source: Calculated from GSDP figures at factor cost-State Domestic Product of Sikkim, Directorate of Economics and Statistics, Monitoring and Evaluation Planning and Development Department, Government of Sikkim, Gangtok, 2001 and http: / / www.mospi.nic.in.

** Annual Growth Rates for 1981-82 to 1992-93 were calculated from GSDP at constant prices(base year-1980-81), For 1993-94 to 1998-99 the base year was 1993-94 and for 1999-2000 to 2006-07, the base year was 1999-2000.*

Table 10.1: Food Grain Output (1975-2002)

(Thousand tonnes)

Crop	*1975-76*	*1980-81*	*1985-86*	*1990-91*	*1995-96*	*1966-67*	*1997-98*	*2000-01*	*2001-02*
Rice	10	10.63	17.05	22.04	21.68	22.06	21.45	21.35	12.9
Wheat	0.15	10.3	11.22	13.08	15.3	14.81	14.2	10.1	5.52
Maize	16.5	28.93	49.25	57.5	56.56	56.63	55.71	59.61	49.38
Finger-millet	3.2	3.84	4.3	4.62	4.75	4.71	4.73	4.23	2.76
Barley	0.5	0.46	1.3	1.18	1.57	1.56	1.51	1.21	0.97
Buckwheat	0.8	1.38	1.38	1.42	1.74	1.61	1.6	1.53	1.74
Total cereals	31.15	55.54	84.5	99.84	101.6	101.38	99.2	98.04	73.28
Urd	0.6	2.92	2.9	3.05	3.22	3.3	3.3	2.74	1.77
Other pulses	0.1	0.2	1.7	2.38	2.7	2.69	2.31	2.41	1.83
Total pulses	0.7	3.12	4.6	5.43	5.92	5.99	5.61	5.15	3.6
Total food grains	31.85	58.66	89.1	105.27	107.52	107.37	104.81	103.21	76.9

Source: Department of Agriculture, Government of Sikkim.

Table 10.2: Agricultural Yield (1975-2002)

(km / hectare)

Crop	*1975-76*	*1980-81*	*1985-86*	*199-91*	*1995-96*	*1996-97*	*2001-02*
Rice	891.3	729.8	1,117.7	1,395.2	1,381.9	1,405.3	1,272.5
Wheat	1,016.1	1,495.0	1,540.6	1,699.5	1,844.1	1,791.4	1,266.0
Maize	588.2	973.3	1,283.1	1,464.2	1,439.2	1,440.6	1,295.8
Finger-millet	677.4	780.3	910.2	958.0	965.2	957.1	741.9
Barley	564.5	805.8	1,320.9	1,332.2	1,477.0	1,440.9	1,159.5
Buckwheat	541.9	508.0	701.1	838.8	807.3	794.1	796.4
Total cereals	669.6	935.2	1,231.8	1,423.0	1,422.5	1,421.6	1,234.6

Calculated by using data on production and area under crops.

Table 10.3: Area Under Different Crops

(*Thousand hectares*)

Crop	*1975-76*	*1980-81*	*1985-86*	*199-91*	*1995-96*	*1996-97*	*2001-02*
Rice	11.4	14.8	15.5	16.05	15.94	15.95	10.30
Wheat	0.15	7.0	7.4	7.82	8.43	8.4	4.43
Maize	28.5	30.2	39	39.9	39.93	39.94	38.72
Finger-millet	4.8	5	4.8	4.9	5	5	3.78
Barley	0.9	0.58	1	0.9	1.08	1.1	0.85
Buckwheat	1.5	2.76	2	1.72	2.19	2.06	2.22
Total cereals	**47.27**	**60.34**	**69.7**	**71.29**	**72.57**	**72.46**	**60.31**

Source: Department of Agriculture, Government of Sikkim.

tonnes in 1975-76 to 55.71 thousand tonnes in 1997-98. The contribution of agriculture to gross state domestic product (GSDP) has continuously been declining though the dependence on agriculture has not been declined over the periods. The share has declined from 48.7 per cent in 1980-81 to just 18.8 per cent in 2006-07 (Fig. 10.1). In addition to this, the average compound annual rate of growth of population since 1980s has outweighed the growth of food grain production and the gap got extremely widened since1990s and onwards (Fig. 10.2). This is bound to create food scarcity within the State. In fact, Sikkim has registered highest per capita PDS purchase (8.6 kg) in the country. The areas where PDS off take were relatively high were not only deficit in terms of cereal production but also tended to be areas of low cereal consumption (Swaminathan, 2003). The work participation rate or the ratio

Table 10.4: Work Participation Rate (1971-2001)

Year	*Labour Force as a Percentage of Population*
2001	39.4
1991	40.4
1981	41.4
1971	53.2

Source: Calculated from Census Reports of 1971, 1981, 1991 and 2001.

Table 10.5: Budgetary Expenditure on Agriculture (*in percentage*)

Year	*Expenditure*
1980-81	0.95
1985-86	3.91
1990-91	2.62
1995-96	0.77
1999-2000	1.22

Source: Government of Sikkim, Department of Agriculture.

of labour force to population has also been declining consistently in the State of Sikkim (Table-10.4). Lower work participation rate reflects difficulty of finding work and increased marginalisation of workers (Patnaik, 2005). The growth of agricultural sector is further being impaired by very low budgetary allocation in terms of percentage. A rise in allocation was observed in the period 1985 to 1991 and there after it started declining (Table-10.5).

SECTION II
FOOD SECURITY IN SIKKIM

It has been observed that Sikkim has made substantial progress in food grain production and productivity, but the question is whether the State has self sufficiency in food grain production or not. Indian Council of Medical Research (ICMR) has prescribed a guideline for the requirement of different food items to improve the quality of health (Table10.6).

Given the above per capita per day food requirement, yearly food requirement for the entire population of Sikkim for the year 1990-91 and 2001-02 was calculated, and it has been

Table 10.6: ICMR's Quantitatives Assessment on Required Food for Health

Food items	*Requirement Per day(gm.) Per head*
Cereals and millets	420
Pulses and legumes	40
Total grains	460
Roots and tubers	75
Vegetables	125
Fruits	50
Milk	150
Fats and oil	25
Meat	25

Source: ICMR 2001.

Table 10.7: Foodgrains Sufficiency in Sikkim (1990-91 & 2001-02)

(in thousand tonnes)

	1990-91			*2001-02*		
	ICMR requirement	*Actual production*	*Surplus/ Deficit*	*ICMR requirement*	*Actual production*	*Surplus/ Deficit*
Cereals	61.33	99.84	38.51	81.60	73.28	-8.32
Pulses	5.84	5.43	-0.41	7.77	3.6	-4.17
Food Grains	67.17	105.27	38.10	89.37	76.88	-12.49

Calculated by using ICMR criteria.

Table 10.8: Sufficiency of Food Items (Other Than Food Grains) (2001-02)

(in thousand tonnes)

	2001-02		
	ICMR requirement	*Actual Production*	*Surplus / Deficit*
Vegetables	24.29	30.17	5.88
Potato	14.57	22.67	8.10
Roots and tubes	9.71	1.72	**-7.99**
Fruits	4.86	9.05	4.19
Oilseeds	5.84	6.38	0.54
Meat	7.77	3	**-4.77**

Calculated by using ICMR criteria.

observed that Sikkim is gradually moving from food surplus State to food deficient State.

From the tables 10.7 and 10.8, it is evident that in the year 1990-91, Sikkim was having surplus of 38.15 thousand tonnes in cereals and 38.10 thousand tonnes in food grains but within 10 years, the surplus disappeared and the estimation says that in 2001-02, the deficit in cereals stands at 8.32 thousand tonnes and there is a deficit of 12.49 thousand tonnes in food grains. In addition, Sikkim have never produced surplus amount of pulses, but the deficit in production is slowly mounting. As it is evident from table 10.7, that in 1990-91, the deficit in production of pulses was 0.41 thousand tonnes and in 2001-02 it reached to 4.1-4.17 thousand tonnes.

According to data available (for 2001-02) for the production of food items other than food grains, it is estimated that Sikkim is enjoying surplus production of vegetables, potato, fruits and oilseeds but in meat, and roots and tubes, the state is facing a deficiency.

Now, the question arises why this deficiency has occurred; is this because of rising population pressure, or fall in productivity, or reduction in cultivable area, or are all these factors together affecting the production? It is observed that fall in cultivable land, fall in productivity and rise in population are among the major factors affecting the food grain production adversely (Chakrabarti, 2009). As a matter of fact, in comparison to 1996-97, in 2001-02, area under cultivation for rice, wheat, maize, finger millet have decreased, and only marginal rise is visible in case of buck wheat although area under high yielding varieties for rice, wheat and maize have been showing a rising percentage since 1975-76. At the same time compound annual rate of growth of population is also showing a rising trend. In 1981-91, the population of Sikkim was growing at 2.5 percent per annum and in 1991-2001, the population grew at 2.9 percent per annum; population in urban areas has grown much faster than rural areas (Table 10.9).

Table 10.9: Compound Annual Rate of Growth of Population In Different Census Periods

		Total	*Male*	*Female*
1991-2001	Total	2.9	2.9	2.9
	Rural	2.7	2.7	2.6
	Urban	4.9	4.5	5.5
1981-1991	Total	2.5	2.3	2.8
	Rural	3.4	3.2	3.5
	Urban	-3.2	-3.5	-2.8
1971-1981	Total	4.2	4.3	4.0
	Rural	3.4	3.5	3.3
	Urban	10.0	9.9	10.2

Source: Calculated from Census Reports, Sikkim, 1971, 1981, 1991 and 2001.

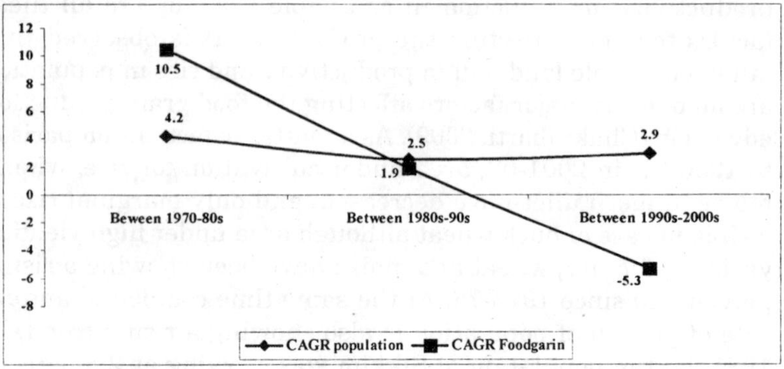

Fig. 10.2: Compound Annual Rate of Growth (CARG) of Population and Food Grain Production In Sikkim

Source: CARG of Population calculated from Census Reports of 1971, 1981, 1991 and 2001and CARG of Food Grains was calculated from data available from Dept. of agriculture, Govt. of Sikkim.

Conclusion

It is evident that though no longer monarchic rule exists in Sikkim, the feudal elements still has its root in agrarian system. Land reform measures seem to be inadequate and have failed to ensure distributive justice for its agrarian society. Food grain production, agricultural productivity or yield, and agricultural growth have started decelerating since 2000. Share of agriculture to Gross State Domestic Product has continuously been declining; however, people depending on agriculture for their livelihood have hardly declined. Growth rate of population has outweighed the growth of food grain production and has transformed Sikkim from food surplus state to a food deficient state. In addition to that plan, allocation in agriculture has also started declining. In view of impending food scarcity, the present practice of importing food grains under Public Distribution Scheme will vigorously be persuaded. This will further reduce the public expenditure on agriculture. In addition, it is bound to increase the incidence of rural poverty, both from nutritional point of view as well as in terms of declining employment opportunities in rural areas. It is indeed true that agriculture is providing sustenance to the majority of the people, but rising demographic pressure on cultivable lands, physical constraints created by the terrain, limitations of terrace farming in terms of productivity, irrigation, cost of production, lack of infrastructural support, declining public expenditure, and complete absence of marketable surplus are working as major obstacles for the agricultural sector. Therefore, attention should immediately be given to raise the agricultural productivity and productio and to do so, institutional changes have become imperative. Serious efforts are to be made to bring more land into cultivation through appropriation of surplus land possessed by big land owners and this will not only increase distributive efficiency but also raise the allocative efficiency[1]. As a result, the State will be able to avert impending food scarcity.

Note

1. By allocative efficiency, we mean the ability of a firm to use the inputs (land, labour, capital, etc.) in optimal proportions, given their respective prices. The role of successful land reform in enhancing allocative efficiency in the agricultural sector is hardly consciously considered. Allocative inefficiency generally occurs when, given the prices of inputs and outputs, a producer cannot optimally allocate his or her resources to minimise the cost of production and subsequently leads to non-realisation of the potential productivity of the inputs used. Such inefficiencies add considerably to the lowering of the capacity of the farmers to generate marketable surplus, thus nullifying the achievement of distributive efficiency. Providing access to land, either through redistribution or through a secure tenancy contract, would have been effective in increasing the productivity of agricultural practices.

References

Acharya, S.S., (1998). "*Agricultural Price Policy and Development: Some Facts and Emerging Issues*", Indian Journal of Agricultural Economics, Vol. 52, No. 1: 1-47.

Census of India (1981). Series-19, Part XIII A and B.

Census of India (1991). Series-22 Census of India (2001), Provisional, Series-21.

Chakrabarti, Anjan (2009). "*Economic Development and Employment in Sikkim*", Authors Press: New Delhi.

Government of India (2001). "*Indian Planning Experience - A Statistical Profile*", Planning Commission, New Delhi.

Government of India (2007), "*Agriculture Strategy for Eleventh Plan: Some Critical Issues*", Planning Commission, New Delhi.

Dasgupta, Manas (1992). *"Sikkim Problems and Prospects of Development"*, Indus Publishing Company: New Delhi

Swaminathan, Madhura. (2003) "Strategies towards Food Security" Social Scientist, Vol. 31, No. 9/10, Sep. – Oct : 58-94

Patnaik,.Utsa (2005). "Theorising Food Security and the Poverty in the Era of Economic Reforms" *Social Scientist*, Vol. 33, No. 7/8, Jul.-Aug : 50-81

Planning Commission (2007). Agriculture Strategy for Eleventh Plan: Some Critical Issues.

11

Reinventing Municipal Administration in Sikkim

Municipal Administration: Legal and Political Background

Local government institutions have always existed in India in one form or another since times immemorial. There are two types of local government– urban local government and rural local government. The limitation of this chapter is that it deals with only the urban local government, or in other words the municipal administration. The municipal administration in our country has a long history. There are references to these in Rig-Veda, Manusmriti and Mahabharata which provide the proof of existence of some form of municipal government in India. In Rig-Veda, for example, there is a mention of *Purapati* whom Manu describes as 'superintendent of all affairs, elevated in rank, formidable, resembling a planet among the stars' (Tinker 1967). Megasthenes, the Greek scholar in his book *Indica* described elaborately the municipal organisation of Patliputra, the capital city of the Mauryan. According to him, six boards or departments looked after the municipal administration of the city. The board of five members entrusted with particular and important departments of human activities, amongst which even the care and entertainment of foreigners was included and the registration of births and deaths was not neglected. The boards also looked after the commercial domains like industries, trade, manufactures and their sale, collection of taxes, etc.

The system of municipal government continued to a great extent during the Mughal period for several centuries without any major changes. During this period, the king appointed the officer called the *Koetwals* to administer the affairs of the bigger towns. The *Koetwals* acted not only as the chief executive officers for all magisterial, police and financial matters, but they were also the chief officials for discharging such functions entrusted to them by the ruler. Abul Fazl in his book, *Ain-e-Akbari,* gives the detailed account of administration of towns and cities of Mughal period. According to him, the duties of *Koetwal* were truly multifarious, severely exacting and frequently unpleaseant, and he was expected to be a man of refined address to make his vigilance reflect credit his administration.

The present form of municipal administration in India however owes its genesis to the British rule. The creation of Municipal Corporation at Madras attributed much to Sir Joshia Child, the then Governor of Madras, who in 1642, obtained a charter from James II for setting up the corporation in the town. Consequently, in 1687, Madras city had the first Municipal Corporation of the country with limited powers and scope of activity (Bhargava and Rao 1978). The corporation was comprises of Mayor, aldermen and burgesses, who were empowered to levy taxes for the building of a guildhall, a jail and a schoolhouse. This was followed by the establishment of similar corporations in Bombay and Calcutta. The corporation excercises the power to levy certain direct taxes and to provide certain amenities like education, sanitary, cleaning the roads etc.

The Charter Act was passed by the British Parliament in 1793. This was the first statutory enactment relating to municipal administration in India. The Act empowered the Governor-General to appoint Justice of Peace for the Presidency towns and vested with judicial and other powers including the collection of taxes. In 1870, the Lord Mayo's Resolution was passed and introduced the concept of elected representatives in the municipalities.The Resolution encouraged the introduction of an elected Chairman in the municipalities.

Another major initiative taken in this direction was the Ripon Resolution of 1882. Lord Ripon is considered the founding father of urban local government as he implanted the concept of municipal authorities as units of self-government. He believed that local self-government was a means of popular and political education. His Resolution adopted on 18 May 1882 dealt with the constitution of local bodies, their functions, finances and powers and laid the foundation of local self-government in modern India. There was a great change made by Lord Ripon by releasing the municipalities from the burden of paying the costs of town police over which they had no control. In the place of such costs, the municipalities were called upon to support education, medical aid, and public work (Mallik 1929). As a consequence of this Resolution, various provincial legislatures in India enacted the Municipal Act for the creation of urban local bodies. The Madras District Municipalities Act and Bengal Municipal Act were enacted in 1884. In 1891, there were 739 municipalities with a population of 13 crore (Mallik 1929) throughout British India. The functions of Indian municipalities comprise the usual services essential for the health and convenience of town dwellers. They cover the construction and unkeep of roads and public buildings, the lighting and watering of roads, medical relief, vaccination, sanitation, drainage, water supply, measures against epidemics, and education (Wheeler 1917).

The Royal Commisison on Decentralisation constituted in 1906 was the next important landmark in the history of municipal administration in India. The Commission in its report submitted to Government of Britian recommended certain measures for strengthening of municipal government in India– firstly, commission recommended that outside the presidency towns, there should be three different form of municipal government. Larger cities with 1 lakh population should have a special form of government with a full time paid executive officer, the towns of the moderate size should have the ordinary forms of government and the semi-urban areas, a town panchayat; secondly, the commission recommended that the municipal boards should control the services which they maintain from their own resources. If the government desired to control any service, it should be provincialised; and thirdly, it recommended that the municipal boards should be relieved of their financial responsibilities in connection with the maintenance of police, famine and such other services.

In 1914, the Government of India passed a resolution with two suggestions–firstly, small towns should be governed by a separate statute. The Chairman and the vice chairman of the town committees should be appointed, and secondly, the resolution said that for the municipal boards the total population of the area should not be less than 5000 and the density of population not less than 1000 sq.m. Likewise, the Indian Local Self-Government Policy of 1915 contemplates the removal of restrictions on the powers of the municipal institutions and laid down certain definite directions for the improvement of those bodies. The Government of India Acts 1919 and 1935 also contains the provision of municipal governance. The first Act introduced the system of diarchy and placed the local self-government in transferred subject under the charge of popular minister of the provincial legislature. The Act among other things increased the taxation power of local bodies and reduced the nominated member of municipalities. The India Act of 1935 established a federal form of government and introduced "fully responsible" government in the provinces. The Act also declared local governemt as a provincial subject.

The Constitution of India which was adopted in 1949 came into effect from 26 anuary 1950 though directs the state under Article 40 to organise panchayats has no any provision for the establishment of urban bodies. The Entry 5 of List 11 of the Seventh Schedule was the only reference to urban self-government. Entry 5 of the State list gives legislative power to the State with regards to municipal laws, establishments, constitution and powers of local governments. Except for recognising local self-government as an essential part of the system of Government, the Constitution does not confer any independent status or powers to local government bodies. The central government after independence constituted and appointed a number of local committees and commissions, including the Local Finance Enquiry Committee (1949), Taxation Enquiry Commission (1953), The Rural-Urban Relationship Committee (1963-66), Committee of Ministers on Augmentation of Financial Resources of Urban Local Bodies (1963), The National Commisison on Urbanisation (1988), etc. from time to time to streamline the structure of local urban bodies in the country.

The Seventy-Fourth Constitutional Amendment Act (CAA) of 1992, was however, the first Amendment Act that accords the constitutional recognition to the municipalities in independent India. It is the first serious attempt to ensure stabilisation of democratic municipal government through constitutional provisions. The Act decreed both the economic and political empowerment of such bodies, and a standardised mode of democratic representation for the denizens of cities across India (Tiwari, 2002). It provided urban local bodies (ULBs) with political, functional, and fiscal empowerment for good governance and seeks to introduce fundamental changes in more than 3,000 urban local bodies existing in the country. Until recently, urban local government was manifested in Municipal Corporations, Municipal Councils, Town Area Committees and Notified Area Committees. However, following the 74th Constitutional Amendment Act, Urban Local Self-Government in India has been classified into three types - Municipal Corporations, Municipalities and Nagar Panchayats. Thus, at present, the municipal governanance in India are largely classified into three groups–(i) larger urban areas (populations of more than 1 million) governed by Municipal Corporations, (ii) medium-sized urban areas (population size of 2,00,000 but less than 1 million) governed by Municipal Councils, and (iii) smaller urban areas in transition from rural to urban areas (population size less than 2,00,000) governed by Nagar Panchayat. All three types of ULBs mentioned above have been classified under the provision of Article 243Q of the Central Act of 1992. The population, population density, revenue generated per annum, percentage of employment in non-agricultural activities, and economic importance of the local body are the five criteria listed by Central Act for constituting the ULBs. These categories are based on the types of governance organisation permitted by laws and regulations. Table 11.1 below shows the state wise number of ULBs in India.

Table 11.1: Number of Urban Local Bodies (UBLs)

State / Union Territory	*Municipal Corporation*	*Municipal Council*	*Nagar Panchayat*	*Total*
Andhra Pradesh	07	109	1	117
Assam	01	29	38	68
Bihar	05	32	80	117
Chattisgarh	06	20	49	75
Goa	-	13	-	13
Gujarat	06	85	58	149
Haryana	01	21	46	68
Himachal Pradesh	01	20	31	52
Jharkhand	01	17	22	40
Jammu & Kashmir	-	03	67	70
Karnataka	06	124	87	217
Kerala	05	53	-	58
Madhya Pradesh	14	86	234	334
Maharastra	19	224	02	245
Manipur	-	08	21	29
Meghalaya	-	06	03	09
Mizoram	-	-	01	01
Nagaland	-	-	08	08
Orissa	02	33	68	103
Punjab	04	97	30	131
Rajasthan	03	11	169	183

State / Union Territory	*Municipal Corporation*	*Municipal Council*	*Nagar Panchayat*	*Total*
Tamil Nadu	06	102	611	719
Tripura	-	01	12	13
Sikkim	**01**	**01**	**05**	**07**
Uttar Pradesh	11	193	417	621
Uttaranchal	01	31	28	60
West Bengal	06	112	04	122
A&N Islands	-	01	-	01
Chandigarh	01	-	-	01
Delhi	01	01	-	02
Pondicherry	-	05	-	05
Daman & Diu	-	02	-	02
Total	**108**	**1440**	**2100**	**3648**

Sources: AIILSG (2002), Chhetri 2010.

Sikkim Scenario in Urbanisation

As per 2001 Census data, the population of India was estimated at 102.70 crore. India's urban population rose from about 30 million in 1901 to 300 million by 2001 and the level of urbanisation also grew steadily from 11 per cent of total population to about 28 per cent during this period. Sikkim, like many other states of India, has been experiencing urbanisation over last few decades at somewhat slow pace and at stable levels, which is evident from the records of successive census documents. Total population in 2001 in Sikkim was estimated at 5.40 lakh with 59,493, that is 11.1 per cent in towns. The percentage of population living in urban areas in the state went up from 1.99 per cent in 1951 to 16.23 per cent in 1981 but declined to about 11.1 per cent in 2001. Sikkim is thus witnessing urbanisation since Census of 1951 and had reached appreciable level in 1981 with urban population of 16.23 per cent but the share of urban population declined in

1991. It is likely that the trend of urbanisation is inevitable consequent on the large-scale migration of rural people to urban areas. However, the drivers of urbanisation are changing – with a shift away from rapid rural population influx in the post-independence era to a rapid growth of existing urban areas (Kundu 2006). This rapid urbanisation is becoming a challenge to the Government and to the administrators in terms of provision of minimum basic amenities to the people.

The urban sector in Sikkim comprises of one Municipal Corporation, one Municipality and five Nagar Panchayats. Urbanisation in Sikkim, like the other parts of the country is linked to the designated cities and towns. Several peculiarities are visible in the urbanisation process in Sikkim. The main reason for urban population growth in the state is the increase in the number of urban areas, and also urbanisation of the peripheral areas of the existing major urban centres. The increase in the density in urban areas is due to the population increase in the state. The rural to urban migration, which accentuates urban problems and urban poverty, is only marginally present in the urban scenario of the state. It is interesting to note that Sikkim's level of urbanisation is relatively low to its town density in comparison to other states. degree of urbanisation is lower than the all India proportion (25.72%). Table 11.2 below indicates the growth of urban population in Sikkim vis-a-vis India.

Table 11.2: Growth of Urban Population in Sikkim and India (in %)

Year	Sikkim	India
1951	1.99	17.29
1961	4.22	17.97
1971	9.37	20.22
1981	16.23	23.73
1991	9.12	25.72
2001	11.1	27.78

Source: Census of India.

Municipal Administration in Sikkim: Historical Overview

Among the two form of local government viz. the rural and urban, the later is very new in Sikkim. There was no urban local body until the enactment of Bazaar Committe Act in 1969. As the Sikkimese society is truely a rural society, the then Chogyal felt no need for the establishment of such body. But the growth of towns in the middle of 20th century in different parts has compelled the government to create a body to look after the affairs of towns, and in this case, the bazaar. The Government of Sikkim, therefore, enacted the Bazaar Committee Act in 1969 for the administration of the Bazaar areas. The main objective behind this Act was the delegation of power to the officers working at the bazaar area. The Government of Sikkim, by notification, declares any area to be a Bazaar area. Under Section 2(1) of the Act, there were seven such bazaar areas in 1969. Table 11.3 shows the district-wise distribution of Bazaar area in 1969.

Table 11.3: District-wise distribution of Bazar Area (1969)

Sl. No.	*District*	*Bazaar Area*
1.	East Sikkim	Gangtok including Deorali
2.	East Sikkim	Singtam
3.	East Sikkim	Rangpo
4.	West Sikkim	Gyalsing
5.	South Sikkim	Namchi
6.	South Sikkim	Jorethang including Nayabazar
7.	North Sikkim	Mangan

Source: Sikkim (1969).

The Committee comprises of six members,that is, a chairman and five members. Of these five members, two were elected from Sikkim subjects and two from non-Sikkim subjects residing in that area. The king nominated one person as a member who exercises same rights and discharges the same duties as any elected member. In the absence of the District

Officer, the Deputy Development Officer acts as the ex-officio chairman of a Bazaar Committee. The committee appoints its own secretary from amongst its members.

The committee was elected for the term of three years but the term of committee may be extended, superseded or dissolved earlier.

The committee meets once in every month but the chairman may call a special meeting if there was a requisition in writing by not less than three members of the committee, or the Executive Officer. The District Officer, and in his absence the Deputy Development Officer presided the meeting of Bazaar committee. The chairman and three members form the quorum of committee meeting.

The Bazaar Committee under section 9 of the Act entrusted with such duties and functions relating to health, welfare and amenities of the residents of the Bazaar area. Some of important functions are:

- Construction, maintenance, repair, improvement and cleansing of roads, bridges, squares, gardens, tanks, ghats, wells, channels, drains, latrine and urinals within a bazaar area.
- Planting trees, bamboos and flowers.
- Maintenance of water supply and the lighting and watering of roads.
- Erection and maintenance of public halls, offices and other buildings required for the purpose of the bazaar committee.
- Maintenance of market.
- Acquiring and keeping of open spaces for the promotion of physical exercise and recreation.
- Establishment and maintenance of free public libraries and reading rooms.
- Taking precautionary measures against incidents of fire;
- Provision of burial and cremation grounds.
- Construction and maintenance of Dharmasala.
- Other works of public utility calculated to promote the

health, comfort or convenience of the inhabitants (GoS 1969).

The Bazaar Committee has also been vested with power to levy taxes on water and conservancy and cattle pounds fees within its area.

The Bazaar Committee Act which was passed in 1969 was the only initiative taken by the government for the creation of urban local body in Sikkim before its merger to India. Sikkim was merged to Indian Union on 16 May 1975 by the Thirty Sixth Amendment Act. The merger of state in 1975 led to establishment of democratic elected government where people can participate in the election process and choose their representive according to their choice. The Bazaar Committee Act that was enacted in 1969 to associate the people residing in the bazaar area in the management of local affairs has been repealed by the Sikkim (Repeal and Miscellaneous Provisions) Act 1985. The new Municipality Act was passed in 1985, which established the municipality in Gangtok. As a result of this Act, the Gangtok Municipality was formed but within a year, the body was dissolved and the management and regulation of affairs of town areas had been transferred to the Department of Local Self-Government, which was later rechristened as Department of Urban Development and Housing.

Thus, the concept of democratic institutions in the urban areas is very new to the majority of the people. Except the resident of Gangtok, where the municipality was created for short period in the year 1985 but dissolve after a year, no such institutions were created in other notified town of the state. Recently, the government has enacted the Sikkim Municipality Act, 2007 for the creation of local urban bodies in consonance with provision of 74th Amendment Act, 1992. The Act has been passed in line with spirit of Central Act, to bring in desired changes in policy environment to facilitate implementation of new measures introduced by the Government of India towards decentralisation of urban governance. The Act establishes the three-tier municipal board – Municipal Corporation in Gangtok, Municipal Council in Namchi, and Nagar Panchayat in five towns of state that is, Singtam, Rangpo, Jorethang, Geyzing and Mangan (Chhetri 2010). As per the provisions of new Act, a municipality is to be divided into territorial constituencies called wards and one Commissioner/ Councillor is to be elected for every ward directly by the voters of every such ward. The election to the municipalities is conducted by the same State Election Commission appointed by the Governor under Article 243K for the conduct of panchayat election. The salient features of the Sikkim Municipality Act, 2007 are :

1. Constitution of three-tier municipalities.
2. Composition of municipalities.
3. Constitution of Area Sabha.
4. Reservation of Seats.
5. Five years fixed duration.
6. Power, authority and responsibilities of municipalities.
7. Apointment of State Election Commission and Finance Commission.

Municipal Structure

The municipal governance in Sikkim under the Municipality Act of 2007 are largely classified into three groups– (i) larger urban areas governed by municipal corporations, (ii) medium-sized urban areas governed by municipal council, and (iii) smaller urban areas in transition from rural to urban areas governed by Nagar Panchayats. These categories are based on the types of governance organisation permitted by laws and regulations. Municipal corporations usually exercise a good degree of fiscal autonomy and powers as they have a larger population and tax base, and deal with state governments directly. Municipalities with smaller jurisdictions have to deal with the state governments through the district collectors.

The basic data about the municipalities at a glance can be seen in Table 11.4.

Municipal Corporation

The Municipal Corporation as a form of city Government occupies the top position among the local authorities, and enjoys a greater measure of autonomy than the other forms of local Government. In almost all the states, the Municipal Corporations have been assigned numerous functions such as

Table 11.4: Municipalities at a Glance: Sikkim

S.No.	*Type of Municipalities*	*Name of Municipalities*	*No. of Wards*	*Total Voters*
1.	Municipal Corporation	Gangtok Municipal Corporation	15	93548
2.	Municipal Council	Namchi Municipal Council	07	11826
3.	Nagar Panchayat	1.Singtam Nagar Panchayat	05	6195
		2.Rangpo Nagar Panchayat	05	10205
		3.Jorethang Nagar Panchayat	05	9623
		4.Geyzing Nagar Panchayat	05	3625
		5.Mangan Nagar Panchayat	05	3609

supply of drinking water, electricity, road transport services, public health, education, registration of births and deaths, drainage, construction of public parks, gardens, libraries, etc. These functions are normally divided as obligatory and discretionary. In Sikkim, there is only one Municipal Corporation (MC) that is in Gangtok, the capital of Sikkim with more than 93,000 populations. MC is constituted for governing the area. It has all elected members. Gangtok MC has at present 15 elected Councillors. Under the amended municipal law, election to the municipal bodies must take place every five years, unless a municipal body is dissolved earlier. The Mayor elected by the members of the Corporation from amongst themselves is the first citizen of the city, and presides over the meetings of the Corporation. The Mayor and Deputy Mayor of Gangtok MC have been given the status of minister and deputy minister respectively. Though the Mayor is the formal head of the municipal corporation, real administrative authority lies with the Executive Authority which is comprises of Chief Councillor, Deputy Councillor and other councillors elected by the councillors of MC. They exercise the executive and financial power of municipality. Their term of office is coterminus with the duration of municipality.

The Gangtok Municipal Corporation also has a Chief Municipal Officer (CMO) and other officers to deal with all or any of the functions relating to finance and accounts, health, sanitation, architecture and town planning, engineering, administration, law, fire services, urban forestry, parks, gardens, playgrounds, promotion of cultural, educational and aesthetic aspects, cattle pounds, prevention of cruelty to animals, and internal audit. CMO is appointed by the state government either on regular basis or on deputation for a term of three years.

Municipal Council

Normally, Municipal Council covers smaller areas than the Municipal Corporation. The municipal acts of the states govern the Municipal Councils. The Governor of a state has the power to notify any area as a smaller urban area for which a municipal council must be set up. Usually, factors such as the population or the economic importance of such an area are considerations for creating a municipal council. The state of Sikkim has only one Municipal Council, that is, Namchi Municipal Council in South district. All the members of municipal councils are elected directly by the people of the area. Namchi MC has seven wards and from each ward people elects one councillor. The head of the municipal council is elected from among the councillors, and is called the Chairperson. The chairperson convenes and presides over all the meetings and (s)he is also required to watch over the financial and executive functioning of the council. The Chairperson is helped in the discharge of his functions by an executive officer usually appointed by the state government. The Chairperson occupies an important position in the municipal administration and enjoys considerable authority and power both in the deliberative and executive organs of the municipality. The chairperson of Municipal Council has been conferred the status of deputy minister by the state government. The powers and functions of municipal councils are almost similar to those of municipal corporations. Municipal councils may also have to discharge duties under some other acts, which may be specified by the state government. All the members of the Municipal Council enjoys the term of five years.

Nagar Panchayat

The Nagar Panchayat is a semi-municipal authority constituted in rural-urban transition areas. In Sikkim there are five Nagar Panchayats established by the Act of 2007 in five different towns. They are– Singtam Nagar Panchayat, Rangpo Nagar Panchayat, Jorethang Nagar Panchayat, Geyzing Nagar Panchayat, and Mangan Nagar Panchayat. The members of the Nagar Panchayats are elected directly by the people. For the purpose of election, the whole area is divided into a ward and from each ward people elects one councillor. The Act of 2007 divided all the Nagar Pachayat of state into five wards, and therefore the total strength of each Nagar Pachayat are five. The President is elected from amongst the members whose term is coterminus with the term of Nagar Panchayat. The President convenes and presided over the meetings of the panchayat and in his absence, vice-president discharge the functions of President.

Area Sabha

The Sikkim Municipality Act, 2007 has a provision to create an Area Sabha in each ward of a municipality. Therefore, at present, each ward of a Municipality has an Area Sabha. The Councillor elected from a ward acts as a chairperson of the Area Sabha for that ward. The composition of the Area Sabha, the representation of various interest groups therein, and the functions thereof, are prescribed by the state law.

Powers and Functions

Most of the states while amending the Municipal Acts included the list of functions enlisted in the 12th Schedule of the Constitution under the provision of Article 243W (see Box 11.1 for the list of functions). But each state has varying degrees of conformity with the legislation in terms of what are obligatory or discretionary functions of municipal bodies within each state. The states of Kerala, West Bengal and Tamil Nadu, for example, have transferred these responsibilities to the ULBs. These states have not restricted to the subject matters as envisaged in the 12th Schedule but also devolved some additional functions to the ULBs.

BOX 11.1

As per the 12th Schedule of the 74th Constitutional Amendment Act of India, 18 new tasks have been defined as in the functional domain of the ULBs, the most important of which are:

1 Urban Planning including town planning
2. Regulation of land-use and construction of buildings.
3. Planning for economic and social development
4. Roads and bridges
5. Water supply for domestic, industrial and commercial purposes
6. Public Health, sanitation, conservancy and solid waste management
7. Fire services
8. Urban forestry, protection of the environment and promotion of ecological aspects.
9. Safeguarding the interests of weaker sections of society, including the handicapped, etc.
10. Slum improvement and upgradation
11. Urban poverty alleviation.
12. Provision of urban amenities and facilities such as parks, gardens, playgrounds
13. Promotion of cultural, educational and aesthetic aspects.
14. Burials and burial grounds; cremations, cremation grounds and electric crematoriums.
15. Cattle pounds: prevention of cruelty to animals.
16. Vital statistics including registration of births and deaths
17. Public amenities including street lighting, parking lots, bus stops and public conveniences.
18. Regulation of slaughter houses and tanneries.

The government of Sikkim has also passed the Municipal Legislation in 2007. The Municipality Act of 2007 in Sikkim provide for functions, duties and responsibilities to be carried out by the municipal government. These are divided in two categories obligatory and assigned functions.

The obligatory functions are:

- Supply of water for domestic, industrial, and commercial purposes.
- sewerage and drainage.
- solid waste management.
- communication systems including construction and maintenance of roads, footpaths, pedestrian pathways, transportation terminals (both for passengers and goods), bridges, over- bridges, and subways.
- transport system accessories including traffic engineering schemes, street furniture, street lighting, parking areas, and bus stops.
- community health and protection of environment including planting and caring of trees on road sides and elsewhere.
- the *bazars*.
- slaughter houses (GoS 2007).

Assigned Functions

In addition to all these core functions mentioned above, the Municipal body performs some other functions assigned to it from time to time by the central and state governments. They are:

- primary education.
- public health and sanitation.
- public transport facilities and supply of energy in municipality area.
- urban poverty alleviation.
- Securing or removing dangerous buildings or places.
- construction and maintenance of public parks, gardens, libraries, museums, rest houses, leper homes, orphanages and rescue homes for women.

Table 11.5: Profile of Women, SCs, STs, OBC and MBCs in Municipality in Sikkim *(as on July 2010)*

Urban Local Body	*Total Seats Elected*	*Women*	*SCs*	*STs*	*OBCs*	*MBCs*	*Unreserved*
Municipal Corporation	15	05	01	04	02	02	06
Municipal Council	07	03	0	02	01	02	02
Nagar Panchayat	25	11	02	05	04	03	11

Source: Chhetri 2010.

- housing for low income groups;
- protection of environment.

Reservation and Women's Participation

The Constitution (Seventy Fourth) Amendment, 1992 has served as a major breakthrough towards ensuring women's equal access and increased participation in urban local government. The Amendment Act aims at constitutional guarantees to safeguard the interests of urban local self government to enable them to function as effective democratic and self governing institutions at the grass root level. This Amendment provides for reservation of 33 per cent of elected seats for women at local government level in urban area. There is also a one-third reservation for women of posts of chairpersons of these local bodies.

In conformity with Central Act of 1992, the Government of Sikkim has enacted the Sikkim Municipality Act in 2007 and Sikkim Municipality (Amendment) Act 2009. Both these Acts, among other things, have the provisions for the reservation of seats for SCs, STs and women in different tier of municipality. Table 11.5 depicts the category-wise distribution of elected members in 2010 election.

The Sikkim Municipality (Amendment) Act 2009 is very important because this particular Act has raised the percentage of reservation of seats for women from 33 to 40 per cent which is more than the reservation provided by the Central Act of 1992. These provisions have provided great opportunities and challenges to women particularly in the local government field. This is of great significance, since this grass-root level participation has considerably broadened the base of women's participation in politics at local level. As a result of the reservation, women's participation in local governments increased quite radically, with the enactment of the legislation providing 40 percent reservation of seats for women in local bodies. The legislation and its implementation have added another level in political participation. Table 11.6 indicates the total number of women elected representatives in urban local bodies in Sikkim.

Table 11.6: Category-wise distribution of Women Elected Representatives (WER) of Municipality *(as on June 2010)*

Urban Local Bodies	*No.*	*Total Member*	*WER (Total)*	*SC*	*ST*	*OBC*	*MBC*
Gangtok Municipal Corporation	01	15	05	01	02	01	-
Namchi Municipal Council	01	07	03	-	01	01	-
Nagar Panchayats	05	25	11	-	06	01	02

Source: *Chhetri 2010.*

Conclusion

The phenomena of urbanisation coupled with globalisation and liberalisation are increasing pressure on service delivery in the towns and cities that are engulfed by vast number of problems. To improve urban governance and delivery of services, there was a need of constitutional amendments as well administrative actions. The 74th Constitutional Amendment Act was therefore enacted in 1992 to empower the urban local bodies in the country. As a result, many states in India have amended their respective municipal legislation to incorporate the provisions of central Act. The Sikkim Municipality Act 2007 which was passed by the government in consonance with the 74th Constitutional Amendment Act 1992 is a great step forward in the development of urban local administrative system in Sikkim. This was the first major Act, enacted by the government for the creation of municipal bodies in post merger period. The Act incorporated all the major provisions of Central Act. Under the provisions of the present Act, all the powers of the Municipalities are vested on the elected bodies. But to make the urban agglomerations prosper with high quality of life of the citizens there is an imperative need to strengthen and empower Urban Local Bodies. More emphasis should be laid on decentralised decision-making, bottom-up planning and timely release of funds among others. Capacity building among officials, non-officials and community leaders, complemented by transparent decision-making and accessible information system, would contribute to greater awareness and participatory environment at urban local level. All these will ease the development process, and help in establishing good Urban Local Bodies in the state.

References

Bharagava, B.S and S. Rama Rao. (1978): *Indian Local Government-A Study*, Calcutta, Minerva Associate Pvt. Ltd.

Chhetri, Durga P. (2010): *Sikkim Chronicle*, Siliguri, Dipali Publisher.

Mallik, S.N. (1929): "Local Self-Government in India", *Annals of the American Academy of Political and Social Science*, Vol. 145, Part 2: India.

Tinker, H. (1967): *The Foundation of Local Self Government in India, Pakistan and Burma,* Bombay, Lalvani Publishing House.

Government of Sikkim (1969): The Sikkim Bazaar Committe Act 1969.

Government of Sikkim (2007): The Sikkim Municipality Act 2007.

Kundu, A. (2006), 'Trends and Patterns of Urbanisation in India', *India Infrastructure Report 2006*, New Delhi, Oxford University Press.

Tiwari, D.P. (2002): "Challenges in Urban Planning for Local Bodies in India." *Map Asia 2002*, Bangkok, Thailand:GIS@Development.

Wheeler, H. (1917): "Local Self-Government in India", *Journal of the Society of Comparative Legislation,* Vol. 17, No. 1/2.

12

Multiligualism and the Development of Limboo Language: Contextualising the Language Policy in Sikkim

SECTION I

Introduction

According to Southworth (1980), multilingualism is an integral part of every social segment of life Multilingualism in India is seen as a normal and natural phenomenon. The existence and use of multilingualism is recorded throughout the recorded history. Even as India is a multilingual nation, the Indian states that constitute India are also equally multilingual. Each state within India has a dominant regional language, but within every state there are around 20% of the total population of that state speaks one or more minority languages (Khubchandani, 1972). Although it was destined that the regional languages of the respective states would be adopted in their region yet the process of adoption of the regional languages and the replacement of English in the states for official purposes was considerably delayed due to various reasons. Disputes over language policy raise a number of different normative questions. The most hotly contested of these typically concern the problems of *public recognition* and *individual linguistic autonomy*. A language enjoys public recognition when it is possible to access public services and/or conduct public business in that language. In recent years, the issues related to the tribal and other minor and minority languages in India have been raised and debated by linguists, educationists and politicians from different perspectives. Spolsky (2004) began by observing that studies of the social life of language are often too 'language-centred'. Any investigation of language that considers only language will be deficient, and inappropriate limitations and restrictions can cripple insights. The Official Language Policy and the constitutional provisions have a direct impact on the development of tribal languages and resolving of the language issues. In the development of any tribal language, there is a need to identify the issues, provide suggestions and make sincere efforts in resolving the issues in the framework of the constitutional provisions and the Official Language Policy. This would help in finding out appropriate model for the development of tribal and minor/ minority languages. The tribal languages are currently on the lowest ring of hierarchy after English, Hindi, other languages in the VIII schedule and languages recognised by the Sahitya Akademi for awards. Ninety percent of the total number of languages falls under this category. They belong to all the language families prevalent in India. In this backdrop, the present chapter endeavours to contextualise the development of the Limboo Language in the broader framework of multilingualism practiced in the Indian State of Sikkim.

Sir G.A. Grierson carried out the Linguistic Survey of India (LSI) between 1866 and 1927. This survey identified 179 languages and 544 dialects. The 1951 Census, the first census after India attained its independence, listed 845 languages including dialects, out of which more than 1,00,000 persons spoke 60 languages/dialects. A comprehensive account of the multiplicity of languages was presented in the 1961 census. This census adopted as its main reference the language classification of the Linguistic Survey of India. The 1961 Census returned 1652 mother tongues and classified them under 193 languages. These languages were identified as belonging to four different language families – Austric (20 languages), Dravidian (20 languages), Tibeto-Burman (98 languages), and Indo-Aryan (54) languages, and one return with a doubtful affiliation. In the 1961 Census, 91% of the population spoke one of the fifteen scheduled languages and this number rose to 95.58% in the 1981 Census. In the 1991 Census, the returns of the mother tongues came to 10,400. These 10,400 raw returns were subjected to thorough scrutiny. This resulted in 1576 rationalised mother tongues, and 1796 names, which were treated as unclassified and relegated to the other mother tongues category. The 1576 rationalised mother tongues were regrouped following the linguistic methods under 114 languages (18 languages that are included in the VIII Schedule of the Constitution of India, and 96 other languages). 96.29% of the total population of India has one of the Schedule VIII languages as their 'mother tongue' and the rest (3.71%) speak the languages not listed in the Schedule VIII of the Constitution of India. 85 mother tongues are grouped under the Schedule VIII languages, and 131 mother tongues are grouped under the other 96 non-scheduled languages. As per the Third All India Education Survey, 58 languages find a place in the school curricula and 47 are used in public administration at one level or another. Newspapers are published in 87 languages and there are radio broadcasts in 91 languages. Sikkim is one of the smaller states in India, however, with a linguistic diversity, warranting a balanced linguistic policy for the development of the various languages belonging to various linguistic hierarchies.

SECTION II
Multilingualism and Linguistic Policy and Politics in Sikkim

Linguistic Policy and Politics in Multi-Lingual Sikkim

Sikkim, has a linguistic diversity. No Linguistic survey was done before the annexation of Sikkim to Indian Union. the first Linguistic survey was done in 1981. As per the said survey, there is variety of languages spoken by the people of Sikkim belonging to two largest language families, that is, Sino-Tibetan and Indo-European Family. The point worth noting is that all the languages belonging to Indo-European Family have domain over the other languages belonging to the Sino-Tibetan Family. English is the associate language, language of elites, bureaucracy, judiciary, tourism, school, colleges and the like. Hindi has been accepted as the National language by the Sikkimese people. Nepali is recognised under the Eight Schedule of the Indian Constitution and the lingua-franca of Sikkim. There are other languages which are recognised by the Government of Sikkim. They include Bhutia, Lepcha, Limboo, Sherpa, Gurung, Newari, Rai, Tamang and Sunuwar. However, Sikkim also has a host of other languages like Thami, Yakha, etc. Fig. 12.1 shows the languages spoken in Sikkim along with the strength of the speakers.

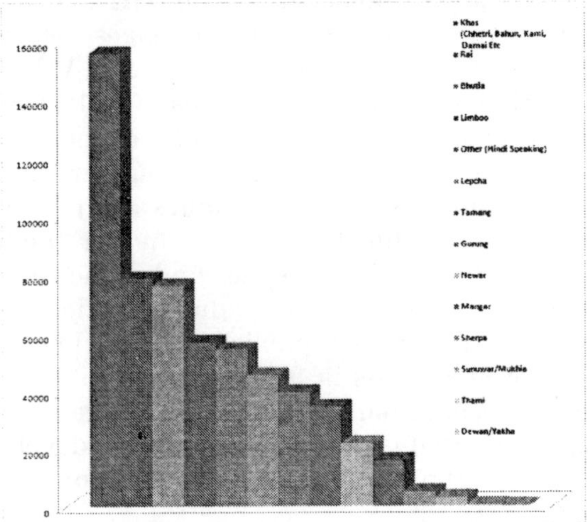

Fig. 12.1: Languages and their Speakers in Sikkim

Sikkim has attempted to keep its multicultural and multilingual nature intact. Consequently, owing to a variety of compulsions not limited to its multicultural concerns alone, the state has gone a long journey in its symbolic recognition of smaller languages. As a result, Nepali, Bhutia and Lepcha languages were recognised as state languages by the Sikkim Official Language Act, 1977. Further, in 1981, the Sikkim Official Language Act 1977 was amended in 1981 to include Limboo in the category of state languages. In 1995, the Act (1977) was further amended declaring seven other languages, viz, Rai (Bantawa), Newari, Gurung, Manger, Sherpa, Sunuwar and Tamang as state languages. However, what is conspicuous is the fact that two other languages, namely, Thami and Yakha languages have not yet been recognised as the state languages on the plea that there are a very few speakers (Thami= 453 and Yakha=194) speaking these languages. The multiculturalism practiced in the state of Sikkim is quite ambivalent in the sense that the languages which are at the verge of extinction with a very few speakers have not been recognised; hence, the opportunity to bring the languages back in suffers. This shows that electoral compulsions, among other things, underpin the process of recognition of languages in Sikkim.

SECTION III
The Development of Limboo Language in Sikkim

Limboo Community in Sikkim

The Limboos are known by different names such as Subba, Limbus, Yakthumgbas, Tsongs, Chang, or Chung. They are the descendents of the ancient Kiratas of the Limbuwan. According to the State Socio-Economic Census of 2006, the population of the Limboos in Sikkim is 56650 persons, spread over the entire of Sikkim, however, with a concentration in areas like Daramdin, Soreng, Hee, Dentam, Lingchum, Khanisherbong, Samdong, Yuksam, Namphok and Mangshila.

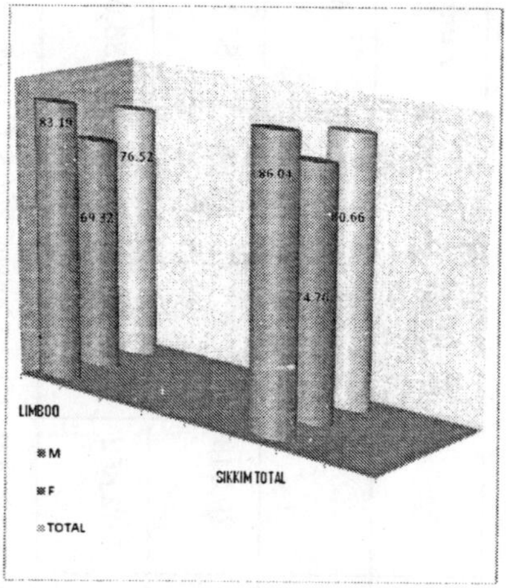

Fig. 12.2: Literacy Rate of the Limboo Community vis-a-vis the State Average

Source: Constructed on the basis of the State Socio-Economic Census, 2006, Government of Sikkim.

Table 12.1: Profile of Limboo Community in Sikkim

	Population			*Literacy Rate (In %)*			*Sex Ratio*	*Household Data*			
Limboo	*M*	*F*	*Total*	*M*	*F*	*Total*		*APL*	*BPL*	*Total*	*HH Size*
	29,343	27,307	56,650	83.19	69.32	76.52	931	7,598	3,074	10,672	5.31
Sikkim State	3,02,852	2,78,694	5,81,546	86.04	74.76	80.66	920	90,212	21,618	1,11,830	5.2

Source: State Socio-Economic Census 2006, Government of Sikkim.

Table 12.1 shows the profile of the community vis-a-vis the state population.

The Limboo community in Sikkim constitutes around 9.74% of the total population of the state, spread over 10,672 households. Approximately 75% of the Limboo households in Sikkim live above poverty line. Of the total limboo population of 56,650, 51.8% are male and 49.2% are females. The Sex ratio of the Limboos is 931:1000 which is slightly higher than the state average of 920:1000. Literacy rate of a community also impinges upon its language and its development. The following figure shows the literacy rate of the Limboos vis-a-vis the state average.

As revealed from the figure above, the literacy rate of the Limboo community, both in case of male as well as female members, is slightly lower than the state average. The difference is hardly of around 4% with that of the state average. This implies that the recognition of the Limboo language way back in 1981 has contributed to the improvement in the literacy levels of the community.

Limboo Language: The Nomenclature, Script and Morphology

The origin of Limboo language is not exactly known. The Limboo language is one of the oldest languages of North Eastern India, Nepal and some other countries. It is known by several names like the Limboo language, the Yakthungpaan, or the Sirijunga. However to bring uniformity in the language, Limboo today called their language only a Yakthungpaan. Limboo language belongs to the Tibeto-Burman Speech Family. G.A. Grierson (1909) has classified this language on the basis of phonetics, grammar, etc. According to his study, Limboo is a dialect of a much complex character or one of the complex pronominalise languages. Due to the extensive use of pronominal prefix, Limboo agrees with Bara and still more with Kuki-Chin language. It is another link in the chain connecting Tibetan and the Himalayan dialects with the Tibeto-Burman languages of Burma (Myanmar) and Assam. Linguists Soren Egerod (1974) has also classified Limboo into Tibeto-Burman Speech family. Robert Shafer (1955, 1966) and Benedict (1972) have also agreed with the Grierson's classification.

The Limboos have their own script called Sirijunga script; it was named in honour of King Sirijunga of Limbuwan. The Limboos believe that King Sirijunga borrowed this script from the Devanagari script based Brahmi script during the period of the Guptas (400-800 AD) Limboos thus have the manuscript written by the Sirijunga Hang himself and same has been revived, propagated and popularised by his incarnate Tye - Ongsi Srijunga (1704-41) which are available in the Indian office Library, London and Archives of Sikkim. It is also known as the Limboo Script. According to the compilation of alphabets made by A. Campbell and Brian Hodgeson, there are 9 vowels, 19 consonants, 6 conjoint letters, 3 clusters and 2 vowel lengths in the Limboo script. However, Baj Bir Tholong and Iman Singh Chemjong (1904-76) have pointed out that there are 29 consonants, 7 conjoint a small letters, 2 vowel lengths and 8 vowels instead of 9 in the script. There were some addition and exclusion of vowels, consonants, etc. B.B. Muringla Nugo, popularly known among the Limboos as the 'modern architect of Sirijunga script', has contributed a lot in giving perfect shape and size to Sirijunga script. Now, the script is designed to contain 25 consonants, 9 vowels, 8 conjoint letters, one glottal stop, 1 vowel length, and I coda consonant.

There are four dialects in Limboo–Chhatharay, Panchtharay, Tammerkholay and Phedappe. In Sikkim only the Panchtharay dialect is used but all the dialects are understandable to the entire Limboo speakers. All the dialects are grammatically similar but few words make difference in meaning. Most of the words of different dialects are reflected in dictionaries, stories, novels, plays, poems, etc. They are used as synonyms. B.B. Muringla Nugo, has done a remarkable job in modernising the Sirijunga script and making Limboo language universally acceptable to all Limboos across the globe.

Development of Limboo language: A Brief Historical Survey

Brian Hudgeson (1840) preserved the limbo manuscripts in India office library, London. R.K.Sprigg brought those preserved manuscripts to Nepal to identify the script and language which was unknown to the scholars and linguist of those days. Kirkpatrick (1811) recommended this language as one of the native languages of Nepal. However, Limboo language had lost its ancient glory before it was revived by Lalshore Sendang (1854), who came to West Sikkim from Athrai of present Nepal in order to revive teaching Sirijunga script, and to propagate Limboo language among the Limboos of different villages of Daramdin, West Sikkim. Campbell (1840) collected around 326 words, G.A. Grierson (1909) 241 words, Major Senior (1908) 3200 words.

In 1928, Subedar Bajbir Tholong published a Limboo Primer Book called 'Tum Yakthung Ningwa? fu Sapla' from Calcutta and circulated to all the Gurkha soldiers serving in India. The second edition of Limboo Primer Book was published by Nirmal Limboo and Jiwan Das Rai in 1929 and continued up to 3rd edition by Ika Bahadur Sereng and C.B.Rai Sangwa of Darjeeling and distributed in Nepal, Bhutan and Sikkim in 1930. In the same year, Sher Bahadur Meyonghang and Mohn Lal Hangam published a Limboo book 'Kirat Varnamala', Kalu Singh Papo also introduced a book 'Yakthung Sewa Samlo'. Subedar Harkajong Makhim published a book called 'Madhpaan Nishedh' and a dictionary. In the same year, a noted writer Iman Singh Chemjong also published one book 'Nissammang Sewa Samlo'. It was a poetry book in Limboo. In 1931, Subedar Budhiraj Phago and Jasman Subba duo wrote a book containing Limboo songs called 'Kirat Samlo Mundhum'. In 1931, Bajbir Tholong and Iman Singh Chemjong published Second Primer book 'Nisigekpa Yakthung Sapla' and Third Primer book 'Sumsigekpa Yakthung Sapla' and a book on mathematics 'Yakthung Hisab Sapla' and another book 'Kirat Itihas' in 1948 and reprinted in 1952 and 1982. In 1938, Inspector Lal Singh Subba established an institution called 'Jambok Memorial' School in the sweet memory of his beloved son 'Jambok'. The abovesaid school was established as a centre of learning and teaching Limboo language. It was ever first school (where the Limboo language was taught) in the history of Limboos. Unfortunately, the school could not contribute much to impart the language education. Till 1950, Sikkim was silent over the use of Sirijunga script; only the Nepali and Roman English were used. The use of Sirijunga script prevailed outside Sikkim only. Iman Singh Chemjong, Padam Singh Subba (Muringla) and Mon Bahadur Khamdhak published 'Tum Yakthung

Ningwa?fu Sapla'in 1951 from Sikkim. After 10 years Iman Singh wrote another book introducing Limboo conjoint letters.

During 1950s, Lal Man Singh Subba (Muringla) of Lingchom, Bharna Dhoj Limboo of Tikjek and Mondal Tilok Singh Subba (Muringla) of Timburbung were continuously putting pressure on the Raja of Sikkim Sir Tashi Namgyal (1894-1963) to start formal education on Limboo language in the schools of Sikkim. Not only this, they also demanded for the reservation of Limboo seat in the council of Minister to the Sikkim Darbar. Partially, their demand was fulfilled in 1958. Mondal Harka Dhoj Mangyung's contribution towards language is note worthy. He was elected as representative from the Limboo Community to Sikkim Darbar in 1967. He requested the then King Palden Thendup Namgyal (1923-82) for formal Limboo language education in Sikkim. The last King accepted his request and order was passed to teach Limboo language as an optional subject in the schools of Sikkim for the first time in the history of Limboo language. Itcha Purna Das Mangyung was appointed as first Limboo language teacher in 1968. He was posted at Bara Samdong School in West Sikkim. Thereafter, the Government of Sikkim appointed many Limboo language teachers. It was a big milestone in the development of the Limboo language.

Mondal Tilok Singh Muringla also wrote a book 'Samaj Sudhar' in 1951 appealing Limboo people for reformation of society, emphasising language, etc. Iman Singh Chemjong left Sikkim in 1952 because of threat from administration. He was appointed as the specialist in the Department of Kirati language (in Nepal 'Kirat' word is added before Limboo) and Culture in Royal Nepal Academy, Kathmandu in 1961. He was an active writer who never stopped writing and publishing books. He wrote 'Kirat Sahityako Itihas' in 1955. He collected Limboo words and prepared 'Limboo-English –Dictionary', one 'Folklore' and 'Kirat Mundhum' in 1961 and 'Kirat Mundhum Khahun' in 1965. He wrote four more books viz. 'Kirat History and Culture in 1967,' Kirat Darshanko Sarangsh'.

A.Weidert and B.Subba (1985), George Van Driem (1987), Boyd Mikhailowsky (n.d.) collected many limbo words for compiling a dictionary. G. A. Grierson has included the language in his linguistic survey and considered it as one of the complex pronominalised languages of north eastern India, George Van Driem wrote 'A Grammar of Limboo' in 1987; A. Weidert along with B. Subba published a Concise Limboo Grammer and Dictionary in 1985.

Apart from the academic matters, Limboo has been introduced in AIR Gangtok in 1983. It broadcasts news, articles, songs, skits, etc. on daily basis.

Recognition of Limboo Language as a State language

The Government of Sikkim recognised Limboo language as one of the Official language of Sikkim in 1981 by amending the Official Language Act of 1977, vide Government Notification Nc. 6/LD/81 dated 31 March 1981. This recognition has fulfilled the long demand of the community who wanted to see their language at par with other three languages viz. Nepali, Lepcha and Bhutia recognised already by the state government in 1977. This measure of government undoubtedly ensures the safeguard not only to the language but also to the culture, customs and traditions of the community. Moreover, the recognition of any language by the government helped to accelerate the development of community as a whole in the field of education, health, human development and the like.

Development of Limboo Language through Literary Activities

Limboo language developed into its present shape mainly through literary activities by a host of limbo literary figures. Iman Singh Chemjong was the first person to write limbo dictionary in Sirijunga script. Kaziman Kondongwa wrote the first dictionary from Nepal. Others in the list include Nor Bahadur Yongyang (2048 BS), Ronsang Nembang (2015 BS), Hasta Lal Sawaden (2041 BS), Krishi Kumar Songbangfe (1992), Hari Chongbang (2050 BS), Bairagi Kaila (2048 BS, 2051 BS, 2053 BS), Birahi Kaila (2050a, 2050b), and Khel Raj Yonghang (2052 BS) who collected words and published there dictionaries from Nepal. B.B.Subba Muringla (1980) was the first to write Limboo-Nepali-English Dictionary and a pedagogical Limboo Grammar from Sikkim. Bajrabihari Kumar, P.S. Subba (Muringla) and B.B.Muringla Nugo (1985) introduced a Hindi-Limboo bilingual dictionary which was published by Hindi

Sansthan, Nagaland. Further, many associations and societies of the Limboos have been engaged in literary and other such activities, contributing towards the development of the language.

The Limboos of Sikkim have ever highest number of registered Associations. They are: (1) Sukhim Yakthung Sapsok Songjumbo (literary society) (2) Sukhim Yakthung Wenchha Chumbho (Youth), (3) Sirijunga Yakthung Sakthim Phojumbho Art and Culture, (4) Sukhim Yakthung Nichhamcha Sapsok Chumbho (student literary society), (5) Namdha Sukhim Yakthung Saplan Chumbho (publication), (6) Teymen Yakthung ma-chumbho (national level), and (7) Kirat yakthungt chumlung (oldest but defunct). All the associations, irrespective of their objectives, give top priority to Limboo language and its development. They sponsor the publication of books, magazines, journals, news bulletins, calendars, etc.

Educational Curriculum and the Development of Limboo language

Education which is the basic human right is perhaps the most vital requirement for inclusive growth, empowering individual, community and society in the development process. It transcends human being from ignorance to enlightenment, from the shade of social backwardness to the light of social amelioration and the nation from underdevelopment towards faster social and economic development. Many world organisations including UNESCO observed that 'illiteracy is a grave hindrance to social and economic development and hence the extension of literacy is a pre-requisite for the successful implementation of national plans for economic and social development'. The recognition of language, among other things, is instrumental in raising the percentage of literacy of community in particular and state in general. The inclusion of language in the curriculum further encourages the children of the community to take admission in the school which in long run help to arrest the drop-out rates. With the recognition of limboo language as official language, the government has included the limboo language in the curriculum of the state at different standard. The Central Board of Secondary Education (CBSE), New Delhi has also included the Limboo language in its curriculum in 1981 as a subject for class ten (X) and class twelve (XII) in 1983 respectively. From academic session 2000-01 vide Reference No. 312/ UG 2000 dated 17 July, 2000, University of North Bengal has introduced Limboo as Modern Indian Language (MIL) at the Undergraduate level. Now, all the colleges of Sikkim are affiliated to the Sikkim University. The Sikkim University has given Limboo equal weight-age with other subjects as an optional subject in its Undergraduate course (which is of 300 marks for 3 semesters and it is one of the Compulsory Regional Language with 100 marks for semester). The introduction of the language at the undergraduate levels by the educational boards and universities has given a fillip to the development of the language in the state.

In school, the teaching of Limboo language was started in1968 which was long before the recognition of language as official language of state. P.T. Namgyal, the then chogyal of Sikkim, issued a Royal Proclamation in 1968, thereby giving an order to introduce the Limboo language as optional subject in the school and appointment of teacher to teach the language. Initially the subject was though introduced only up to class II but with the increasing demand from the leaders and social activists of community the subject was introduced later on up to XII standard. Presently, in Sikkim 1134 schools are there of which 780 are government schools and remaining 354 are private schools. Out of 780 government and 354 private schools,

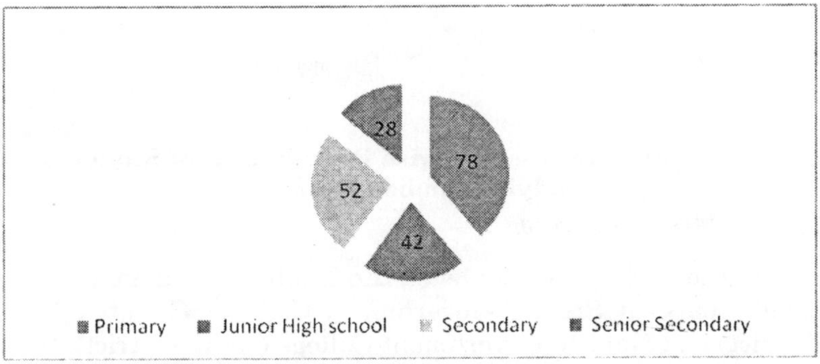

Fig 12.3: Number of schools that taught Limboo Language
Source: State Socio-Economic Census 2006, GoS.

the Limboo language is being taught respectively in 200 government and 14 private schools. Of this 200 government schools, 78 are primary, 42 junior high schools, 52 secondary and 28 senior secondary. Percentage wise, 39% are primary, 21% are junior high schools, 26% are secondary, and 14% are senior secondary (see Fig. 12.3).

With the increase in the number of schools where Limboo language is being taught, there is also increase in the number of students who have opted to this language as their one of the subject. In current academic session of 2010, there are total 8180 students in 200 government schools who are studying Limboo language. Majority of the students (5,330) are from west district followed by east district with 1049 students. South and North district has 1,141 and 660 students respectively who are presently studying Limboo languages in different schools (see Fig. 12.4).

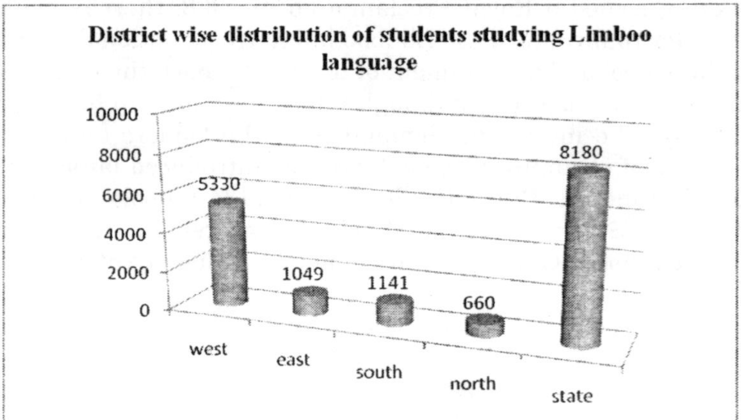

Fig 12.4: District-wise Distribution of Students studying Limboo Language

Source: HRDD, GOS 2010.

At the undergraduate level, the Limboo language is being taught only in Sikkim Government College, Gangtok (east district) and Namchi Government College (south district). Both the colleges are under the Sikkim University, the only university of state which was established in 2007. Initially the language was introduced in the curriculum of undergraduate as MIL but this was made later on an elective subject of 300 marks. With the introduction of Limboo language as an elective subject in the syllabi of college, many students from this community took this subject as their elective paper. In Sikkim Government College, Tadong, though only 13 students took admission in 2000-01 but their number increased to 37 in the next session that is in 2001-02 which is the highest of all the sessions. Thereafter, the number of students decreases gradually and it was only in 2009 the enrolment was increase to 36. The Figure 12.5 below shows the session wise number of Limboo student enrolled in Sikkim Government College, Tadong and Namchi Government College from 2005 to 2010.

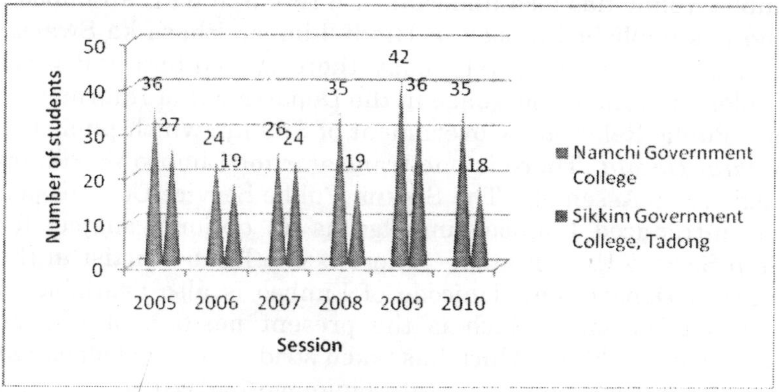

Fig 12.5: Number of Limboo students enrolled in two Colleges of Sikkim

Source: Department of Limboo Language, SGC and NGC

As revealed from the figure above, the Namchi Government College (NGC) which is located in south district of Sikkim has highest number of Limboo reading students than the Sikkim Government College (SGC) located at state capital Gangtok. In 2005, for instance, NGC has 36 Limboo reading students whereas SGC has only 27. Similarly in 2009, NGC has 42 students which are the highest of all session (2005-10), the SGC has only 36. SGC, though situated at state capital, has got limited number of Limboo reading students than NGC. There are two reasons for this– firstly, the majority of students who were taking admission in SGC preferred to take English and Nepali as their language elective paper rather than Limboo, and secondly, the students from west, which has highest number of Limboo population in Sikkim and highest number of student studying Limboo languages in schools, takes admission in NGC and they opted to Limboo language as their elective subject.

SECTION IV
Concluding Observations

There are many scholars who are pursuing their studies on the Limboos language, Limboo Society and Limboo Culture. Dr. Gopal Prasad Dahal, a scholar and linguist from Sikkim has done research on 'Paschim Sikkim Chhetrama Boliney Limboo Bhasikako Varananatmak Adhyayan. Dr. (Mrs) Shova Subba Yolmo has also undertaken a research on the Limboos, and has published a book in Hindi 'Limboo Bhasa ka Swarup Vikash' (2008). Moreover, today there are editors and proof readers on Limboo language in the Department of Information and Public Relations, Government of Sikkim, which publishes *Sikkim Herald*. There is one translator for Limboo in Sikkim Legislative Assembly. The Sikkim Public Service Commission has introduced Limboo language as an optional subject for Civil Service Examinations. There is one Limboo artist in the Culture Department. Unicode of Limboo is also available in Internet Websites. Such is the present position of Limboo language in Sikkim, which has taken strides in its development since its recognition as a state language in 1981.

References

Chemjong, I.S (ed.) (2015 BS). Limboo- Nepali- English Dictionary, Royal Nepal Academy Kathmandu.

Dahal, Gopal Prasad (2000). Paschim Sikkim Chhetrama Boliney Limbo Bhaisikako Varnanatmak Adhyayan.

Driem, Goerge Van (1987). A Grammer of Limbu, Mounton de Gruyter, Armsterdam.

Grierson, G.A. (2006). Language of North Eastern India- A Survey, Vol. I, Gyan Publishing House, New Delhi.

Marak, C.R.,and Shangpliang, J.S.(ed) (2008). Growth and Development of Khasi and Garo Language, Sathitya Acadamy.

Muringla Nugo, B.B. (2004). Yakthung Sappanlen Maaram Tamepmo. Kwality Store, Gangtok.

Risley, H.H. (1894). The Gazetteer of Sikkim, Sikkim Nature Conservation Foundation, Gangtok.

Sinha, A.C. (1975). Politics of Sikkim: A Sociological Study, Thomas Press, (India) Ltd.

Southworth, F. (1980). "Function Aspects of Bilingualism", International Journal of Dravidian Linguistics G (1).

Spolsky, Bernard (1989). Remarks Made at Fourth International Conference on Minority Languages, Ljouwert.

Subba, B.B. (1985). Concise Limboo Grammar and Dictionary, Lobsters Publication, Armsterdam.

Subba J.R. (2002). History and Development of Limbo Language, Ambika Printers, New Delhi.

13

Development of Education in Sikkim: The Changing Scenario

Introduction

Until the early seventies, the small and beautiful place Sikkim was an independent kingdom ruled by the *'chogyals'* on hereditary basis. With the 35th amendment of the Indian Constitution in 1974, Sikkim became the 'associate' state of India. It became the 22nd state of the Indian Constitution with the 36th amendment of the Indian Constitution in 1975.

The mosaic of Sikkimese society consists of three ethnic communities - the Lepchas,the Bhutias and the Nepalese, and some plainsmen from different parts of India. The Lepchas are believed as the original inhabitants of Sikkim. They are of Mongolian origin. They migrated from Assam and Upper Burma to this region. They are peace loving people. With them in Sikkim there was existence of some Limboos of Nepali community during that period. Until the Bhutia immigration, the Lepchas were ruled by local Lepcha chiefs.

The Bhutias entered in Sikkim from Tibet. They also have Monoglian features. They ruled here through 12 succeeding *chogyals* and wanted to spread Buddhism all over Sikkim. With the influence of the Bhutias, majority of the Lepchas converted into Buddhism who used to practice animism earlier.

The Nepalese is the third ethnic group and constitute more than 80 per cent of population. They are mainly Hindus.

Few of the Nepali tribes are Buddhists and some are converted to Christianity.

Along with these three ethnic communities, there are some plainsmen from different parts of India who entered this region during the period when J.C.White was appointed the first British Political Officer in Sikkim. Now they are settled in different parts of Sikkim with diversified occupation mainly in trade and commerce. All the communities maintain peace and harmony, and their peaceful co-existence gives Sikkim an unique feature.

Educational Development

Before the 17th century, there was no historical evidence which show the existence of any educational system in Sikkim. The first education system was religion based monastic education which was started after the Tibetan immigration in the State during the early 17th century. This type of education was restricted to the Lamas only and not for the common people.

During the British period or in 1830s, modern formal education began in the State when a Scottish missionary named Reverend McFarlane established a missionary school in 1883 in Gangtok. Two other schools named Bhutia Boarding School and Nepali Boarding School were also established in 1906. Both these schools later combined into one high school called Tashi Namgyal Higher Secondary School in 1924, which was named after the then Maharaja of Sikkim –Tashi Namgyal. Christian missionaries also established one girls' school during that period. Since 1944, education and educational institution were brought under the direct control of the then Maharaja Tashi Namgyal.

To impart formal education in a planned and systematic manner, the first Education Directorate was set up in 1954. Since then, the standard of education has been improved. There were only 86 educational institutions which include 82 primary schools, 2 upper primary and 2 secondary schools in Sikkim in the mid nineties. In 1975, the number increased up to 264. By the end of 2004, there were 783 government schools including schools opened and upgraded under Sarva Siksha Abhiyan.

Education: Pre and Post-Merger Periods

There is a popular saying in Nepali-*'Pari Lekhi Kay Kam, Hollow Joti Khao Maam'* means to make two ends meet, you have to plough the field. Then what is the use of reading and writing? Traditional education system of Sikkim was based on that saying. People used to gather knowledge from their day to day experience of life. Hence, traditional education was very practical need based type. Though the royal and elite family members were very interested to spread education within this region, the then political turmoil did not allow the growth and development of education.

Before the British administration started in Sikkim, the lamaistic education imparted in the monasteries prevailed in this region. This type of education was restricted to the lamas and it imparted religious education only. To become a monk, the lamas used to get training on different skills like painting, paper making, etc. But for the common people, educational facilities were very negligible.

Britishers wanted to bring educational reformes in Sikkim. Their intension was to make the future *chogyal* or ruler modern English educated who would follow their ideology and support British policy of reform. The Britishers tried to create loyal people who would not oppose them to finalise the future successor of Sikkim.

Before starting the modern English system of education in Sikkim, the first British political officer, Claude White wanted to educated the royal prince and children of some influential persons like the lamas and kazis who used to help them in admistration. To fulfill that objective, 18 children from elite family were sent to Darjeeling for education. Later, Kumar Sidkeong Tulku was sent to Oxford University in England for further studies.

J.C.White was also interested to establish an English boarding school at Gangtok. He thought that in this way, the government could save the money which it spends on educating the local boys outside Sikkim. Within the two consecutive years – 1906 and 1907 – two boarding schools namely Bhutia Boarding School and Nepali Boarding School were established respectively. After completion of education from these schools, children used to be sent to Darjeeling with financial support for higher studies.

Kumar Sidelong Tulku returned from England in 1908 and became the Vice-President of the State Council. He was given the charge of education, forest and monasteries. He had shown keen interest in spreading modern English education all over the State and gave new dimension to education in Sikkim. Durning that period a number of schools were established. Before that education was confined only within the children of the elitist section but he encouraged the common people to send their boys and girls to the newly established schools which impart modern English education. In 1909, he established Enchey School in Gangtok as a monastic school which at present has been continuing as one of the government higher secondary school. In 1912, three government schools in three different places Namchi, Rhenock and Pathing statred functioning, which was the brain child of Kumar Sidkeong Tulku. From the period of Kumar Sidkeong Tulku, female education in Sikkim got priority. In 1913, a girls' school mainly for the daughters of the kazis was opened. Subjects like Tibetan, Hindi and knitting were taught there. Only 5 girls enrolled their name in that school. In 1915 the number of the students increased to 13. In 1918, the curriculum was revised and subjects like spinning and lace making were also introduced. Girls of the common people were not allowed to this school.

In the late 19th century, Christian missionaries were also interested to spread modern education in Sikkim. But the then maharaja Tashi Namgyal did not favour Christian missionary activities in Sikkim. Few school of Christian missionaries were handed over to Scottish missionaries. The Scottish missionaries also established different schools in the State. Sikkim had 21 schools including 6 government schools, 13 mission schools and 2 schools under landlords by the year 1920. Female education got priority when the Scottish mission established a girls' school in 1923. A Scottish missionary Mary Scott opened a girls' school for the common people at Gangtok. It was the first full fledged girls' school. The state government extended financial support for this school. Apart from English education, girls of all classes used to get training on cooking, first aid, needle work, etc. Before 1939, it upgraded up to middle school level. In 1941, it was decided by the Sikkim Durbar to build a new school building with hostel facility in the memory of the Maharaja Kumar Paljor Namgyal, who was killed while serving in the Royal Indian Air Force. In 1945, it was recognised as a high school by Calcutta University, and at present it has been continuing as Paljor Namgyal Girls' Senior Secondary School at Gangtok, but it is not a fully government school now. It has autonomous body but state government provide financial assistance to this school. Gradually, the Thikadars and common people started understanding the importance of modern education and took initiatives to establish more schools in Sikkim.

In the post-merger period, a large educated workforce became indispensable for the state to maintain administration and welfare. Therefore, the state government started giving emphasis on educational development. Till now, the education sector has been receiving greater priority in the state.

Existing Education Systems

School education system in Sikkim is divided into four stages – (a) Primary (Class I-V), (b) Junior high (Class VI-VIII), (c) Secondary (Class IX-X), and (d) Senior Secondary (Class XI-XII) level. Before the primary stage, pre-primary stage is there. To join the pre-primary stage, children should be 4+.

Examination of class V and class VIII level is conducted by the Sikkim Education Board itself; at secondary and senior secondary level, children appear examination conducted by Central Board of Secondary Education (C.B.S.E.), Delhi because all government schools in Sikkim are affiliated to the C.B.S.E. English is the medium of instruction instead of mother tongue. Mother tongue of different Sikkimese ethnic communities i.e. Nepali, Bhutia, Lepcha are taught as second language. Some other languages or dialects which are used by different caste groups of Nepali people like Rai, Gurung, Mukhia, etc. are also have been introduced in school level and Limboo, Lepcha and Bhutia languages have been introduced upto college level. As a compulsory language, Hindi is taught from class IV to class VIII.

In senior secondary level, there are three main streams – Science, Humanities and Commerce. Apart from this, recently vocational education, as a stream, has been introduced in school level. Subjects like Tourism, Floriculture, Horticulture, Poultry, Information Technology etc. are taught in vocational streams.

Majority of the government senior secondary schools in Sikkim have only Arts or Humanities stream. With that, some schools have commerce stream and some have Science stream. But there are only few schools where entire three streams are available. Vocational stream is available in 40 government schools. Besides, there are some private schools where children can study upto senior secondary level. After completion of school education, for higher study students may join in Government College of Tadong (East district), or Namchi (South district), or Rehnock (East district). There is one Law College in Gangtok, three B.Ed Colleges, one Sanskrit Mahavidyalaya at Gyalshing (West district), and one Tibetan Institution called SHEDA. For technical education, there are two polytechnics at Bardang (East district) and Chisopani (South district), and one Industrial Training Institute at Rangpo (East district).

With the support of the state government, Sikkim Manipal University, which is situated in Gangtok, has two constituent colleges - one at Majhitar which is an Engineering College and another at Tadong (East Sikkim) which is a Medical College. In the year 2007, one Central University has been established in the State. Construction work for the University is going on at Yangyang (South Sikkim).

To make education accessible to all sections of the society, Government of Sikkim is extending financial support,especially to the weaker section of the society. A large number of private schools are also coming up in the State to meet the rising demand for better education.Though the demand for a full-fledged university which was a long felt need, came into reality recently, the number of colleges and technical institutes are not sufficient to meet the demands of the increasing number of students.

Literacy Rate

The overall literacy rate of this State is very encouraging. Since 1971, there has been a sharp increase in literacy rate. While in 1971 the literacy rate of Sikkim was only 17.74 per cent which was almost half of the national level, by 1981, the literacy rate has increased at a much faster rate. In 1981, it was 34.05 per cent followed by 56.94 per cent which is about 5 per cent higher than the national average. The data shows gradual progress of the State in the field of education. Over the decades, the state's achievements related to literacy rates are furnished in Table 13.1.

Table 13.1 : Literacy Rate in Sikkim and India 1971-2001

Item	*Year*	*Unit*	*Sikkim*	*India*
Literacy Rate	1971	Percentage	17.74	34.45
	1981	"	34.05	43.56
	1991	"	56.94	52.21
	2001	"	69.68	65.38

Source: Sikkim: A Statistical Profile 2002, Government of Sikkim.

Table 13.2 shows the area-wise decadal progress in literacy rate by districts.

Table 13.2: District-wise Percentage of Literates to Total Population 1981-2001

Year	*Sikkim*	*North*	*East*	*South*	*West*
1981	34.05	29.74	41.39	32.49	23.62
1991	56.94	42.43	53.95	43.87	36.82
2001	69.68	69.11	75.57	68.12	59.31

Source: Sikkim: A Statistical Profile 2002, Government of Sikkim.

The above table shows that from 1981 onwards for continuous two decades, district-wise literacy percentage is highest in the East district and lowest in the West district. In the year 2001 also, the literacy rate of the West district is lowest,that is, 59.31% compared to 75.57% in the East district which is highest among the all 4 districts. Though the table indicates educational development in Sikkim, there is vast disparity in rural-urban educational scenario and male-female literacy rate.

Table 13.3: Rural Urban Disparity regarding Literacy Rate in Sikkim

State / District	*Literacy Rate*					
	Rural			*Urban*		
	Person	*Male*	*Female*	*Person*	*Male*	*Female*
Sikkim	67.67	75.11	59.05	84.82	88.61	80.19
North	68.78	77.16	57.15	79.41	81.98	75.06
East	72.89	80.15	64.13	84.86	88.64	80.29
South	67.43	73.92	60.30	88.92	93.25	83.74
West	59.02	66.94	50.46	77.98	82.90	71.30

Source: Sikkim: A Statistical Profile 2002, Government of Sikkim.

Table 13.3 shows the overall rural-urban disparity regarding literacy rate in Sikkim on the whole, there is 17.15 per cent of rural-urban disparity. In rural areas the overall literacy rate is 67.67 per cent whereas in urban areas it is 84.82 per cent. The disparity in the West district is about 2 percent (1.81%) more compared to the state level. While literacy rate in the rural areas of West district is 59.02 per cent, it is 77.98 per cent in the urban areas of West district.

Womenfolk of Sikkimese society have shown a remarkable achievement in their literacy rate. Compared to the national average, the female literacy in Sikkim is higher. Table 13.3 above presents district-wise female literacy rate in rural and urban areas. Though the development with regard to literacy made by Sikkimese women is praiseworthy, still rural-urban gap in female literacy is very shocking. In the state level, gender disparity regarding literacy rate in rural areas is about 16 per cent (male literacy-75.11%, female literacy-59.05%) whereas in urban areas the gap is 8.42 per cent (male literacy -88.61%, female literacy-80.19%). It reveals that the gender disparity is just double in rural areas compared to urban areas. Similarly, West district also shows a very dismal picture related to female literacy. The gender disparity regarding literacy rate between rural and urban areas is 5 per cent in West Sikkim.

Educational Institutions

State government of Sikkim is taking various initiatives to improve the educational system and to provide quality education in the State. After merger there has been a substantial increase

Table 13.4: District-wise and Category-wise Government Schools

Category of schools	*East*	*North*	*South*	*West*	*Total*
Primary	146	60	142	157	499
Upper primary	47	16	47	41	151
Secondary schools	30	11	28	23	92
Sr. secondary schools	19	3	9	10	41
Total	242	90	226	225	783

Source: Annual Report of Sarva Siksha Abhiyan 2004-05.

Table 13.5: District-wise Educational Institutions in the State

Dist.	*Govt. School*	*Private School*	*Pre-Primary**	*Monastic Schools*	*ICDS*	*JNV/KV***	*College*	*Total*
North	90	18	90	18	88	1	0	215
South	226	53	225	20	115	1	2	417
East	242	120	242	28	150	1	5	546
West	225	55	225	13	122	1	1	417
State	783	246	782	79	475	4	8	1595

Source: Report of S.S.A. 2005

Note: *Pre-primary class is attached with all government schools from primary to senior secondary schools as such theses are not included in total.

**Jawahar Navodaya Vidyalaya/Kendriya Vidyalaya.

in the number of schools.Tables 13.4 and 13.5 presents district-wise educational institutions in the State including government, private, monastic, I.C.D.S., J.N.V., K.V., colleges.

Along with the total government schools, there are private schools, monastic schools, ICDS, JNV/KV, colleges, etc. Therefore, the total number of education institutions in the State was 1595 by 2005.

Teachers

With the expansion of educational institution in Sikkim, the number of teachers has also increased. Before the merger, due to lack of local qualified teachers, the recruitment of teachers was done from different parts of India. But recently the scenario has been changing. The number of local educated youth is increasing, and to protect these educated people in service sectors, recruitment of teachers upto senior secondary level in government schools are reserved for local people. Sometimes, due to non-availability of local teachers, recruitment of non-local teachers is done on ad-hoc basis.

Table 13.6 shows that there has been a steady increase in the number of teachers during 1975-91 in primary to senior secondary level, though the number of female teachers have not increased in the same rate.

Table 13.7 reveals sex-wise primary and upper primary teachers from all four districts. The percentages of trained and untrained teachers at primary level are 71.93 per cent and 28.07 per cent respectively. In upper primary level 50 per cent teachers are trained. The table reveals a dissatisfying feature in both primary and upper primary level. Compared to the male- trained and untrained teachers in both primary and upper primary level, the number of female teachers is less in all four districts.

Table 13.8 reveals that in the elementary level total number of teachers during 2003-04 was 5,567, whereas, it was 5,587 in 2004-05. The table shows that there is an increase of 20 teachers only. Taking three districts (South, West and North) into account, there was an increase of 93 male teachers and decrease of 8 female teachers during 2004-05.

Table 13.6: Teachers in Institutions by Stages (1975-76 and 1990-91)

Year	Teacher											
	Number				Trained (%)				Women (%)			
	Pry	Mid	Sec.	Sr. Sec.	Pry.	Mid.	Sec	Sr. Sec	Pry	Mid	Sec	Sr. Sec
1975-76	625	306	-	175*	26	24	-	37	-	41	-	37
1980-81	1106	472	604	317	47	53	45	37	23	26	40	44
1985-86	1878	1167	1115	584	49	43	45	42	27	25	37	40
1990-91	2245	1565	1322	759	50	41	43	41	28	31	40	40
	(2465)*	(1585)	(1291)	(856)	(48)	(41)	(41)	(47)	(27)	(32)	(42)	(50)

Source: Mahajan et.al: 1995

**Figures for senior secondary include secondary and senior secondary stages.*

***Figures in parentheses denote status in 1992-93*

Note: Pry = Primary; Mid. = Middle; Sec. = Secondary; Sr.Sec. = Senior Secondary.

Table 13.7: District-wise and Category-wise Teacher Position: Trained/Untrained Teachers in Government Schools (2004-05)

District	*Primary*			*Upper Primary*			*Primary*		*Upper Primary*		*Total*
	Male	*Female*	*Total*	*Male*	*Female*	*Total*	*Trained*	*Untrained*	*Trained*	*Untrained*	
North	182	126	308	69	46	115	222	86	45	70	423
South	737	372	1109	167	147	314	980	129	141	173	1423
East	908	768	1676	428	307	735	1226	450	436	299	2411
West	631	387	1018	198	114	312	529	486	225	187	1330
State	2458	1653	4111	862	614	1476	2957	1154	737	739	558

Source: Annual Report of S.S.A. 2004-05.

Table 13.8. Number of Teachers at Elementary level (2003-05)

District	*2003-04*			*2004-05*		
	Male	*Female*	*Total*	*Male*	*Female*	*Total*
East	-	-	2476	1336	1075	244
West	772	492	1264	829	501	1330
South	889	510	1399	904	519	1423
North	230	198	428	251	172	423
Total	-	-	5567	3320	2267	5581

Source: Annual Report of S.S.A. 2004-05.

Total number of teachers during 2002-03 was 8010, whereas West district itself had recorded total 2,197 teachers including 1071 trained and 720 untrained teachers of all categories. Table 13.9 shows category-wise number of teachers in West district during 2003. Total 491 teachers from West district, in the academic year 2003, are under training through the initiative taken by the H.R.D.D., Government of Sikkim.

Table 13.9: Number of Teachers (Category-wise) 2003

Category of teachers	*Trained*	*Untrained*	*Under training*	*Total*
PGTs	33	34	6	73
GTs	64	228	93	385
PRTs	824	322	392	1538
School mothers	150	51	Nil	201
Language teachers	-	85	-	-
Total	1071	720	491	2197

Source: District Profile 2003 and Annual Report of State Mission Authority, 2002-03.

Teacher-Student Ratio

The distribution of teacher-student ratio in Sikkim at various levels is highly uneven, though it is good at the primary level (1:19) compared to the all-India ratio of 1:46 in 1995. The teacher-student ratio of humanities sections of some of the senior secondary schools is far higher than the teacher-student ratio of science section. It could go upto 1:80 which may affect the teacher's effectiveness badly. In 2005, the teacher-pupil ratio in the West district of Sikkim was 1:21. Year- wise teacher-pupil ratio at different levels of school education is furnished in Table 13.10.

Table 13.10: Teacher-Student Ratio (Government)

Sl. No.	*Item*	*1997-98*	*1998-99*	*1999-2000*	*2000-01*	*2001-02*
1	Pre-primary	-	1:29	1:30	1:30	1:29
2	Middle	-	1:14	1:14	1:14	1:14
3	Secondary	-	1:04	1:05	1:05	1:05
4	Senior secondary	-	1:03	1:03	1:03	1:03

Source: Sikkim : A Statistical Profile 2004-05, Government of Sikkim.

Concluding Observations

The growth of any state depends on the holistic development of its various sectors in society and 'education' is one of the key instruments in this process. The last two decades have shown enormous improvement in the literacy scene in the state which is reflected clearly in the average literacy figures. The scenario of educational progress in Sikkim began to change rapidly after the formation of democratic government in 1975 by replacing a century old monarchical system. A host of major initiatives taken by the government in the field of education had a deep impact on the improvement of education sector. The progress that the state has made during the last three decades has been remarkable. However, the issues like dropout rates, inadequate infrastructures, quality education etc. still remain the matter of concern in education scenario. Thus in order to achieve an inclusive education in the state, it needs more concerted effort by the government and officials concerned.

References

Annual Report 2002-2003, State Mission Authority, Department of Education, Government. of Sikkim, Gangtok.

Annual Report and Statement of Accounts, 2004-05, State Project Office, Sarva Shiksha Abhiyan, Human Resource Development Department, Gangtok.

Bareh, H.M. (2001). *Encyclopedia of North-East India, Vol. VII- Sikkim,* New Delhi.

Basnet, Lal Bahadur (1974). *Sikkim-A Short Political History,* New Delhi, S. Chand and Co. (Pvt.) Ltd.

Bhadra Madhumita (1992). *Sikkim-Democracy and Social Change,* Calcutta, Minerva Associates (Publications) Pvt. Ltd.

Bhasin Veena (1946): *Ecology, Culture and Change Tribals of Sikkim Himalayas,* New Delhi, Inter-India Publications.

Bhattacharya Aparna (2001). "The Cultural Pattern of the Tribal Women in Sikkim: Tradition and Modernisation", *Journal of Indian Anthropological Society*, Vol. 36, No. 2-3 Jul/Nov.

Census of India (1991). Series-22, Sikkim Part XII A and B District Census Handbook, Directorate of Census Operations.

Census of India (2001). Sikkim Series, Government of India.

Choudhury, Maitreyee (2005). *Human Resources Culture, Amenities and Quality of Life in Sikkim: A Critique,* Occasional Paper, Centre For Himalayan Studies, North Bengal University.

Datta, Amal (1991). *Sikkim Since Independence, Study of Impact of Education and Emerging Class Structure,* New Delhi, Mittal Publication.

Datta, Karubaki (1991). "A Note on the Present State of the 'Histories' of Sikkim", *The Himalayan Miscellany,* Vol. 5, No. 1, Centre for Himalayan Studies, N.B.U.

Desai, Mamata (1988). *Eco-system and Ethnic Constellation of Sikkim,* Calcutta, Best Books Publication Department.

Joshi, H.G. (ed.) (2004). *Sikkim Past and Present,* New Delhi, Mittal Publications.

Kharel, M.P. (2002). *Socio-Economic Conditions of Sikkim Under Colonial Domination (1889-1947) An Authenticity Discourse,* Ph.D. Thesis, Department of History, North Bengal University.

Lahiri, Ashok Kr. *et al.,* (2001). *Sikkim– The Peoples' Vision,* New Delhi, Government of Sikkim in association with Indus Publishing Company.

Lama, M.P. (2001). *Sikkim Human Development Report,* Delhi, Government of Sikkim and Social Science Press.

Mahajan, Baldev *et al.,* (1995). *Educational Administration in Sikkim, Structure, Process and Future Prospects*, New Delhi, Vikas Publishing House Pvt. Ltd.

Sarma, Nilotpal (1991). *Plainsman in the Hills A Sociological Study in Sikkim,* Ph.D. Thesis, Centre for Himalayan Studies, North Bengal University.

Shukla, Satyenda R. (1976). *Sikkim: The Story of Integration,* New Delhi, S. Chand & Co. (Pvt.) Ltd.

Sikkim: A Statistical Profile 2002. Directorate of Economics, Statistics, Monitoring and Evaluation, Government of Sikkim.

Sikkim: A Statistical Profile 2004-05. Directorate of Economics, Statistics, Monitoring and Evaluation, Government of Sikkim.

Sikkim Coronation (n.d.). Coronation Souvenir Book Committee, Gangtok, Sikkim.

Sinha, Awadhesh Coomar (1975). *Politics of Sikkim A Sociological Study,* Haryana, Thomson Press (India) Limited, Publication Division.

Subba, T.B. (1983). *Caste Class and Agrarian relations in the Nepalese society of Darjeeling and Sikkim,* Ph.D. Thesis, Department of Sociology and Social Anthropology, University of North Bengal.

14

Geography of Unmet Need for Family Planning and Factors Non-Use of Contraception

Objectives and Methodology

The main objectives of the present paper is to estimate the total unmet need for family planning which is observed in two folds–unmet need for spacing and unmet need for limiting. In addition to this, the role of education and socio-economic traits in family planning are also observed. Moreover, an attempt is also made to identify the major factors that are responsible for non-use of contraception. The research design is essentially descriptive which is mainly confined in North Sikkim. The present investigation has been carried out with the single tribal community (Lepcha) living in Dzongu, which is located in Northern part of Sikkim.

Using purposive sampling an interview schedule was administered by individual questionnaire among the woman aged 15 to 45 which is considered as reproductive age. The acquisition data related to this investigation is from the area of small village; Lingthem, Lingdong, Hegyathang, Sangdong, and Gour located in Dzongu, North Sikkim a reserved area only for the Lepcha tribe. The field study was carried out in 2006 from lower belt of Dzongu where populations are distributed very sparsely. Only 120 total number of household are found in this area, and among this total number of household, 98 ever-married women of reproductive age were found who were interviewed for the estimation of total Unmet Need for Family Planning.

Introduction

Unmet need generally refers to that proportion of currently married women of reproductive ages who either want no more children, or always want to avoid their pregnancy, or want to postpone their child bearing stage for specific period of time but are not practicing any means of contraception. In other words, the unmet needs simply means specially the need of fecund woman to compose their family size of their own liking but are not able to meet with such desire of need. There are several factors to be discussed in this context, which are responsible for the unmet need. Before that the vital thing to know about some elements of unmet need is essential as the unmet need for family planning clearly bespoke about the difference between such reproductive preferences and actual practice of birth control.

Concept and Approaches

The total unmet need is the sum of both 'unmet need for spacing' and 'unmet need for limiting'. Spacing refers to that proportion of currently married women of reproductive age who is fecund, do not want any additional children for at least three years, and are not using any means of contraception. Similarly, limiting includes those fecund women of reproductive age who have already reached their desired family size, do not want any more children or want to avoid their pregnancy but are not using any means of family planning, (Subedi 1998). So, normally there are two ways of unmet need of fecund woman who are capable of produce their young ones, that is their intension to have interval between any additional children, and want no more children at all after they have reached their desired family size. The estimation of unmet need include all married woman of reproductive age with the reproductive intention of their own irrespective of real or perceived objections from their husbands about their intension. There are different literatures which suggest about the various approaches to the estimation of unmet need. Bongaarts (1991), among those literatures, has elucidated some of the approaches that included conventional approach, instantaneous KAP – gap, (knowledge, attitude, an actual practicing of contraception) total unmet need and alternative approach.

Conventional approach: Conventional approach to unmet need is based on two basic components–the recent practice of contraception and desire for more additional children by the woman of reproductive age. Thus, conventional KAP – gap or unmet need is the total number of currently married women of reproductive ages who wants no more children, or desire for limiting for their child bearing capacity but are not using any method of contraception.

Instantaneous KAP – gap: It is another approach to unmet need which is an improvement over conventional approach that includes information about the preferences of fecund women to postpone their child bearing and the risk factor such as pregnancy, infecundity, and breast feeding status. The instantaneous KAP – gap can be defined as the proportion of currently married woman of reproductive age who at the time of survey are exposed to the risk of being pregnant, want no more children or want to avoid their pregnancy or postpone pregnancy, and are not using contraception.

Some calculation of instantaneous KAP – gap also include those woman who are not sexually active in the month prior to the survey and those who are unsure about their want to stop child bearing stage (Westoff 1988).

The total unmet need refers to the increase in contraceptive use that would have reduced fertility to intended level. Some unintentionally pregnant and amenorrheic women, at one point in time, would have been current users if their demand at the time of conception had been met. Westoff (1988) with this assumption has denoted in the estimates of total unmet need, included women who were currently pregnant or amenorrheic if their pregnancy were unwanted or mistimed.

Alternative approach: The introduction of alternative approach to unmet need is mainly taken into account of the shortcoming of three approaches as mentioned above, i.e. conventional approach, instantaneous KAP – gap and total unmet need approach (Westoff's Method). This approach includes the adjustment factor and corrects for the reduction in the need for limiting that is resulting from satisfying the demand for spacing and the overestimations of need for spacing. The adjustment is based on the fact that satisfying demand for spacing will reduce some proportion of demand for limiting. Hence, Bongaarts (1991) proposed alternative approach for a maximum and a minimum estimate of the total unmet need. A maximum estimate is calculated as:

$$Umax = L + S - A$$

where:

L = unmet need for limiting based on Westoff's Method.

S = unmet need for spacing based on Westoff's Method.

A = adjustment factor equal to the reduction in the need for limiting

Resulting from satisfying spacing demands.

The assumption in calculating the adjustment factor is that fulfilling the unmet need for spacing reduces the unmet need for limiting by an equivalent amount among women who will have a need for limiting. Therefore, the size of adjustment factor is assumed to equal to the proportion of married women who are complete reproducers with an unmet need for spacing.

Using the concept and approach dealing with unmet need (Subedi 1998) in this section is an attempt to investigate about the present position of unmet need for family planning in Lepcha society of North Sikkim. The current investigation for this purpose comprised of very few family within the Lepcha Community. This paper mainly deals with the socio-economic condition of the Lepcha Tribe and unmet need for family planning being associated with the social structure, it is essential to deal with the objectives. There is no any secondary source of data which are used to estimate for this objective. The study is mainly based on the primary source of data through surveying the each households of study area interviewed by questionnaire approach with ever married women of 15-45 years of age. The eligible women for the responsibility of such questionnaire were married women of reproductive age, i.e., 15-45 years of age, who live together with their husband and entered into the sexual union the night before the survey time.

A distinction is made between "Limiters" or intention of women to postpone their child bearing, for the analysis of unmet need and estimation of demand and unmet need for both 'Spacing' and 'Limiting' has been done. It is purely based on the information obtained from each individual respondent woman through questionnaire in field survey. Moreover, there are several factors that contributed to the non-use of contraception, and such information is also collected by applying some method during survey. So, the exact estimation of unmet need absolutely depends upon the authenticity of information provided by the respondents.

All these estimations of unmet need are based on the research framework designed for the study of unmet need in Nepal by Subedi (1998). There are basically two components for the estimation of total unmet need–one is desire for Spacing and another is desire for Limiting. The unmet need for spacing is defined as the proportion of currently married fecund women of reproductive ages who are (i) neither pregnant nor amenorrheic, not using any method of family planning and want to have interval of two or more years for their next additional child, (ii) currently pregnant and whose pregnancy was mistimed, and (iii) amenorrheic women whose last birth was mistimed (amenorrheic are those who have not experienced the resumption of menstruation after last birth).

Fecundity is measured by the evidence of menopause. Infecund women are those who reported themselves to be menopausal and had not experienced menstruation for the last six or more months at the time of survey. This assumption applies to the currently married women of reproductive age who are neither pregnant nor are postpartum amenorrheic. Similarly, the unmet need for limiting on the other hand is defined as the proportion of currently married fecund woman of reproductive age who are (i) neither pregnant nor amenorrheic, want no more children but are not using any method of family planning, (ii) currently pregnant and whose pregnancy was unwanted, and (iii) amenorrheic and whose last birth was unwanted.

Fig. 14.1 shows the details about the components of unmet need with corresponding percentages of currently married woman of reproductive ages (15-45 years) based on field survey. Firstly, a distinction is made between the users and non-users of contraception. The further classifications among the non-users of contraception are followed by pregnant or amenorrheic and not pregnant or non-amenorrheic, and those pregnant women are divided into intended mistimed and unwanted pregnancy. The intended pregnancies are excluded from calculation because such categories are out of estimation of unmet need. Likewise, a distinction is made between fecund and infecund women among not pregnant women and those infecund are excluded from calculation, as it also does not come under the unmet need. Even among fecund women some

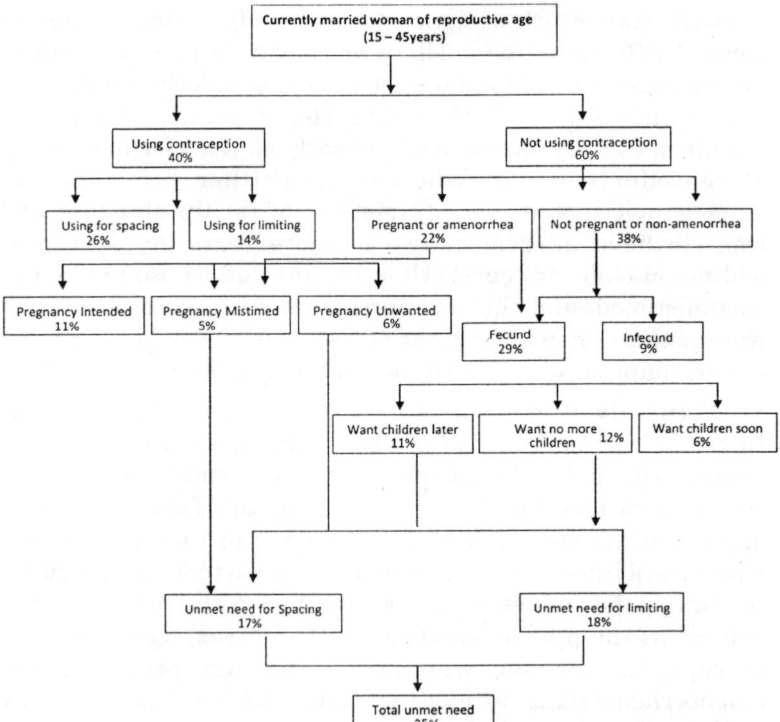

Fig. 14.1: Components of unmet need for family control with corresponding percentages of currently married woman of reproductive age (based on field survey 2002)

are excluded if they fall under the category of 'want children soon'. So, from rest of the women with unmet need for spacing and limiting are identified and eventually the total unmet need is calculated. The figure shows that 35% of total unmet need is found adding with 17% for spacing and 18% for limiting.

According to the information obtained from household survey, the current demand for family control is high. It is near about 78% of total woman who are liable to produce their young ones and demanding for family control. Among which, 48% are demanding for spacing, which is little high in comparison to 44% demanding for limiting. Regarding satisfied demand, only 44% are found satisfied among which 27% demand for limiting was satisfied whereas the satisfied demand for spacing was found 31.5%. In aggregate, the consequence upon the unmet need is estimated as 34.5%. There was 18% of the unmet need for limiting whereas 16.5% are found demanding for spacing. The proximity in the percentage of demand satisfied between limiting and spacing is only the difference of 1. There is found only a difference of 2% in unmet need for spacing and limiting. In this paper, there are total 86 women of reproductive age who is included for the study of their unmet need for family planning.

Table 14.1: Demand and Unmet need for Family Planning in Dzongu

Sl. No.	*Description*	*Spacing*	*Limiting*	*Total*
1.	Demand	41%	37%	78%
2.	Demand Satisfied	3.5%	27%	30.5%
3.	Unmet Need	16.5%	18%	34.5%

High Demand, i.e., 78% for family planning is due to the fact that almost women of reproductive have already passed through their desired family size at the time of survey. Another factor for this is social traits in which they are engulfed, as their society is more conscious about civic value. They are found intended on family control but are not much practicable. Their demand for family planning is rarely satisfied as reported by the concerned woman as they are not self reliant. There is increase in demand for family planning due to their high level of educational attainment.

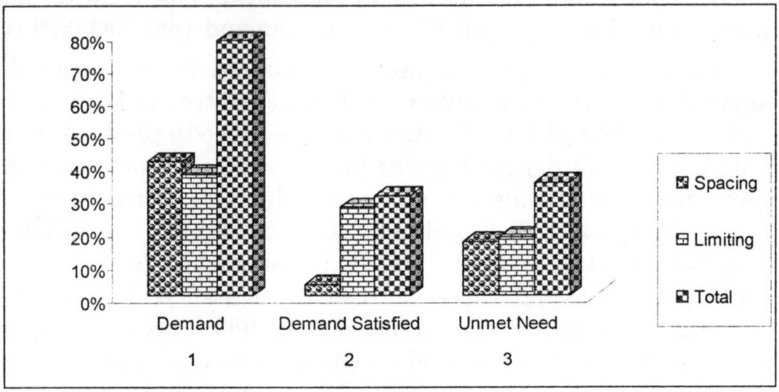

Fig. 14.2: Demand, Demand Satisfied and Unmet Need for family planning

There are several causes which are responsible for the unmet need for the family control in the Lepcha Society of Dzongu area. The composition of family size depends upon the woman's associated household characteristics, which are determined by the reproductive preference of women, knowledge attitude and practice of family planning and husband's background. So, there is found their own reproductive history in the Lepcha Society. According to the data collected from each household survey in Dzongu area, the recent contraceptive prevalence rate (CPR) is 40% (field survey 2006).

Unmet need by Educational Attainment of Women

Educations play a significant role for family control. The women having higher education have more demand for family planning in comparison to the uneducated women. Within the surveyed area, the percentage of women who had ever attended school is very high of 74% among the total respondents. Among them, 32% had attended Primary Level and 44% were secondary level and above. There are large numbers of women with high level of educational attainment. The total demand increases with an increasing level of educational attainment. So, the demand seems to be highest among those women having

Table 14.2: Unmet Need for Family Planning by Educational Attainment (in %)

Sl. No	*Educational Attainment*	*Demand*			*Unmet Need*		
		Spacing	*Limiting*	*Total*	*Spacing*	*Limiting*	*Total*
1.	No Education	8.9	8.9	17.8	40	50	90
2.	Primary	28	27	55	18	19	37
3.	Secondary and above	42.8	32	74.8	23	22	45

secondary education and above, whereas in woman with no education the demand is almost low. The following table shows clear picture about the level of demand, demand satisfied and unmet need with the level of educational attainment. In this way the demand satisfied is also found highest among women having secondary education and above while lowest among the uneducated women. However, the percentage of demand unsatisfied is also high among women of educational attainment as compared to no education. It is high because the total demand is also high in this category.

The total unmet need is those proportions that are demanding for family control and are unable to meet with their desired family size. So the above data shows the tabular representation of percentage wise distribution of demand and unmet need with respect of their educational attainment. The table shows that the total unmet need is lowest among women with no education as compared to women of having some educational attainment which has higher rate of unmet need. This low level of unmet need among women with no education and high among the women with educational attainment is owing to the high and low level of demand among educated ones and uneducated respectively. The percentage of demand satisfied is though high among educated women, the demand among them is too high to be fulfilled. Thus, the difference between demand and contraceptive prevalence of educated women remain high as compared to those women with 'no education'.

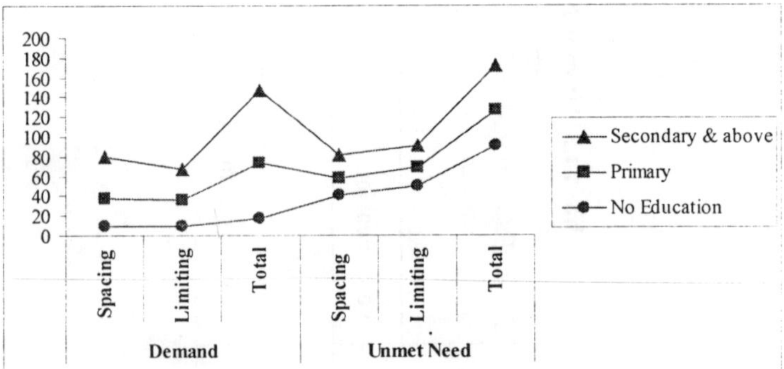

Fig. 14.3 Unmet Needs and Demand for Family Planning with the Level of Education of Woman

Biologically, woman are similar everywhere in terms of their reproductive system, as all are involved in the process of producing young ones but their reproductive preference may differ from one another. Such preferences mostly depend upon their attitude, knowledge and perception of an individual. The reproductive preferences can also be stated as demand either for spacing or limiting in order to compose their desired family size. Moreover, their role of education in the level of unmet need is significant one. As the level of education increase, the demand for family planning also increases simultaneously. With an increase in the level of education, the unmet need for both spacing and limiting are found increased progressively. However, there is an increase in the demand for both spacing and limiting with an increase in the level of education. Since, the percentage of demand satisfied for spacing and limiting are almost equal but the increase in demand not satisfied is rather high in the higher level of educational attainment.

Factors for Non Use of Contraception

There are several factors that lead to the non-use of contraception–firstly, the concerned area (Dzongu) for this study is recognised as the separate Kingdom only for the Lepcha people where this people are not influenced by cultural traits of other communities. So, for the lack of socio-cultural interaction with other groups, they are least aware about the means of family planning; secondly, they are not much familiar with several means of contraception by knowledge, and in addition to this, the unavailability of those means nearby their social milieu to which they are acquainted with. The total number of women with educational attainment is found more than those women with no education, and it is obvious from those premises that the role of education is an influential factor for practicing method of family planning. Nevertheless, the use of contraception seems to be negligible and thirdly, there is gap in knowledge, attitudes and actual practice of contraception and those who have knowledge of contraception are also not using it because of their social attitudes. So, the conditions above are the factors resulted for non-use of contraception.

Conclusion

Unmet need for family control is an outcome of no use of contraception according to the reproductive preferences. Need here refers to the demand to have exact desired family size. When a gap between such demand and actual practicing of contraception exist then the level of unmet need also arises. The high level of unmet need among the woman of reproductive ages in Lepcha community of Dzongu shows a large gap between preferences and performance of birth control. At first was no intension of woman about the birth control and the couples desired to have more children which ultimately led to have large family size. But now there found large proportion demanding for family planning in order to have small family size. The level of unmet need among the Lepcha society in Dzongu is recorded to be high as compared to other societies (Field Survey). It is due to the fact that this tribe is more isolated and is not exposed to the influence of any social phenomenon of other social groups. Increase in the level of unmet need for limiting is due to the lack of practicing permanent methods of birth control, as sterilisation both male and female is found almost absence thereof, as well as the absence of temporary method of family planning led to the increase in the level of unmet need for spacing. With the changes in social structure, attitude towards the birth control seems to be high within this tribe, and hence, the demand for family planning is found increasing slowly and steadily.

References

Subedi B.P. (1998). "Geography of Unmet Need for Family Planning and Factors Non use of Contraception" T.U. Journal Vol. 21, 51-68.

Bongaarth John and Judith Bruce (1995) "The Causes of Unmet Need for Contraception and the Social Content of Services" *Studies in Family Planning*. Vol. 26(2): 57-75.

Castgerline, John B, Aurora.E, Perez and Ann. E. Biddlecom (1996). *Factors Underlying Unmet Need for Family Planning in the Philippines,* Population Council Working Papers No. 84, New York: The Population Council.

Westoff F. Charles (1988) "The Potential Demand for Family Planning: A New Measure of Unmet Need and Estimates for Five Latin American Countries" *International Family Planning Perspectives,* Vol. 14(2) 45-53.

Westoff. F.C. and Pebley (1981) "Alternative Measures for Unmet Need for Family Planning in Developing Countries" *Family Planning Perspectives,* Vol. 7(4).

15

Sikkim: The Nathu-La Silk Trade Route: A Cradle of New Relationship between India and China

Sikkim an amasing place of hidden valleys, mystical monasteries, temples, churches, mosques, historical monuments, snow fed lakes, and a mountain setting covered with flowers and rare fauna. Sikkim is a veritable paradise on the East and a tourist destination for all season. The flora and fauna of Sikkim is a treat for nature lovers. The bio-diversity of the flora and fauna naturally covers a wide and myraiel spectrum tropical to alpine.

Sikkim has 4,500 species of flowering plants, 5,125 species of orchids, 36 types of rhododendrums, 23 varieties of bamboos, 362 types of ferns and its allies, 60 species of Primula, 552 types of birds, 690 types of butterflies, and 48 species of fish. Magnificent parasitic orchids cling to the moist mass which thickly clothes the dripping bush of the tall oaks, ilex and magnolias, and long tuffs of stringy lichens hang from the branches in fantastic shapes, and stream in the wind like hoary beards[2]. The most popular orchids of Sikkim are Nobile Cymbidiums, Cattaleya and Dendrobium. The Rhododendron grande grows over 10 m tall, whereas the Rhododendron Nivale grows barely a few inches above the ground[3]. Rhododendron is the state tree and 'Nobile orchid' is the state flower. Moreover, several species of medicinal plants and herbs are found throughout Sikkim.

The lower altitude is home to prowling jungle cats, agile mongoose and others. While in the temperate zone swing the common langurs, leopards, red panda, musk deers, the Himalayan black bears and the flying squirrels, at high altitudes roam the yaks, mules, snow-leopards, shapi, blue sheep and the Tibetan wild ass, some of which are extremely rare and endangered. The 'Red Panda', a sluggish yet cuddly little arboreal animal is the state animal cf Sikkim.[4] Sikkim boasts about 30% of the birds found in India; here nestles about 550 species of them, from the tiny 3.5 in. long olive grand warbler to the gigantic bearded vulture with over loft of wing span. In Sikkim fly numerous birds like king fisher, whistling thrushes, bulbuls, magpies, falcons, and many more[5] Interestingly, a bird from Sikkim, the handsome monal pheasant shares its name with lady lmpey, the wife of the first Governor General of Bengal, who is said to have been so much fascinated by it that she pioneered its breeding in England. The 'blood red pheasant' is the State bird of Sikkim.[6]

Sikkim also offers a voyage of adventure and discovery one who wishes to undertake trekking, rafting, mountaineering or mountain biking. Beside these, the attractive culture patterns of the Sikkimese ethnic communities – Lepchas, Bhutias and the Nepalis, are well projected in a number of festivals round the year. The gourmet can taste a variety of cuisine. Sikkim, joined the national mainstream on 16 May 1975. It is dedicated emotionally to the cause of national integration. There is a complete peace and tranquility amongst the Sikkimese. Gradually, various initiatives are being undertaken by the Government to develop Sikkim as one of the ultimate eco-tourism destinations. Moreover, Sikkim can generate more than 8,000 MW of hydel power; it is declared as an organic state and strategic planning is being done to make Sikkim, the 'Switzerland of the East'.

The Nathu-La Silk Trade Route

The interest and attention of the entire world was the center of attraction on the reopening day of the Nathu-La, the pass for trade between the two powerful Asian Giants on 6 July 2006. On this significant day, the two ever growing civilisations of the world were going to change the history of mankind[7]. The two powerful giants were coming together. The cold was is now history and we are in war of trade. Here, no more artillery power shall win. It is the competitiveness, quality and devotion of the trade, industry and commerce that will bring success. The world rejoiced that now, peace shall prevail and Asia will lead the torch of peace the world over. The world will thank those great personalities who had worked for golden day as well as beginning of new era. Now, Nathu-La has been opened for border trade, and it will finally culminate in the International trade.[8]

Historically, this trade route emerged gradually to finally become one of the most viable and widely used routes from across the Indian sub-continent. Though the concept of barter trade remained for long, it really picked up to become a trading system with all modern practices and amenities, after four and a half decades or so.

Dr. Pawan Chamling, the Chief Minister of Sikkim in his welcome address said that it was a historic day for the people as the route that linked the two great civilisations from the time immemorial was being reopened. Chamling stressed that the reopening of this route has been possible only because of the farsightedness, vision and determination of the leadership of both India and China.

This route has the rarest distinction of bringing together nomads and city dwellers, pastoral–People and farmers, merchants and monks, soldiers and pilgrims, and scientists and literary figures.

The background for trade between British India and Tibet via Nathu-La and the neighbouring Jelepla was established after colonel Francis Edward Younghushand led a military mission to Tibet in 1903-04. Subsequently, the historic trade convention signed between the colonial rulers, and Tibet in 1904, made the former a key player in Central Asia.[9] Fifty-eight years later in 1962, the Indo-China trade relations came to an abrupt halt; the conflict created a dead end on both sides of the border, thus heralding a period of economic atrophy in the whole Himalayan region particularly in Tibet.[10] The closure disrupted an entire economic system that has brought prosperity to many parts of the eastern Himalayas including Sikkim, the hill areas of West Bengal, Tibet and the neighbouring areas of China. The tradition of common culture practices, intellectual exchanges and other activities including diplomatic missions was also discontinued. Much has changed over the last four decades on both sides of the Himalayas. Tibet is now Tibet autonomous Region (TAR). China has become a military and economic powerhouse and is demonstrating its capitalist might on the Nathu-La trade issue while the Indian response to it remains joded.[11]

Geographically, Nathu-La pass divides the international border between the Asian giants – India and China (Tibet). Etymologically, Nathu-La in the Tibetan language can be explained as 'na' means ear, 'thu' means listen and 'la' means pass. So, its literal meaning is "the pass of ear or whispering". This pass of the listening ear has for centuries been a natural gate between India and China (Tibet). It once witnessed a flourishing border trade in wool, machine parts and other goods[12]. The 4310 m pass served as the trade route between British India and Tibet beginning around 1860s through Sikkim flourishing the trade between the two countries–India and China.[13]

In olden days, trade was conducted in four routes in Sikkim viz., via Namchee and Chadam to the Great Rangeet; and also via Zeme to Goke and Tramdue to Colbong. The Tibetan merchants entered Darjeeling by routes starting from Chola, Yekla, Nathey, Cumra and Dangsa. All these net in Sikkim through which they entered Darjeeling via Gangtok and Dikling. The report was thoroughly examined by the Bengal Government. The Deputy Commissioner of Darjeeling was instructed to keep the road to the Great Rangeet and also that to the Teesta (Made by the British force in Sikkim in 1861) in good repair[14] in days to come.

The spiritual Hindu and Buddhist devotees of the Indian sub-continent will get a chance to have a glimpse of lake

Mansarovar and Mount Kailas once the route opened for Tourism in 2011. Lakhs of devotes will travel through Sikkim to attain Moksha (Salvation) at the abode of Lord Shiva at Mansarovar. The tourist flow of 3 lakhs in Sikkim per year was projected to triple by 2011 A.D. leading to a new set of economic activity and enterprises benefiting the local populace of Sikkim.[15]

The trade through Nathu-La started in a small scale, however, the passage of time will get this transformed into a massive operation. The infrastructural development plan for the next four years will bring an excellent two lane strong road between Siliguri and Nathu-La to match the finishing touches being given by the Chinese on their side by providing rail and road links upto Chumbi. The entrepreneurs who remain active through this difficult period of trial and error will ultimately reap the rich benefits. The youths of Sikkim who constitute 50% of the population need to understand this and make their life style accordingly, and thereby, win the battle of trade and tourism.[16]

On 6 July 2006, the inaugural ceremony at the international border at Nathu-La consisted of ribbon cutting by Chief Minister of Sikkim, Pawan Chamling and the Chairman of TAR, Champa Phuntsok. Also present on the occasion were Vice-Chairman of TAR, Hao Peng and Sum Yuki, Ambassador of the People Republic of China to India. Chamling in his welcome address welcomed all the delegates on behalf of Government of India and he said that it was historic day for the people as the route that linked the two oldest great civilisations from the time immemorial was being responded. He also, said that the reopening of this route has been possible only because of the far sightedness, vision and determination of the leadership of both India and China[17].

1000 traders from Sikkim crossed the border to trade in Renquingang on the inaugural day, while traders from TAR also came to Sherathang for the same. The border trade mart shall remain open from 1 June to 30 September every year, and trade market will open from Monday to Thursday every week from morning 7.30 am to 3.30 pm in the afternoon as per Indian time, and 10 am to 6 pm as per Chinese time. A permit will be issued costing Rs. 50/- each that will be levied for every vehicle entering Sikkim and fee of 5 yens (Rs. 25) will be levied the trade mart point at Renquingang. 29 items that will be exportable to China from India and 15 items that are importable from China to India[18] are shown as under:

Exportable items to China from India

Dry fruits, Dry and Fresh Vegetables, Tea, Coffee, Rice, Tobacco, Milk processed products, Liquour, Stationery, Canned food, Hardware, Palm Oil, Agricultural implements, Blankets Copper Products, Clothes, Cycle, Bareley, Flour, Vegetable Oil, Gur and Misri, Snuff, Spices, Shows, Kerosene oil, utensils, wheat cigarettes and local herbs.

Exportable items to India from China

Goat skin, Sheep skin, wool, seribelyipe, goat Kashmiri, Horse, Raw Silk, Common Salt, China clay, Yak Hair, Yak Tail, Borax, Goat, Sheep and Butter.

While speaking at a function held in Sherathang on 6 July 2006, Pawan Chamling said that event of the reopening of the Nathu-La Trade Route marks the beginning of a new era in the even flourishing Indo-China relations. He added that the two giants can together change the entire course of economic orientation and patterns of growth and development at the global level. Reiterating the fact that people of India particularly of Sikkim would like to really make use of this trade route as major avenue for both economic growth and multifaceted development. He felt that over the years, Sikkim could be a major trading zone like Singapore and therefore, he emphasised that the Government was proposing to setup a special Economic Zone where many of the small and medium enterprises from both India and abroad could be located.[19]

The Trade Mart at Sherathang is equipped with adequate number of sheds for offices, Post Office, Cyber Cafe, Customs and Immigration offices, Banks, Power, etc.; on the other hand, the Chinese Trade Mart has also provided facilities for display of commodities, ware houses, banking, foreign banks, immigration, post office and adequate supply of drinking water and power,[20] etc.

NEW TRADE SEASON

2007

Starts : May 1

Ends : November 30

2006

Started on : July 6

Ended on : September, 30

Christy Fernandes, Additional Secretary in the Ministry of Commerce and Industry, Government of India, referring to the aspirations of the people on both the sides said that it becomes necessary to expedite the concept of border trade as it stands today. The concept of Border Trade is that the neighbouring places on both sides will be allowed duty free trade. Fernandes also mentioned that it is important to inform the traders about the quarantine artification by authorities of both the countries and urged the traders to follow these formalities meticulously to avoid any hassles. He further assured that those procedures are little tedious at present, an endeavour will be made to simplify these measures and it shall be made more pragmatic for the People of both countries. Regarding immigration, hundred traders will be allowed to visit the trade mart from both sides. Concluding his address to the Press, Fernandes said that the mission may be very successful and the people and diginitaries from TAR of China were pro-active and supportive throughout. The delegation was received by the Governor of TAR of China and accorded grant hospitability during their stay in China, the Deputy Governor, TAR of China saw off the delegations through Nathu La.[21]

This was the trade route that linked vast masses of South-Asian sub-continents with China and Central Asia. This cultural high way once triggered a chain of religious contacts, commercial exchanges and sharing of mountain commonly and the representatives of King Ashoka in India and traveller-scholars like Factlien and Hiven Tsang from China were the harbinger of such contacts this route has the rarest distinction of bringing together nomads and city dwellers, pastoral people and farmers, merchants and monks, soldiers and pilgrims, scientists and literary figures.[22]

It is through this trade route, we together share our artistic-traditions, together managed to conserve the ecologies, Sanctity, Pristine glory of nature, further boosting world peace and harmony. The travellers like Doughlas Freshfield, David Robertson, DTF Newall and John Clarke provide us with beautiful and nostalgic accounts of situations surround this trade route. We have a rich heritage of folk songs and folk literature based on the movement of the People, their cultural exchanges and exhibitions of social habits and expressions on this route.[23] In 1890, the exports from India to (China) Tibet and from (China) Tibet to India were as under:

India - Export Products

Superfine clothes, watches, snuff boxes, Indigo, Pocket knives and scissors, chant shells and cloves.

(China) Tibet Export Products

Yak Tails, Gold dust, Talents of silver, Musk, Tincan and goats wool.

By 1950s, there was a significant change in the trade lists. The exports between the two countries were as under :

India - Export Products

Petrol, Rolex watches, Parker Pen, Food, Vegetables, Candles, Pashminas, Vaseline, Tweed Cloth, Shoes, cigarette and religious items like and Butter Lamps.

(China) Tibet Export Products

Chinese Silver Dollar (also known as 'Dyangs'), Gold, Salt, and Bundles of Raw wool.

We have travelled a long way the means of transport also saw a major change. The mule Caravans of the 19th Century were gradually replaced by the early 20th century 'Tharkas' (2 wheel axle) strapped on the back of the mules that ran through the flat terrain of the Tibetan Plateau. Banks, post offices and trade marts also came into being on both sides.[24] And now in the 21st century, we shall have the most sophisticated vehicles to transport the goods on both sides of the border. In other words, this route symbolises the fading of creaking sounds of burdensome mules caravan and virtual extinction of 'Postal Runner'. It heralds the beginning of a modern means of transport and communication. Culture ticked with strong sense of mutual interdependence and collective survival.[25]

The reopening and restoration of this trade route through Nathu-La deeply justifies the historical statement of mutually share this great moment, brings over joys and happiness in great measures between two countries on 6 July 2006. The formal reopening of this great Himalayan Pass after a long gap of 44 years (since 1962) of closing down angurs well for the collective well being of both the countries.[26] Historically, this trade route emerged gradually to finally become one of the most viable and widely used routes from across the Indian Sub-continent. Though the concept of barter trade remained for long, it really picked up to become a trading system with all modern practices and amenities.[27]

Sikkim is a growing example of how road map of sustainable development could be drawn and reached at. Hence, nature and people have a harmonious cohabitation and also culture and trade traditionally complemented each other and continuity and change endlessly supplemented each other. And this trade of the 21st century is believed to be conducted through Nathu-La in the broader framework of sustainable development. It has a great vision of integrating trade and tourism because it is thought that Sikkim is the point of central tendency in the entire Panorama of Buddhist circuit tourism among Bhutan, Nepal, Lhasa, Mayanmar, Arunachal Pradesh, Bihar, and Sikkim. This is undoubtedly going to be the most fascinating attractive tourism hub and heritage sites in the world. Sikkim has the great interest in making this route as the cultural highway that brings these cradles of ancient civilisations closer and closer. That is why Sikkim proposes a 'Sikkim Lhasa Bus Service' at an appropriate and favourable time.[28]

The reopening of this historic trade route between India and China through the Nathu-La route in Sikkim also reopens a vast range of possibilities and opportunities. This is more so for the neighbour locked North East Region. This trade route reopening is an absolute impossibility even a decade back, but five major factors have steadily converged to make this happen.

First, the far sightedness and dynamism of the Sikkimese leadership the consistent arguments of Chief Minister of Sikkim Pawan Chamling over the past decade led to the sensitising of all segments of Sikkimese society bringing in knowledge and expertise to indicate potential gains; second, a significant realisation on the part of China that its national security could be ensured more durably through a policy of better relations with periphery nations. This gradually and successfully implemented in the form of local integration in Asia-Pacific and cultural Asian Regions,[29] third, globalisation triggered opportunities and issues of market expansion and integration became a central theme in India and China relations. Hence, economic ties and compulsions of wider integration have opened the vistas of new approaches to resolve the long standing boundary disputes,[30] fourth, the development of a more realistic analysis and favourable public opinion created by both national and local media.[31] Fifthly, another land mark development between these two countries is the recognition of Sikkim by the Chinese Government as one of the integral constituents of the Indian Union after the abolition of the Institution of Namgyal dynasty for 332 years of theocratic regime on 16 May 1975.[32]

The projected volume of trade is to the tune of Rs. 206 crores by 2007, Rs. 2.266 crore by 2010 and Rs. 12,203 crore by 2015 AD.[33] It was during the visit of then Prime Minister, Atal Behari Vajpayee to Peoples Republic of China, this historic Memorandum of India and the Government of the People's Republic of China on expanding Border Trade was signed at Beijing on 23 June 2003[34].

The text reads as under :

> "The India side agrees to designate changer of Sikkim State as the venue for border trade market", the Chinese side agrees to designate Renquinggang of the Tibet Autonomous Region as the venue for border trade market" (Article 1)[35]
>
> This has brought a significant politico-strategic gain to India as China formally recognised Sikkim as a Constituent State of India. During an official visit of Premier, Wen Jiabao to India in April 2005, he formally

presented a map showing Sikkim as a Constituent State of India. Prime Minister, Man Mohan Singh and Premier, Jiabao decided to establish a strategic and cooperative partnership for peace and prosperity.[36]

Further, the study group has mentioned that on a very simple assumption, the charges on tourists visiting Sherathang and Nathu-La could generate a revenue of Rs. 1.81 Crores in 2006 and Rs. 3.47 Crores in 2010 AD. The income and employment affects on road side hotels and restaurants, handicrafts and transport and communication and many other backward and forward linkages are likely to be immense.[37]

Border Trade Resumed for the second time. The second phase of border trade between India and China through Nathu-La border was resumed on 1st May, 2007, a month earlier compared to last year. The trade period has been extended and stretched upto November as against September last year[38] (i.e. 2006. As per the original schedule, the trade period was 1 June to 30 September, which is now rescheduled from May 1, to November, 30. On the reopening day this year, 20 Indian traders and 29 Chinese traders crossed Nathu-La border. 15 Indian items and 28 of Tibet Autonomous Region of China have been put in to the trade basket this time. A demand to increase the number of items and value of daily trade from Rs. 25,000/- to Rs. 1,00,000/- and other demands are still pending for Delhi's nod as told by S.K. Sarda, President of Sikkim Chamber of Commerce. However, the traders express their happiness with the stretch of trade period as Sarda said.[39]

Among the various issues that have been placed before the center are review of the import-export item list, permission for Indian traders to stay at Renquingang for at least two days, issuance of IEC Code for Sikkimese traders without PAN, issuance of dollars for traders for trade purposes and extension of CFS and CITES offices at Sherathang Trade Mart; and improvement in the road connectivity, especially the National Highway 31A.[40]

No doubt, Nathu-La could become a bigger revenue

generate than dairying, agriculture, horticulture, communication, transportation industries, lotteries or even hydro-electricity projects and promoting tourism and hospitality industries. For traders, well, Nathu-La will mean freedom from charging usurious profits because the Sikkim market is so small. It will open up a whole new venue and could be bigger than the trade of the fifties. On the other hand, 2006 was declared as the year of 'Indo-China Friendship' and we shall leave no stone unturned to march shoulder to shoulder with the authorities to achieve the desired goal in strengthening the policies of the Government of India[41]. Further, we are determined to see that the Silk Route gets its old glory back. The trade here will certainly lead to massive developments and bring attitudinal changes in the growing minds of North-East as well as nation as a whole. Ultimately, it will work as an integrating force with futuristic vision, mission, norms and objectives resulting to booming the economy at the global level to promote international relation and understanding.

Finally, the restoration of Sikkim trade after 44 years will be a continuous trade which is between India and China (Tibet) through Sikkim, and it will continue forever to improve the economy of not only Sikkim but also India.

Notes and References

1. Verma, Rajesh, "*Sikkim, Darjeeling, Bhutan*" (A Guide and Hand Book), Gangtok, Rajesh Verma – Publication (12th ed.), 2004, p. 21.
2. Waddel, L.A., "*Among the Himalayas*", Kathmandu (Nepal), Ratna Pustalk Bhawan Publication, 1978, p. 24.
3. Verma, Rajesh., *op. cit.* p. 21.
4. Sikkim, *Sikkim-Nathu-La-Culture-Adventure*, Gangtok, Sikkim Association of Adventure Tour Operators Publication, 2004, p.19.
5. *Ibid.*, p. 19.
6. *Ibid.*, p. 19.
7. Sarda, S.K., *Opening of Nathu-La*, Panorama, (Monthly New Magazine of North-East) Vol. XV, No. 6, September 2006, Shillong, Hill Pub. (P) Ltd., p. 36.

8. *Ibid.*, p. 36.
9. Gurung, Bijay, *Light and the End of Nathu-La*. The Statesman (North-East) Extra, Friday, June 6, 2006, Siliguri, the Statesman Publication, p. 2.
10. *Ibid.*, p. 2.
11. *Ibid.*, p. 2.
12. Sikkim, *Sikkim and Nathu-La; then and Now*, Gangtok, IPR Publication (GOS), 2006, p. 2.
13. *Ibid.*, p. 2.
14. Sikkim, *Now Focus: Sikkim Matters*, Gangtok, Published by Pema Wangchuk, Baba Press (Gangtok) Tadong, 2006, p. 11.
15. Sards, *op. cit.* p. 36.
16. *Ibid.*, p. 36.
17. Sikkim, *Sikkim Today* (Quarterly-April-June) 2006, Gangtok, IPR Publication (GOS), p. 4.
18. *Ibid.*, pp. 4-5.
19. *Ibid.*, pp. 6-7.
20. *Ibid.*, pp. 8-9.
21. *Ibid.*, p. 9.
22. Sikkim, Chamling Pawan, Address on the Historic occasion of Reopening of Nathu-La Trade Route Between Sikkim (India) and Tibet Autonomous Region (China), Gangtok, IPR Publication (GOS) dated : 3 July 2006, p. 2.
23. *Ibid.*, p. 2.
24. *Ibid.*, p. 2.
25. *Ibid.*, p. 3.
26. *Ibid.*, p. 3.
27. Cited in the Address of Pawan Chamling, *op. cit.* p. 2
28. *Ibid.*, p. 4.
29. "Blender", *Outlook* (the weekly Magazine) Maheshwar Puri Publication (Pvt) Ltd., New Delhi, dated : 17th July 2006, p. 28
30. *Ibid.*, p. 28.
31. Lama, Mahendra P., *Beyond Nathu-La* Sikkim Shows the way", the stateman (North-East) Vol. C, XXXX-149, dated : Monday, 26th June, Siliguri, the Statesman Publications, Ltd., p. 1.
32. *Ibid.*, p. 1.

33. *Ibid.*, p.1.
34. *Outlook*, *op.cit.* p. 28.
35. Sikkim, "*Nathu-La Trade Route*" (Barbinger of Greater Peace and Development), Gangtok, Department of Commerce and Industries, Government of Sikkim, 2006, p. 10.
36. *Ibid.*, p. 10.
37. *Ibid.*, p. 30.
38. Sikkim, *Sikkim, Nathu-La Trade Route* (Harbinger of Greater Peace and Development), Gangtok, Department of Commerce and Industries, Government of Sikkim, 2006, p. 27.
39. *Weekend Review* (North Eastern) Gangtok, Choice International, Vol. 6, no. 18 dated 3-10 May 2007, p. 1.
40. *Ibid.*, p. 1.
41. "Nathu-La Beckons Second Time". *Sikkim Express*, Vol. XXXI, No. 15, dated 1st May 2007, Gangtok, Choice, International, p. 1.

Contributors

A.B. Subba is Assistant Professor and Head, Department of Language (Limboo) at Sikkim Government College, Tadong.

Anjan Chakrabarti is a well appreciated young, energetic and committed researcher, and presently teaching Economics at St. Joseph College, Darjeeling, West Bengal. He has published several papers in national and international journals, and authored a book on 'Economic Development and Employment in Sikkim'. He also has to his credit publications in the *Economic and Political Weekly.* He is associated with a number of professional organisations in different capacities.

Chandrani Chhetri is a Post Graduate Teacher of Sociology at Buriakhop Senior Secondary School, West Sikkim. She did her M.A. and Ph.D. from North Bengal University.

Durga P Chhetri is Assistant Professor in Political Science at Southfield College, Darjeeling, West Bengal. His areas of academic interest include 'decentralisation', 'governance', 'gender studies', 'rural development', and social exclusion and inclusion.

K.R. Chakravarti is a retired Principal of Rhenock Government College, East Sikkim. He has a number of publications in referred journals to his credit.

Maitreyee Choudhury is presently Professor and Director, Centre for Himalayan Studies, University of North Bengal, Darjeeling, West Bengal. Prior to joining the Centre for Himalayan Studies, she taught Geography at Sikkim Government College, Gangtok and served as the Head of the Department of Geography for seven years. During her long tenure of teaching and research, she has published numerous research papers and articles in several Indian and international journals. She has to her credit four books: Sikkim: Geographical Perspective (2006), Himalayan Studies in India (ed) (2008), The Himalayan Miscellany: An Anthology of Select Articles on Bhutan and Tibet (ed) (2003) and Women Empowerment, and Gender Insecurities: A South Asian Perspective (2010).

Mohammad Yasin is Professor of Political Science at the University of North Bengal, Darjeeling, West Bengal. He is also a Director, Department of Adult, Continuing Education, Extension and Field Outreach. He has rich experience in teaching, research and extension activities for more than two decades. He has guided many M.Phil. and Ph.D. students. He has published several research papers in national and international journals. His published work includes Indian Politics: Protests and Movements (2003), and Indian Politics: Processes, Issues and Trend (2004). Presently, he has assumed the Office of the Director, Aligarh Muslim University Centre, Murshidabad, West Bengal.

Navin Pandey is Assistant Professor in the Department of Geography at Sikkim Government College, Tadong.

Padam Nepal is working as Assistant Professor of Political Science at St. Joseph College, Darjeeling, West Bengal. He has had brilliant academic career and participated in and presented papers at national and international conferences/seminars in India. He is the author of Environmental Movement in India (2009) and co-author of An Introduction to the Politics (2009).

Suresh Gurung is the Principal of Damber Singh College, Gangtok, East Sikkim. He is the author of book Sikkim: Ethnicity and Political Dynamics (2010).

Vibha Arora is Associate Professor in the Department of Humanities and Social Science at Indian Institute of Technology, Delhi. She did her M.A. and M.Phil. from University of Delhi. She had her doctoral studies at the Institute of Social and Cultural Anthropology, University of Oxford on 'Just a Pile of Stones! The Politicisation of Indigenous Knowledge, Identity and Sacred Landscapes among the Lepcha and Bhutia Tribes of Contemporary

Sikkim, India'. She has participated in and presented papers at national and international conferences/seminars in India and abroad. She has a number of publications in referred journals to her credit.

Vimal Khawas is currently an Executive Fellow at Sikkim University, Gangtok, East Sikkim. He has co-authored a book 'Gender Issues in Development: Concerns for the 21st Century'. His other works are published in various professional journals.

Y.P. Nepal is the Principal of Government Senior Secondary School, Namchi, South Sikkim.

Index